Passing by the Dragon

Passing by the Dragon

The Biblical Tales of Flannery O'Connor

J. Ramsey Michaels

With a foreword by Thomas Howard

CASCADE *Books* · Eugene, Oregon

PASSING BY THE DRAGON
The Biblical Tales of Flannery O'Connor

Cascade Books
An Imprint of Wipf and Stock Publishers
199 W. 8th Ave., Suite 3
Eugene, OR 97401

www.wipfandstock.com

ISBN 13: 978-1-62032-223-9

Cataloging-in-Publication data:

Michaels, J. Ramsey.

Passing by the dragon : the biblical tales of Flannery O'Connor / J. Ramsey Michaels ; with a foreword by Thomas Howard.

xii + 212 pp. ; 23 cm. Includes bibliographical references.

ISBN 13: 978-1-62032-223-9

1. O'Connor, Flannery—Criticism and interpretation. 2. Christian Fiction, American—History and criticism. I. Title.

PS3565.C57 M5 2013

Manufactured in the U.S.A.

For Carolyn

Contents

Foreword

FLANNERY O'CONNOR'S STORIES, SET most of the time in seedy hamlets and backwoods regions, have, since the 1950s, stirred up hilarity, exultation, contempt, perplexity, and even sometimes fury, among readers. Critics and readers whose outlook has been formed by late-twentieth-century literary and moral categories find these tales incomprehensible; but rather than admitting defeat, they roll out all the machinery of positivism, Freudianism, structuralism, post-structuralism, gender studies, and even New Age, in the effort to fit her work into some acceptable literary category—or else to damn it.

The effort, of course, is a compliment to Miss O'Connor, since it admits that *something* ought to be said on the topic. If her work were of no importance, the obvious tactic would be to ignore it. But this hasn't happened. We all worry at her conundrums and outrages like puppies with mice.

Readers who share both her fierce Catholic orthodoxy and her bemused and admiring fascination with the fundamentalist faith of good country people—"white-trash," they were often called—will quickly see what she is up to and find themselves bewitched. Presently, if they develop any sympathy at all with her vision, they will find themselves sharing Flannery's attitude.

A quality which a ponderous critical mind might miss altogether, but which is crucial to any grasp of her mind, is her humor. One might almost say that this irrepressible drollery is the very starting point of her art, nay, of her whole imagination and approach to our mortal life. Everything amused her. But far from tincturing her work with mockery, this amusement turns out to be the fountainhead of her obvious affection for her characters. She scorns no one. She looks at humbug, stupidity, and ignorant sententiousness with a wry wince, as though she recognizes all such postures as the very cockade of the poor humanity for which Christ died. She never dissociates herself from her characters. She never patronizes them.

Foreword

What we have in this present volume is an approach to her work that would make her heart glad. Ramsey Michaels sees everything with great good sense. For one thing, he shares her outlook entirely. This "entirely" touches on a certain pleasant irony since Michaels is a Baptist scholar. On the surface of things, this might easily have placed him in a very guarded position vis-à-vis her work, since not only is she a Catholic (which is li'ble to mean mos' anything these days), but a stupendously knowledgeable and ebullient Catholic. She is wholly and energetically at home with the most rigorous of Catholic moral, philosophical, and dogmatic claims. It is from this point of view that she observes the world.

There would be, therefore, a hundred points at which a Protestant scholar might wish to demur: the Marian mystery, the canon of Scripture, the Mass, the operations of grace, Thomism, the Magisterium of the Church—that sort of thing. But Michaels' judiciousness, urbanity, perspicacity, and *catholicity* of spirit govern the whole work. When an explanation for non-Catholic readers seems apt, he supplies it with grace. Where Miss O'Connor's work draws implicitly (or explicitly) on Scripture, Michaels, being a distinguished biblical scholar, is able to throw vastly helpful light on things. Indeed, his bibliocentrism, far from placing him at a distance from this Catholic writer, is the very avatar of the value he places on her work.

I would have to confess that, having read any number of essays and books on Flannery O'Connor (besides her own work, of course), I find Ramsey Michaels' study to be the most intelligent, sympathetic, and rewarding of any such study that I know of. My sense of duty in having been asked to write this Foreword very early found itself transmuted into sheer, mere pleasure. I kept thinking as I read, "Flannery would love this, Ramsey!"

Thomas Howard

Preface

IFIRST HEARD OF Flannery O'Connor in the early 1970s, in a guest lecture at Gordon-Conwell Theological Seminary by Beatrice Batson of Wheaton College. Before that I may have thought she was a man. An Irish novelist perhaps? It wasn't until I picked up a second-hand paperback entitled *Three by Flannery O'Connor* at a Florida flea market outside Lakeland in the summer of 1975 that I truly discovered her work. We had just moved my wife's parents from Michigan to Florida and were staying with them for a couple of weeks, so I had time on my hands and read it all in less than a week, the *Three* consisting of two short novels, *Wise Blood* and *The Violent Bear It Away*, and her first collection of stories, *A Good Man Is Hard to Find*. I found her use of biblical themes both jarring and invigorating, just as in the Bible itself, but only rarely in books about the Bible, where they are routinely tamed and domesticated. Back in New England and teaching New Testament in the seminary, I found time to nourish my O'Connor fixation, filling in the gaps in my reading with *The Complete Stories* (which first appeared in 1971), and later with a healthy sampling of her collected letters in *The Habit of Being* (1978).

Religion and Literature is something of a luxury in theological seminaries, but I managed to talk the Dean into letting me offer seminars twice on "Biblical Themes in Flannery O'Connor." Rarely are seminary courses offered on just one person (other than Jesus and Paul!), and the only precedents I knew of at Gordon-Conwell were C. S. Lewis and Dietrich Bonhoeffer. Never before on a woman. But the students seemed to enjoy them, and I know I did. After I moved to Southwest Missouri State (as it was known then), I offered two mini-courses on O'Connor, team teaching once with a young English instructor, and once with a local Rabbi on Malamud, Roth, O'Connor, and Updike. And during those Missouri years I published a couple of short pieces on O'Connor in *The Flannery O'Connor Bulletin* and *Daughters of Sarah*, and attended a 1987 conference at Conception Abbey, a Benedictine monastery in northern Missouri, where I met such O'Connor luminaries as Paul Engle, her first mentor at the University of Iowa, and Sally Fitzgerald, at that time the custodian of her letters and her legacy.

In retirement, even amid meeting deadlines for the publication of various New Testament commentaries, I finally had the opportunity to indulge my O'Connor habit to the full. In 2006 I presented a paper at a conference on "Flannery O'Connor in the Age of Terrorism," at Grand Valley State University in Grand Rapids, Michigan, a paper that eventually found its way into a 2010 volume with the same title published by the University of Tennessee Press. In 2007 I applied for a grant from the National Endowment for the Humanities to spend a whole month in Milledgeville, Georgia, Flannery O'Connor's home town, at the O'Connor library and archives at Georgia College and State University, O'Connor's alma mater. To my delight my daughter, Carolyn Michaels Kerr, also applied, and we both were awarded stipends of $3,000 for the July 2007 Summer Institute, "Reconsidering Flannery O'Connor," with lectures, seminars and opportunities for our own research in Milledgeville. I was the oldest participant by at least a decade, but the experience opened the door to more publication in *The Flannery O'Connor Review*, and finally to the decision to write this book. I taught one more course in retirement on O'Connor, at Bangor Theological Seminary in Portland, Maine, providing me with the opportunity to create a viable structure for a book on O'Connor and the Bible. Much has been written of the religious and theological dimensions of her fiction, but little on her use and interpretation of the Bible, and that only in passing.

So, I have people to thank. Deans and department heads in the early days who let me step out of my field of specialization and try something new. Later, the O'Connor specialists who welcomed me warmly into their discipline. Among the latter I would single out Avis Hewitt at Grand Valley State, and Sarah Gordon and Marshall Bruce Gentry at Georgia College and State University. Many others are too numerous to name, especially the lecturers and participants in the 2007 NEH Summer Institute. Above all, my daughter Carolyn, who has both joined and inspired my journey in retirement, and who now has major publications of her own on O'Connor, in *Christianity and Literature* and *The Flannery O'Connor Review*. In one sense, this book is for her. In another, it is for anyone with a passion either for the Bible on the one hand, or for Flannery's fiction on the other. I have found the task of bringing the two together not too difficult and altogether rewarding.

Flannery's Bible

FLANNERY O'CONNOR'S BIBLE DOES not give evidence that she was a constant or inveterate Bible reader, for it is neither well worn nor heavily marked. It is in fact still in its dust jacket even today. Her friend William Sessions cautions us that "Her Bible reading—a late experience in her life, in fact—was never primary for plumbing Christian meaning." What was primary, he claims, was "the Eucharist, the Catholic Mass," because "Nothing, certainly not the Bible, would supersede what O'Connor considered the Real Presence" (Sessions, 205). True enough, and yet O'Connor's Catholicism and her biblicism were inseparable and interchangeable. She once characterized one of her most memorable Protestant characters as "a crypto-Catholic. When you leave a man alone with his Bible and the Holy Ghost inspires him, he is going to be a Catholic one way or another even tho he knows nothing about the visible church. His kind of Christianity may not be socially desirable, but it will be real in the sight of God" (Collected Works, 1183).

No surprise, then, that her Bible is the Roman Catholic Bible, a small fat Douay version published in London in 1956 by the Catholic Truth Society, and available to researchers in the O'Connor collection at Georgia College and State University in Milledgeville.[1] And it does have a few markings. It is signed "Flannery O'Connor 1959," and on the dust jacket stands the notation "No. 12:8." Inside, the imprint of a paper clip is

1. That this 1956 Bible was not her first is evident in a 1952 letter to Sally Fitzgerald, asking her to send along a Bible she had left in Connecticut when she returned home to Georgia to be diagnosed with the lupus that eventually took her life. "Thanks for sending the Bible—just in time for *Bible Week*!" she wrote. "All the local churches are going in big for Bible Week" (*Habit of Being*, 43).

visible on the page in the New Testament where the text that gave her the title of her second novel is found: "And from the days of John the Baptist until now, the kingdom of heaven suffereth violence and the violent bear it away" (Matt 11:12). Less noticeable are several markings in Genesis. At Genesis 15:12 a simple letter D in pencil calls attention to the words, "And when the sun was setting, a deep sleep fell upon Abram; and a great and darksome horror seized him." At 28:12, where Jacob "saw in his sleep a ladder standing upon the earth, and the top thereof touching heaven; the angels also of God ascending and descending by it," a pencilled D2 has been placed in the margin. At 31:11, another D stands beside the words, "And the angel of God said to me in my sleep: Jacob? And I answered: Here I am." At 31:24, where Laban "saw in a dream God saying to him: Take heed thou speak not any thing harshly against Jacob," a half crossed-out letter that looks like a D appears in the margin. At 37:6, the notation D5 highlights the words about Joseph, "And he said to them: Hear my dream which I dreamed.", and three verses later, at 37:9, D6 marks the notice that "He dreamed also another dream, which he told his brethren, saying: I saw in a dream, as it were the sun, and the moon, and eleven stars worshipping me." At 37:19 there is nothing with a D, but only a check mark alongside the ominous words of Joseph's brothers, who "said to one another: Behold, the dreamer cometh." It is a fair guess that D stands for dreams, and this is confirmed by another pencil mark highlighting the Douay version's editorial note at Genesis 37:5: "A dream: these dreams of Joseph were prophetical, and sent from God; as were also those which he interpreted, Gen 40 and 41; otherwise generally speaking the observing of dreams is condemned in the Scripture, as superstitious and sinful. See Deut 18:10; Ecclus 34:2, 3."[2] In the twelfth chapter of Numbers, a simple line in the right margin points to Numbers 12:5–9, a passage worth quoting in full:

> The Lord came down in a pillar of the cloud, and stood in the entry of the tabernacle calling to Aaron and Mary. And when they were come, He said to them: Hear my words: If there be among you a prophet of the Lord, I will appear to him in a vision, or I will speak to him in a dream. But it is not so with my servant Moses who is most faithful in all my house. For I speak to him mouth to mouth, and plainly: and not by riddles and figures doth he see the Lord. Why then were you not afraid to speak ill of my servant Moses? And being angry with them he went away.

2. *The Holy Bible: Douay Version*, 47. Unless otherwise noted, all quotations from the Bible in this book will be from the Douay version.

This marking explains "No. 12:8" on the dust jacket as a reference to this text, focusing on the words, "For I speak to him mouth to mouth, and plainly: and not by riddles and figures doth he see the Lord" (v 8). In context, it is the Lord's resounding *No* to the question of Mary (that is, Miriam) and Aaron at the beginning of the chapter: "Hath the Lord spoken by Moses only? Hath he not also spoken to us in like manner?" (Num 12:3).

Whatever else it may be, this small guided Bible study, apparently from O'Connor's own hand, can be read as her private affirmation of the authority of Scripture over against all visions, dreams, riddles, and figures. She seems to have shared the Church's ambivalence about dreams that came to expression in her Bible's editorial note on Genesis 37:5 about "superstitious and sinful" reliance on dreams. "The word 'dreams' . . . always terrifies me," she wrote in 1957 to her friend Betty Hester. "The artist dreams no dreams. That is precisely what he does not do, as you very well know. Every dream is an obstruction to his work" (*Collected Works*, 1031). And yet in her lecture, "Catholic Novelists and Their Readers," drawing on the very passage in Numbers that she marked in her Bible, she freely acknowledges that "The Lord doesn't speak to the novelist as he did to his servant, Moses, mouth to mouth. He speaks to him as he did to those two complainers, Aaron and Aaron's sister, Mary: through dreams and visions, in fits and starts, and by all the lesser and limited ways of the imagination" (*Mystery and Manners*, 181). The comment is part of an attempt in that lecture to distinguish between seeing with one's own eyes as a fiction writer, and seeing through the eyes of the Church. "It would be foolish to say that there is no conflict between these two sets of eyes," she writes. "There is a conflict, and it is a conflict which we escape at our peril, one which cannot be settled beforehand by theory or fiat or faith. We think that faith entitles us to avoid it, when in fact, faith prompts us to begin it, and to continue it until, like Jacob, we are marked" (*Mystery and Manners*, 180). Here too O'Connor is in Genesis, wrestling like Jacob with the Lord until daybreak (Gen 32:24–28). "Like a very doubtful Jacob," her Catholic novelist "confronts what stands in his path and wonders if he will come out of the struggle at all" (*Mystery and Manners*, 183).

O'Connor is caught here between her aspirations and her limitations. "The tensions of being a Catholic novelist," she writes "are probably never balanced until the Church becomes so much a part of his personality that he can forget about her—in the same sense that when he writes, he forgets about himself." And because this is a condition "seldom achieved in this life, particularly by novelists," O'Connor views herself more like "those two complainers, Aaron and Aaron's sister, Mary, through dreams and visions, in fits and starts, and by all the lesser and limited ways of the imagination" (*Mystery and Manners*, 181). In the end, though, she allows herself a trace of optimism, though only a trace: "I would like to think that in the future there will be Catholic writers who will be able to use these two sets of eyes with consummate skill and daring; but I wouldn't be so reckless as to predict it" (*Mystery and Manners*, 181). While the explicit issue in her lecture was the relationship between her "prophetic vision" and the authority of the Church, the text from Numbers to which she appealed hints at a comparable tension between Holy Scripture, with its "mouth to mouth" revelations to Moses, and any Christian writer's "lesser and limited ways of the imagination." In another lecture, "Novelist and Believer," she makes this explicit, warning the writer not to think "that the eyes of the Church *or of the Bible or of his particular theology* have already done the seeing for him" (*Mystery and Manners*, 163, emphasis added). What she says about the Catholic writer and the Church applies as well to any writer, Catholic or Protestant or Jewish, in relation to the Bible, or whatever it is that shapes their faith.

Still, O'Connor was a Roman Catholic, and the Bible that she read, or more often, heard read in church, was the Roman Catholic Douay version. This is immediately evident in the title of her second novel, *The Violent Bear It Away*, taken from Matthew 11:12 in the Douay version, not the King James,[3] and less obviously in her frustration at being unable to find any reference to an almond tree in Jeremiah 1:11, where the Douay version speaks of "a rod watching" rather than the King James version's "rod of an almond tree" (*Habit of Being*, 530; she theorized in another letter to the same person "that that almond tree verse may be in one of the minor prophets???"(*Collected Works*, 1191). O'Connor's canon of Scripture, consequently, is the Roman Catholic canon, embracing the additional Old Testament books that Protestants call the Apocrypha. And some of these additional books were close to her heart. In the front of her paperback reprint of C. S. Lewis' *The Problem of Pain*, she once wrote in pencil, "I am the mother of fair love, and of pain, and of knowledge, and of holy hope," with "Eccles" as the reference. "Eccles" stands not for Ecclesiastes, a book found in every Christian Bible, but Ecclesiasticus, a book found in her Douay version but not in the King James or in most Protestant Bibles. There, in Eccesiasticus 24:24, can be found the words, "I am the mother

---

3. As for other titles, "A Temple of the Holy Ghost" is taken from 1 Corinthians 6:19, where the Douay and the King James agree, and "Why Do the Heathen Rage?" comes from the King James version of Psalm 2:2 (the Douay has "Why have the Gentiles raged?").

of fair love, and of fear, and of knowledge, and of holy hope"[4]—word for word the same, except that O'Connor has changed "fear" to "pain," evidently to conform both to Lewis' title, *The Problem of Pain*, and to her own life, a life lived not in fear but most emphatically in pain for most of her adulthood, pain from the lupus that was to take her life finally at the age of thirty-nine. And at the bottom of page 97 in the same book, in a context in which Lewis is writing about fear, she copied the same text again, this time exactly as it stands in the book of Ecclesiasticus. The voice in the text is that of divine Wisdom, personified as a woman (as is frequently the case both in Ecclesiasticus and in the book of Proverbs), and identified finally as "the book of life and the covenant of the most High, and the knowledge of Truth" (Ecclesiasticus 24:32), that is, as Holy Scripture. In Catholic tradition, the text has been made into a Novena to the Virgin Mary as "Our Lady of Hope," but O'Connor's reference to "Eccles" suggests that she took it not from the Novena, but directly from her Bible.

The Roman Catholic canon is at work within O'Connor's stories as well. She glances at the book of Tobias, or Tobit, for example, in commenting on Mr. Head's assumed role as guide and mentor to his grandson Nelson in "The Artificial Nigger" (210).[5] In "A Circle in the Fire," her final image of three boys burning Mrs. Cope's farm (251) evokes the story of the three young men in the fiery furnace as told not in the Protestant King James version of the book of Daniel but in the Roman Catholic version, with its substantial additions. And in *The Violent Bear It Away* the Protestant reader will look in vain for any biblical reference in the image of Francis Marion Tarwater being "lifted like Habakkuk by the hair of his head" (385). Nothing like it is found in the Old Testament book of Habakkuk, but the Catholic reader will find it in the longer Roman Catholic version of the book of Daniel. The irony in all of this is that the characters in her stories are mostly Bible Belt Protestants, who know their Bible well, but in the cadences of the King James version. They would have known nothing of Tobias, or a longer version of Daniel. The narrative voice in the stories,

4. Protestants who look for this text in what they call the Old Testament apocrypha (in the book called *Ecclesiasticus, or the Wisdom of Jesus Son of Sirach*) will find it, if at all, only in a footnote (at 24:18 rather than 24:24), because the Latin text of the verse is based on Greek manuscripts judged to be secondary (see "The Apocryphal/ Deuterocanonical Books of the Old Testament," 119, in *The New Oxford Annotated Bible*. So too in the Roman Catholic *Jerusalem Bible*, and ironically, the most recent Catholic translations (the *New American Bible* and the *New Jerusalem Bible*) omit the verse altogether.

5. Here and in following chapters, unless otherwise indicated, quotations or references to O'Connor's fiction are drawn from her *Collected Works*.

by contrast, is a Roman Catholic voice, even when it pretends to speak for one of her Baptist or Methodist or Pentecostal characters. This is less surprising than it might seem, given O'Connor's stated conviction that most of them were in some way "crypto-Catholics" (*Collected Works*, 1183), but it also raises the intriguing question, Was O'Connor herself unaware that some parts of her Bible would have been unfamiliar to the fundamentalist characters in her stories?

O'Connor's book reviews, unlike her fiction, were written for a Catholic audience in her diocesan newspapers, *The Bulletin*, *The Georgia Bulletin*, and *The Southern Cross*. They reflect not only her Roman Catholicism and her love for the Bible, but also her perspectives on the biblical scholarship of her day, both Catholic and Protestant. Four months before her death, she commented in a letter to a friend on a blunt warning from C. S. Lewis, "Go among the Biblical scholars, says he, as a sheep among wolves" (*Habit of Being*, 572, from Lewis, *Miracles*, 197), and she seemed to agree. And yet her reviews of contemporary biblical scholarship are largely positive. In them she repeatedly deplores the neglect of the Bible among Catholics generally. In one, she takes issue with Bishop John Wright, who attributes Catholic neglect of the Bible to "an awe, reverential and profound, which makes them feel humble in the presence of this mighty compendium of divine revelation and sacred mysteries." This view O'Connor dismisses as "looking at our sins through stained glass windows," adding bluntly that "Catholics who are not articulate about their love for the Bible are generally those who do not love it, since they read it as seldom as possible." This she attributes either to "laziness or indifference or the fear that reading it will endanger their faith, not their Catholic faith but faith itself" (*Presence of Grace*, 25; *The Bulletin*, September 1, 1956). She goes on to acknowledge that "In the scientist atmosphere of this century, the Bible can be a stumbling block to the faith of those who are not equipped with an adequate knowledge of the nature of inspiration and prophecy, the dates of the books and gospels, and the literary modes of the authors, their use of allegory, metaphor and history" (*Presence of Grace*, 25). She agrees with John L. McKenzie, SJ that "the biblical scholar cannot, nor should be expected to, resolve every line-by-line difficulty, for the Bible should be read first in the security of the faith which the Church has given," yet "Granted this, the biblical scholar is in a better position than the spiritual writer to aid the faithful in returning to frequent Bible reading" (*Prescence of Grace*, 33–34; *The Bulletin*, January 9, 1957).

O'Connor was optimistic about the direction of Catholic biblical studies in her day. "Nineteenth century Biblical scholarship, which wrecked the faith of so many," she writes, "has been almost entirely discredited and the historical value of many Biblical texts attested to by chronologies worked out by radio-carbon dating and the comparison of cultures. There is a healthy sense in these books[6] that as our knowledge of the past grows, the mystery of it grows likewise" (*Presence of Grace,* 126; *The Bulletin,* December 9, 1961). In reviewing Bruce Vawter's *The Conscience of Israel,* she comments, "Fr. Vawter restores [the prophets] to their exotic Oriental culture where they were seen by their contemporaries as inspired men, in communication with 'that otherness that men have always associated with the divine.' In this setting alone it is possible to understand an Isaiah walking naked as a warning to Egypt, and Hosea agonizing over his prostitute wife or an Ezekiel baking his bread over dung to symbolize the destruction to come" (*Presence of Grace,* 141; *The Bulletin,* March 17, 1962). This, as we will see, is exactly the kind of Old Testament prophetic vision that shaped many of her own stories.

O'Connor reviewed Protestant works as well. In Karl Barth's *Evangelical Theology: An Introduction,* she finds "little or nothing in this book that the Catholic cannot recognize as his own" (*Presence of Grace,* 165; *The Southern Cross,* October 24, 1963). As she confided to her friend Maryat Lee in an unpublished letter in the O'Connor collection at Georgia College (February 12, 1962), "all the more important Catholic theologians admire Barth. He gave Protestantism one swift kick away from Schleiermacher et al. Also he is a real theologian. When he talks theology it is theology, not history or culture or social science. I like him because he throws the furniture around." She is far more guarded in her assessment of Rudolf Bultmann, whom she characterized as

> one of the most interesting of the new Protestant theologians. Bultmann's concern is to make a real Christianity acceptable to the man of the modern world—real Christianity as distinct from that purely liberal Protestantism that eventually ends in a system of ethical values, but not real Christianity as the orthodox know it. Bultmann wishes to preserve the central Christian message of the cross but to take away everything unacceptable to modern science, thus discarding every intervention of the Divine into human life. He calls this demythologization. He

6. That is, the two books she was reviewing, *The Bible and the Ancient Near East,* edited by G. E. Wright (Doubleday, 1961) and *The Old Testament and Modern Study,* edited by H. H. Rowley (Oxford Paperbacks, 1961).

would judge the Christian message as found in the gospels by its relevance to an existential philosophy" (*Presence of Grace*, 92; *The Bulletin*, July 23, 1960).

By contrast, O'Connor quotes with unqualified approval these words of Jean Levie, in *The Bible: Word of God in Words of Men*: "God, who alone sees the ultimate connection between the doctrinal passages scattered throughout Scripture, gives to his Church, enlightened by the continual presence of the Spirit, the privilege of progressively gaining a deeper insight into the dogmatic synthesis he intended and willed from the beginning" (*Presence of Grace*, 156; *The Southern Cross*, March 2, 1963). This appeal to the authority of the Church sets her against such existentialist theologians as Bultmann, but also against some of her own characters from the Bible belt, for example the evangelist Onnie Jay Holy in *Wise Blood*, who had his own "Holy Church of Christ Without Christ" which he claimed was "based on the Bible. Yes sir! It's based on your own personal interpitation of the Bible, friends. You can sit at home and interpit your own Bible however you feel in your heart it ought to be interpited." This, he added, was "just the way Jesus would have done it" (86–87).

Still, all satire aside, O'Connor respected most of the fundamentalist characters she created. She agreed with Gustav Weigel, SJ that Catholics are "doctrinally closer to Protestant fundamentals than to those liberal Protestant theologians who have created a naturalistic ethical culture, humanism, and labeled it Christianity" (*Presence of Grace*, 77; *The Bulletin*, August 22, 1959). In one of her last lectures, "The Catholic Novelist in the Protestant South," she wrote:

> Unfortunately, where you find Catholics reading the Bible, you find that it is usually a pursuit of the educated, but in the South the Bible is known by the ignorant as well, and it is always that *mythos* which the poor hold in common that is most valuable to the fiction writer. When the poor hold sacred history in common, they have ties to the universal and the holy, which allows the meaning of their every action to be heightened and seen under the aspect of eternity. The writer who views the world in this light will be very thankful if he has been fortunate enough to have the South for his background, because here belief can still be made believable, even if for the modern world it cannot be made admirable (*Mystery and Manners*, 203).

In a 1962, in an interview with Joel Wells, editor of *The Critic*, as he drove her from Rosary College in River Forest, Illinois to give a talk at Notre Dame, she said more:

> The Bible is what we share with all Christians, and the Old Testament we share with all Jews. This is sacred history and our mythic background. If we are going to discard this we had better quit writing at all. The fact that the South is the Bible Belt is in great measure responsible for its literary preeminence now. The Catholic novelist can learn a great deal from the Protestant South. (*Conversations*, 87)

If these book reviews, letters, lectures and interviews were all we had, Flannery O'Connor would emerge simply as a well-informed and very perceptive pre-Vatican II laywoman, a traditional Catholic at home in the rural Protestant South, yet ready for Vatican II and most of the changes it introduced in Catholic biblical scholarship and in the Church. There is reason to believe that if she had lived longer she would have welcomed the contributions of a Raymond E. Brown, a Joseph Fitzmyer, a John P. Meier, or for that matter a Joseph Ratzinger, Pope Benedict XVI—not to mention any number of moderate to conservative Protestant theologians. But if these reviews and remarks were all we had, there would be no particular reason to write a book about her. What is extraordinary about Flannery O'Connor is her ability to transform a love for biblical narrative into unforgettable narratives of her own, set in a world very different from that of the Bible, and yet in a strange way very much like it as well. This she has done in her fiction, where she seems at times so secure and at home with Holy Scripture that she feels free to treat it almost playfully, turning its imagery upside down, introducing variations on its themes, letting her characters misquote it and misuse it,[7] yet in the end rendering it the kind of homage that only she can render.

Flannery O'Connor's stories can be looked at in two ways in relation to the Bible, not mutually exclusive. That is, either as her own *reading*, and consequently her interpretation, of the Bible, or (more provocatively) as narratives in some way analogous to the Bible itself, a kind of *rewriting* of Scripture, intended not to replace the sacred text but to restate its ancient

7. Nor were her own recollections of Scripture always infallible. In a letter to a young man who feared he might be losing his faith (*Collected Works*, 1163), she quoted the text, "Lord, I believe. Help my unbelief," as "the foundation prayer of faith," but mistakenly attributed it to Peter (evidently while trying to walk on the water), rather than to the father of the epileptic son in Mark 9. Ralph Wood, citing her letter, charitably corrects her mistake (*Contending for the Faith*, 4).

truths in her own time and her own way for her own, largely unbelieving, audience. In one of her letters she speaks of someone who "said that
the best of my work sounded like the Old Testament would sound if it
were being written today—in as much (partly) as the character's relation
is directly with God rather than with other people" (*Collected Works*, 963).
Although she found the comment "interesting," it is surely no more true of
O'Connor than it is of the Old Testament itself, or of the New. Neither in
Scripture nor in O'Connor's world do we meet characters whose relation is
"directly with God rather than with other people." Even though God spoke
to Moses "mouth to mouth, and plainly," the world of the books that bear
his name was a social world not all that different from our own. Biblical
characters meet God directly, to be sure, but also in subtler ways, in their
relationships with each other, in signs and wonders, and in the everyday
events that come their way. In O'Connor's stories both God and the Devil
(not always easily distinguishable) act largely through other people, often
the ones we least suspect, the freaks and lunatics who inhabit her pages,
and sometimes even through the subhuman: a rogue bull, a tacky piece
of statuary, or a tattoo. She called this the "anagogical vision," which she
defined as "the kind of vision that is able to see different levels of reality
in one image or one situation." It was a method used in the Middle Ages
for interpreting Scripture, as O'Connor well knew from reading Thomas
Aquinas,[8] but to her it was "also an an attitude toward all of creation and
a way of reading nature" (*Mystery and Manners*, 72–73). Her stories, she
insists, are above all literal, "in the same sense that a child's drawing is
literal. When a child draws, he doesn't intend to distort but to set down
exactly what he sees" (*Mystery and Manners*, 73). O'Connor intends the
same, but "in, with and under" the literal, visible, always mundane and
often grotesque tales she tells are glimpses of an invisible world above,
hints of redemption, glory, and final judgement through Jesus Christ.

Another word for "anagogical," perhaps, is "sacramental." O'Connor's
life and her theology centered on the Eucharist, but alongside her reverence for the Blessed Sacrament was her conviction that in some sense all
creation, even that which we judge mundane or grotesque, is sacramental,
at least potentially. Or, in Gerard Manley Hopkins' words, that "The world

8. In Aquinas' own words, "so far as the things of the Old Law signify the things of
the New Law, there is the allegorical sense. But so far as the things done in Christ, or
so far as the things which signify Christ, are types of what we ought to do, there is the
moral sense. But so far as they signify what relates to eternal glory, there is the anagogical sense" (*Summa Theologica* I.10, in *Great Books of the Western World*, 19.10).

is charged with the grandeur of God."[9] The difficulty O'Connor faced right from the start was getting her readers to see it.

9. "God's Grandeur," *The Poems of Gerard Manley Hopkins* (London: Oxford Paperback, 1970) 66.

2

Her Wayward Readers

IN THE SAME INTERVIEW in which she acknowledged that "The Catholic novelist can learn a great deal from the Protestant South," Flannery O'Connor added a most revealing comment about her hopes for the future: "Maybe in fifty years, or a hundred, Catholics will be reading the Bible the way they should have been reading it all along. I can wait that long to have my fiction understood" (*Conversations*, 87). This from a woman who had about two years to live, and probably knew it! The comment is revealing in two ways. It demonstrates, first, that as late as 1962 she still did not think her fiction was well understood, even by her fellow Catholics. She was content for it to be a time bomb set to explode in future generations. Second, she felt that the Bible was not well understood either, and she saw that as a key to understanding her work. Anyone who leafs through the early reviews of her fiction will have to agree with her on the first count.[1] Many of the earliest reviews saw her work as just another example of so-called "Southern Gothic" in the tradition of Erskine Caldwell, reveling in violence, lacking in compassion for her characters and satirizing the excesses of fanatical backwoods fundamentalism. Then, in the decade after the publication of *Wise Blood*, critical respect for her fiction steadily grew, though rarely with much appreciation for its religious dimension or its use of the Bible.

Now fifty years more have passed. Religious interpretations of O'Connor have flourished, and even come to dominate the world of O'Connor criticism. This is attributable in part, as she hinted, simply to

---

1. See Scott and Streight, eds., *Flannery O'Connor: The Contemporary Reviews*, especially Irwin H. Streight's Introduction, xv–xlvi.

the passage of time, but not, as she hoped, to any great revival in biblical understanding. While biblical literacy has grown (modestly) among Catholics and in some branches of Protestantism, quite the reverse is true in the public at large. Rather, the change in the way her work is perceived has been largely fueled by her own pronouncements, in public lectures or private correspondence, about her authorial intentions. She embarked on her task as a writer confident in what she wanted to do yet fearful that she would be misunderstood. Her fears were justified, as she found her work disliked—or worse yet, admired—for all the wrong reasons, and her tendency was always to correct what she saw as misunderstandings, to set her readers straight—at least those with whom she corresponded—as to what she was up to.

Much has been written, not always with approval, of O'Connor's attempts to control the interpretation of her stories in the face of what she regarded as persistent misreadings. A typical example is Clara Claiborne Park's verdict in 1982, in some ways a throwback to earlier, more secular readings. Park comments that O'Connor

> was committed to Southern fiction. Yet her stories left Southern readers indifferent, while feeding every Northern stereotype of Southern degeneracy and fanaticism. She was committed to Catholic fiction. Yet Catholic readers could not recognize sainthood in the backwoods Protestants she put forward as prophets, or the operation of grace in the violence she thought necessary to counter the sentimentality of the religious—nor could Catholic or Protestant understand, in the harsh universe she presented as Christian, the invisibility of hope.

Park worries that when stories so carefully put together "consistently require the ministrations of their author, something has gone wrong" (Park, "Crippled Laughter," 249–50).

And yet in this respect O'Connor stands in a tradition as old as literature itself. From Plato to John Updike, writers have feared being misunderstood, and with good reason. Plato, as if in answer to Ms. Park, once wrote that "every word, when once it is written, is bandied about, alike among those who understand and those who have no interest in it, and it knows not to whom to speak or not to speak; when ill-treated or unjustly reviled it always needs its father to help it; for it has no power to protect or help itself" (Plato, *Phaedrus 275 d–e*, in *Loeb Classical Library*, 1.565, 567). Updike, speaking of his own books, humorously recalls moments when he "sees a stranger scowling into one on an airplane or in a hospital ward," and when that happens, he confesses, "My instinct is to tear the book from the reader's hands," because "The stranger, with his or her grimy fingers and glassy gaze, is so clearly not the ideal reader, all-forgiving and miraculously responsive, whom I courted as I wrote" (Updike, "Me and My Books," 759–60). O'Connor would have understood. In the middle of a lecture on "Some Aspects of the Grotesque in Southern Fiction" at her alma mater, Georgia College for Women, she once ad libbed, "When I sit down to write, a monstrous reader looms up who sits down beside me and continually mutters, "I don't get it, I don't see it, I don't want it." Some writers can ignore this presence, but I have never learned how."[2]

What has all this to do with Flannery O'Connor and the Bible? First, as we have seen, the Bible was to her a book whose Author had sent along just the sort of "father" or interpreter that Plato thought necessary: in Jean Levie's words, "his Church, enlightened by the continual presence of the Spirit" (*Presence of Grace,* 156), or more concretely, the teaching magisterium of the Church. Second, within the pages of the Bible itself (especially the New Testament) care is taken, not always, but every so often, to try to ensure understanding, or at least prevent misunderstanding. In the Gospel of John a series of parenthetical comments or narrative asides by the Gospel writer tries to ward off possible misreadings. When Jesus said "Destroy this temple; and in three days I will raise it up," he was referring to his own body, not the temple in Jerusalem (John 2:21); although he is said to have baptized, he himself baptized no one; his disciples did (4:2); when he spoke of being "lifted up," he was referring to his death (12:33), and so on. John in the book of Revelation has an angel at his side to explain to him certain things he has seen but not understood (see Rev 17:1, 21:9). In the first three Gospels Jesus speaks in parables, and while most of his parables are allowed to stand alone—make of them what you will!—a few are supplied with interpretations from Jesus' own lips, interpretations which have shaped the church's understanding of them ever since.

Modern scholars tend to doubt the authenticity of these appended interpretations, suggesting that they represent the Gospel writers' attempts to control the reception of Jesus' enigmatic words. Yet there they are, now undeniably a part of the literary (and for Christians, canonical) text that the serious reader must take into account. Within the narrative world of the Gospels, the parables were part of Jesus' public proclamation, while the interpretations were private, given only to a small circle of disciples. Yet as soon as the Gospels were written down and circulated, the interpretations

2. Cited in Gooch, *Flannery,* 86. Understandably, the words were not included in the lecture as published.

became just as public as the parables themselves, all on the same page for
everyone to see. A curious analogy presents itself, coincidental perhaps,
but illuminating, between Jesus' parables and their interpretations on the
one hand, and the stories and letters of Flannery O'Connor on the other.
Her stories were public, like the parables of Jesus, even more so in that they
were written and published. Her letters, by contrast, like Jesus's interpretations of his parables, were private pieces of correspondence with personal
friends, distant acquaintances, and occasional strangers, often in response
to questions about the meaning of her stories. But they too, many of them
at least, "went public" fifteen years after her death, with the publication of
The Habit of Being, edited by her friend Sally Fitzgerald, in 1979, and more
saw the light of day in 1988, when her *Collected Works* were published in
the Library of America series.

Even before that, in the second edition of *Wise Blood* in 1962, she
went public with a prefatory notice that Hazel Motes, the hero of the novel,
far from being a nihilist or atheist, was "a Christian *malgré lui*," whose
integrity lay in not being able to "get rid of the ragged figure [Christ] who
moves from tree to tree in the back of his mind" (*Collected Works*, 1265).
And in 1964, the year of her death, someone (probably in compliance with
her wishes), saw to it that in the paperback collection, *Three by Flannery
O'Connor*, the ten stories in *A Good Man is Hard to Find* were republished
with the epigraph,

> The dragon is by the side of the road, watching those who pass.
> Beware lest he devour you. We go to the father of souls, but it is
> necessary to pass by the dragon. *St. Cyril of Jerusalem.*

The same quotation (from Cyril's *Procatechesis* 16), worded a bit differently,
appears eight years earlier in a letter she wrote to her friend Betty Hester
(*Collected Works*, 979; January 1, 1956), and again in 1957 in her lecture,
"The Fiction Writer and His Country," where she added, "No matter what
form the dragon may take, it is of this mysterious passage past him, or into
his jaws, that stories of any depth will always be concerned to tell, and this
being the case, it requires considerable courage at any time, in any place,
not to turn away from the storyteller" (*Mystery and Manners*, 35). These
notes from the author, both added after the first edition, sent clear signals,
not just to a private acquaintance but to every reader, as to how O'Connor
wanted her works read. The reader is now given to understand that Hazel
Motes was a believer *malgré lui*, or in spite of himself, not only at the end
of *Wise Blood*, but right from the start, despite all his protestations to the
contrary. And the reader is encouraged to look for the Dragon somewhere

in each of the ten stories that comprise *A Good Man is Hard to Find*, the latter an appropriate follow-up to a note she sent to her friends Sally and Robert Fitzgerald some months before the first edition appeared that the book would be dedicated to them: "Nine stories[3] about original sin, with my compliments" (*Collected Works*, 927; December 26, 1954).[4]

In her lectures and throughout her private correspondence, O'Connor defended freely, sometimes fiercely, her own interpretations of her stories. In contrast to her good friends Andrew Lytle and John Hawkes, she claimed that the grandmother in her most widely-read story, "A Good Man is Hard to Find," was emphatically "not pure evil and may be a medium for Grace." This in contrast to Lytle, who "insists that she is a witch, even down to the cat" (*Habit of Being*, 389). She cautioned her readers to "be on the lookout for such things as the action of grace in the Grandmother's soul, and not for the dead bodies" (*Mystery and Manners*, 113). Later she wrote to Hawkes that "when I read this story aloud I get over my interpretation of it—as against yours and Andrew's—fairly well, but I have an unfair advantage, since I sound pretty much like the old lady" (*Habit of Being*, 412). Surely a classic example of Plato's author, or "father"—in this case, mother—coming to the rescue of her written words.[5] If, as Park and others have argued, O'Connor was trying to control the reception of her novels and stories, she was in the long run largely successful. But Park subverts her own case by playing off the letters against the fiction. To her, "the letters shine," in that they reveal a kinder, gentler O'Connor than what comes across in her fiction, and she insists that "we must put the letters first," taking them "as primary and the fiction as a gloss upon them, the black repository of all that the letters do not say, of the rebellion and disappointment and anger which the letters show so thoroughly surmounted that we might almost believe they were never felt" (Park, "Crippled Laughter," 254). On the contrary, the letters are if anything a gloss upon the fiction,

3. "Nine" rather than ten because she had not yet decided to include "A Stroke of Good Fortune."

4. Interestingly, the Cyril quotation in the *Nicene and Post-Nicene Fathers of the Christian Church*, 2nd series (Grand Rapids: Eerdmans, 1978), VII.5 speaks of a "serpent" rather than a dragon, evoking the imagery of Genesis 3 and the serpent in the garden of Eden and linking the stories to "original sin."

5. Even more classic is her reply to an anonymous professor of English who theorized that the climactic action in the story takes place only in the imagination of the old woman's son Bailey. O'Connor's answer begins, " The interpretation of your ninety students and three teachers is fantastic and about as far from my intentions as it could get to be," and ends with the words, "My tone is not meant to be obnoxious. I am in a state of shock" (*Habit of Being*, 436–37).

not the other way around. The question that must be asked is whether the "rebellion and disappointment and anger" which Clark finds in the fiction are surmounted only in the letters, or already in the fiction itself. Has O'Connor read into her violent stories an action of grace or mercy which is not there? In short, has she interpreted her own work correctly, or not?

Even more basic is the question of whether it was ever O'Connor's intention in her letters and lectures to "interpret" her stories. In a letter to Betty Hester she insisted to the contrary that "you cannot read a story from what you get out of a letter" (*Collected Works*, 1000). And she once stated in an interview what interpretation does *not* mean: "So many students approach a story as if it were a problem in algebra: find X and when they find X they can dismiss the rest of it" (*Conversations*, 73–74). Even her introductory note to the second edition of *Wise Blood* was supplied reluctantly and with hesitation. Several months before that edition appeared she wrote to Betty Hester, "You ain't convinced me that there should be an introduction to *Wise Blood*, particularly one that announces the religious significance of the book. I would want no more said about that than that the book is seen from the standpoint of Christian orthodoxy. 'Explanations' are repugnant to me," she concluded, "and to send out a book with directions for its enjoyment is terrible" (*Habit of Being*, 442; June 10, 1961). Even though in practice she freely supplied "explanations" for friends and inquirers, she herself understood that no explanation or interpretation can ever replace the text. It must never "solve the equation," to the degree that the story becomes dispensable. The story itself always trumps the interpretation, however convincing or valid the latter might be. O'Connor's stories are what they are. Whatever she or anyone else has said about them, the reader can always go back to them afresh and allow them to speak again.

The same is true of the parables of Jesus. In one sense, of course, the analogy breaks down because we are comparing oral stories with written ones, but in another sense it stands, because even Jesus's parables have come down to us as literature, the product of Gospel authors who have put into writing both parable and interpretation. But here again the so-called "interpretations" do not truly interpret, least of all to the degree of making the parables themselves redundant. Only a very few of Jesus's parables are supplied with any kind of interpretation,[6] and the so-called

---

6. They come down to just four: the parable of the sower (explained in Matt 13:18–23, Mark 4:13–20, and Luke 8:11–15), the parable of the weeds of the field (explained in Matt 13:36–43), the parable of the net (explained in Matt 13:49–50), and the parable about what defiles (explained in Matt 15:15–20 and Mark 7:17–23). Even though Mark

"interpretations" are never called that within the text itself. None of them are even attempts to tell what the story as a whole means or what its application might be. They serve merely as a kind of scorecard, or cast of characters. For example, in the parable of the sower (Matt 13:3–9//Mark 4:1–9//Luke 8:4–8), they identify the different kinds of soil into which the seed falls, the varying results and the reasons for the results, but they do not identify the sower, much less the kingdom of God, and without such identifications the meaning of the parable is scarcely transparent. In the parable of the weeds of the field (Matt 13:24–30), the interpretation (so-called) does identify the sower as "the Son of man," the field as "the world," the good seed as "the sons of the kingdom," the weeds as "the sons of the evil one," the enemy as "the devil," the harvest as "the end of the age," and the harvesters as "angels" (see Matt 13:36–43). Yet the heart of the story, in which the servants (who remain unidentified) ask the sower whether or not they should uproot the weeds and are told to let wheat and weeds grow together until the harvest, is left untouched. That exchange is what the parable is actually all about, and the so-called "interpretation" says nothing about it. Much the same is true of the parable of the net (Matt 13:47–48). In each case the appended explanations, whether from Jesus himself or from the Gospel writer, seem intended more to reinforce what the first-century readers or hearers already believed about "the end of the age" than to interpret the story.[7] If the explanations are no less the words of Jesus than the parables themselves, then he seems to have explained just enough to prompt the reader or hearer to look further at the parable itself and explore its mysteries. Most of the time, he provided no additonal comment at all. If those critical scholars are right who assume that the explanations were added by the Gospel writers or their sources after the fact, then whoever added them seems to have respected Jesus's own intention to leave his parables largely uninterpreted, and both his immediate hearers and subsequent generations of readers faced with the challenge, "Whoever has ears to hear, let him hear" (Mark 4:9).

As for O'Connor, she too in the end lets go of her stories as every author must, for reading or misreading at the hands of good and bad readers alike. She stated this explicitly once in a letter to Eileen Hall, the editor

---

knows of an occasion when Jesus "explained everything privately to his own disciples" (Mark 4:34), these are the only concrete examples.

7. The parable about that which defiles (Matt 15:11//Mark 7:15) is somewhat different, in that, although the disciples call it a "parable" (Mark 7:17), it is arguably a riddle, which can in fact be "solved for X," although in the nature of riddles still not thereby dispensed with.

of her Diocesan newspaper, apparently in response to a question as to whether she worried about "scandalizing the little ones" (presumably the Catholic faithful): "When you write a novel, if you have been honest about it and if your conscience is clear, then it seems to me you have to leave the rest in God's hands. When the book leaves your hands, it belongs to God. He may use it to save a few souls or to try a few others, but I think that for the writer to worry about this this is to take over God's business" (*Collected Works*, 987; March 10, 1956). The comment is just as relevant to her secular readers as to the scrupulous Catholics about whom she was asked. It is perhaps her most explicit answer to the worries of Plato, Updike, and all those in between about their less than ideal readers. In the same letter, evidently with the violent behavior of some of her own characters in mind, she cites a well-known biblical incident:

> If a novelist wrote a book about Abraham passing his wife Sarah off as his sister—which he did—and allowing her to be taken over by those who wanted her for their lustful purposes—which he did to save his skin—how many Catholics would not be scandalized at the behavior of Abraham? The fact is that in order not to be scandalized, one has to have a whole view of things, which not many of us have (*Collected Works*, 987).

For any critic, reviewer or biographer of someone like Flannery O'Connor, the fear of misunderstanding her is, and should be, just as great as her fear of being misunderstood. Like T. S. Eliot's Prufrock, one cannot help asking,

> Would it have been worth while
> If one, settling a pillow or throwing off a shawl,
> And turning toward the window, should say,
> "That is not it at all,
> That is not what I meant, at all."[8]

The risk of misunderstanding is indeed great, yet O'Connor herself seems to have assumed that those who are familiar with the Bible in all its earthy realism and dark violence are those least likely to be shocked by her fiction, and best equipped to understand it.

With this in mind, my assumptions are, first, that despite what some critics have said, O'Connor *is* a reliable guide to the intent and meaning of her own fiction; second, that her explicit comments do not begin to exhaust the meaning of her stories, any more than Jesus's appended

8. "The Love Song of J. Alfred Prufrock" (Eliot, 6).

"interpretations" in the Gospel narratives actually interpreted his parables; and third, that she knew they did not. Helpful as her comments are, they leave us with the task of interpretation still before us, and with the conviction that the Bible is, if not the only, at least one essential "instrument to plumb meaning—and specifically Christian meaning" from her stories (*Collected Works*, 858). Moreover, they remind all of us who venture to "interpret" O'Connor's fiction that our treasured "readings" of her stories are no substitute for the stories themselves, which should always be kept close at hand, right alongside the present volume. In this book, I have undertaken readings of both her novels, *Wise Blood* and *The Violent Bear It Away*, plus all but two of the stories in her two main collections, *A Good Man Is Hard to Find* and *Everything That Rises Must Converge*. The two exceptions are "A Stroke of Good Fortune" and "A Late Encounter with the Enemy," simply because the biblical themes, if present at all, are so remote that making a case for them would sound like special pleading. O'Connor once described "A Stroke of Good Fortune" as "in its way, Catholic, being about the rejection of life at the source" (that is, in raising the issue of abortion), and yet "too much of a farce to bear the weight" (*Collected Works*, 939). "A Late Encounter with the Enemy," by contrast an affirmation of life at its end, is also something of a farce and a very good one, a satire on Civil War pageantry outside of any apparent theological framework.

3

A Christian *Malgré Lui*

FLANNERY O'CONNOR'S FEAR OF being misunderstood is nowhere more evident than in connection with her first novel, *Wise Blood*. In a long letter to a reviewer named Carl Hartman, she explained at some length what she intended in the novel (*Collected Works*, 919–22; March 2, 1954).[1] Two years later she confided to Betty Hester that Hartman "reviewed Wise Blood and found it dandy and a kind of manifestoe [*sic*] for all us atheists." Humorously comparing her efforts at control to those of the Vatican, she continued, "In time I got into correspondence with him and with a number of Bulls and Enclycals [*sic*] set him straight as to my intentions if not as to my accomplishments. So if he knew it was affirmative, he knew it owing to my having told him so. But he's a nice man" (*Collected Works*, 999; August 24, 1956). Later, in her "Note to the Second Edition" in 1962, she calls it not only a novel "about a Christian *malgré lui*," but "a comic novel," and "as such, very serious, for all comic novels that are any good must be about matters of life and death" (*Collected Works*, 1265). That *Wise Blood* was both "affirmative" and "comic" was not self-evident to its early readers, nor is it to most students today. While the first and second editions are otherwise identical, it makes a difference whether one reads it with or without the prefaced "help to the reader."

1. For Hartman's original review, see Scott and Streight, eds., *Flannery O'Connor: The Contemporary Reviews*, 19–22.

The Failed Nihilist

Even with that help, *Wise Blood* is a difficult starting point from which to introduce students to O'Connor, particularly if one is interested in religious or biblical themes. The latter are present, but seem to be there only to be negated, for Hazel Motes' way is a way of negation. The "gospel" he preaches to the people of Taulkinham is that "there was no Fall because there was nothing to fall from and no Redemption because there was no Fall and no Judgment because there wasn't the first two," and his "Church Without Christ" is the polar opposite of a biblical kingdom of God, in which "The blind see, the lame walk, the lepers are cleansed, the dead rise again, the poor have the gospel preached to them" (Matt 11:5). It is a church "where the blind don't see and the lame don't walk and what's dead stays that way" (59). Such a gospel might have been "good news" indeed to a people who wanted no part of God or Christ or Redemption, yet Hazel is dismissed as just another preacher: "'He's a preacher,' one of the women said, 'Let's go.'" Hazel Motes is a nihilist preaching to nihilists, but with little success. One reason is that none of it matters to them one way or the other, while to him just the opposite is true: "Nothing matters but that Jesus don't exist" (29). Another is that his nihilism, while convincing to most of O'Connor's early readers and critics, is unconvincing to the other characters in the book. They see him just as O'Connor sees him, as a young man obsessed with Jesus. O'Connor, in her letter to Hartman, calls him "a Protestant saint" (919), "the ultimate Protestant" even, yet one who transcends a Protestant world she describes as "the society that reads the Bible and the Sears Roebuck catalogue wrong" (921). Without quite saying so, she identifies him as a crypto-Catholic—a kind of Catholic *malgré lui*.

Hazel's life can be summed up in the words of T. S. Eliot, "In my beginning is my end," and "In my end is my beginning."[2] As the story opens, Mrs. Wally Bee Hitchcock on the train stares at his eyes, "the color of pecan shells and set in deep sockets. The outline of a skull under his skin was plain and insistent" (3), and as it closes, Mrs. Flood, his landlady, sees that "The outline of a skull was plain under his skin and the deep burned eye sockets seemed to lead into the dark tunnel where he had disappeared" (131). His life, like all life, is lived toward death, just as the existentialists were reminding O'Connor's generation. His dreams in the upper berth on the train to Taulkinham are dreams of death. The berth seemed like a coffin, and he remembered the deaths of his grandfather, his two younger

---

2. The first and last lines respectively of Eliot's "East Coker" (Eliot, 123, 129).

brothers, his father, and (later) his mother, all of them put in a box with the lid shut down on them (see 9–10, 14). And his own preaching in the streets of Taulkinham smacks of existentialism as much as nihilism: "Where you come from is gone, where you thought you were going to never was there, and where you are is no good unless you can get away from it. Where is there a place for you to be? No place," and "You needn't to look at the sky because it's not going to open up and show no place behind it. You needn't to search for any hole in the ground to look through into somewhere else" (93). Taken literally Hazel's words convey existential despair, yet in a strange way their cadences also echo the Apostle Paul: "Say not in thy heart: Who shall ascend into heaven? That is, to bring Christ down; Or: Who shall descend into the deep? That is, to bring up Christ again from the dead. But what saith the scripture? The word is nigh thee, even in thy mouth and in thy heart. This is the word of faith which we preach" (Rom 10:6–8; see also Deut 30:11–14). Small wonder that Hazel Motes is repeatedly mistaken for a Christian preacher!

As for the sky over Taulkinham, O'Connor has already glimpsed it for us, "underpinned with long silver streaks that looked like scaffolding and depth on depth behind it were thousands of stars that all seemed to be moving very slowly as if they were about some vast construction work that involved the whole order of the universe and would take all time to complete" (19). Here if anywhere in the novel, God is at work. The sky, with its "vast construction work" evokes the book of Revelation ("Behold I make all things new," Rev 21:5), eloquently contradicting Hazel's sermon, but O'Connor is quick to add, "No one was paying any attention to the sky." Nor, it seems, to Hazel's sermons.

"In my beginning is my end" implies not only a life lived toward death, but in Hazel's case a life lived in the shadow of Jesus. In his half sleep on the train, he remembers his grandfather, "a circuit preacher, a waspish old man who had ridden over three counties with Jesus hidden in his head like a stinger" (9–10). Like John the Baptist, who believed that "God is able of these stones to raise up children to Abraham" (Matt 3:9), his grandfather used to tell the people of Eastrod, Tennessee, over and over again that "They were like stones!"

> But Jesus had died to redeem them! Jesus was so soul-hungry that He had died, one death for all, but He would have died every soul's death for one! Did they understand that? Did they understand that for each stone soul, He would have died ten million deaths, had His arms and legs stretched on the cross and nailed ten million times for one of them? . . . Did they know

that even for that boy there, for that mean sinful unthinking boy standing there with his dirty hands clenching and unclenching at his sides, Jesus would die ten million deaths before He would let him lose his soul? He would chase him over the waters of sin! Did they doubt that Jesus could walk on the waters of sin? That boy had been redeemed and Jesus wasn't going to leave him ever. Jesus would never let him forget he was redeemed. What did the sinner think there was to be gained? Jesus would have him in the end! (10–11)

The image of Jesus stayed with him, "moving from tree to tree in the back of his mind, a wild ragged figure motioning him to turn around and come off into the dark where he was not sure of his footing, where he might be walking on the water and not know it and then suddenly know it and drown." Haze did not want to walk those waters, nor like Peter have to call on Jesus to rescue him. The way to avoid Jesus, he thought, was to avoid sin, and he had confidence in his ability to do that. "When he was eighteen and the army called him, he saw the war as a trick to lead him into temptation, and he would have shot his foot except that he trusted himself to get back in a few months, uncorrupted." He planned to be gone four months, but he was gone four years, and "didn't get back, even for a visit" (11).

When Haze went off to war, he took with him "a black Bible and a pair of silver-rimmed spectacles that had belonged to his mother," and it was the only book he read: "He didn't read it often but when he did he wore his mother's glasses." His reading of the Bible through his mother's glasses was resolutely Protestant. It helped him say no to save his soul when his buddies wanted him to go to a brothel with them. They told him that "nobody was interested in his goddam soul unless it was the priest and he managed to answer that no priest taking orders from no pope was going to tamper with his soul." But his mother's glasses "tired his eyes so that after a short time he was always obliged to stop." When his buddies "told him he didn't have any soul and left for their brothel," he finally decided to believe them, seeing "the opportunity here to get rid of it without corruption, to be converted to nothing instead of to evil. The army sent him halfway around the world and forgot him. . . . He had all the time he could want to study his soul in and assure himself that it was not there" (12). And so, as the novel begins, he is on his way to Taulkinham not as an evildoer but as a nihilist and atheist, by no means a demonic or Satanic figure, but like most of O'Connor's nihilists a candidate for grace.

His grandfather's words, "Jesus would have him in the end," are prophetic. He never escapes them.

When Haze arrives in Taulkinham, the people he meets keep seeing him not the way he sees himself but the way his grandfather saw him. A taxi driver mistakes him for a preacher because of his black hat and "a look in your face somewheres" (16). A blind man (Asa Hawks, not yet named) says, "I can hear the urge for Jesus in his voice" (27), and later calls him a "Jesus-hog" (62). His sidekick Enoch Emery tells him, "I knew when I first seen you you didn't have nobody nor nothing but Jesus. I seen you and I knew it" (33). Leora Watts, the prostitute he first stays with, exclaims "That Jesus-seeing hat!" as she reaches for his black hat and puts it on her own head (34). Their voices, not Hazel's own, are the reliable narrative voices in the story, and they confirm O'Connor's intention to present him as "a Christian *malgré lui*" and "a Protestant saint." Even his blasphemous denials of Jesus are subverted by what sound like remnants of a very orthodox theology. In almost the same breath in which he says, "I don't believe in sin," and "Nothing matters but that Jesus don't exist," he says "If I was in sin I was in it before I ever committed any. There's no change come in me" (29), words that could as easily have come from some seventeenth-century Puritan divine speaking of original sin. Later he explains further to an uncomprehending truck driver: "There's no person a whoremonger, who wasn't something worse first . . . That's not the sin, nor blasphemy. The sin came before them," only to add the obligatory words of blasphemy, "Jesus is a trick on niggers" (43).

Traces of a rather conventional morality also appear to have survived intact, finely honed in fact, when Sabbath Lily Hawks tells him she is a bastard: "'A bastard?" he murmured. He couldn't see how a preacher who had blinded himself for Jesus could have a bastard" (66). When she insisted that "I am a bastard and a bastard shall not enter the kingdom of heaven,"[3] he turned pale and replied, "You must be mixed up. Your daddy blinded himself," and "You mean in his youth he didn't believe but he came to? . . . Is that what you mean or ain't it?'" (67). He cannot let go of it. Even when he tries to resume his blasphemy he is thwarted. When he tells Sabbath Lily, "I believe in a new kind of Jesus," and "My church is the Church Without Christ," she asks him, "Can a bastard be saved in it?" and he tells her, "There's no such thing as a bastard in the Church Without Christ," because "Everything is all one. A bastard wouldn't be any different from

3. "A bastard shall not enter the kingdom of heaven!" appears to be based on Deuteronomy 23:2 in the King James Version (the one Sabbath Lily would have known): "A bastard shall not enter into the congregation of the Lord, even to his tenth generation." Instead of "bastard" the Douay Version has "a mamzer, that is to say, one born of a prostitute" (which would have made little sense to Sabbath Lily!).

anybody else." Yet his own answer fails to satisfy him, "for something in his mind was already contradicting him and saying that a bastard couldn't, that there was only one truth—that Jesus was a liar—and that her case was hopeless" (69). In the end, his "Church Without Christ" seems to have more in common with conventional morality than with the biblical kingdom of God, where "many that are first shall be last; and the last shall be first" (Matt 19:30) and, as Jesus told the Pharisees, "the publicans and the harlots shall go into the kingdom of God before you" (Matt 21:31). Ironically, the voice in his head speaking up for conventional morality merely accents his conviction that "Jesus was a liar."

Enoch and the New Jesus

The story line in *Wise Blood* is driven to its horrific conclusion—Hazel Motes's self-blinding and eventual death—by three increasingly surreal episodes told in fairly rapid succession: first, Enoch Emery's theft of a "new jesus" to satisfy Haze; second, Haze's murder of Solace Layfield, his fraudulent double; and third, the loss of his car at the hands of a rogue patrolman. In short, it is driven by "wise blood," Enoch's first and then Haze's own, and only then by a dramatic intervention from without—whether from hell or heaven is left to the reader to decide.

It all begins with Enoch, who is in the story mainly to show Hazel Motes the true implications of what he has been saying. From the start, Enoch's naïve literalism trumps Haze's nihilism, and in his own way Enoch knows it. The first reference to the book's title comes when Enoch tells Haze, "You act like you think you got wiser blood than anybody else," but claims, "I'm the one has it. Not you. Me" (33). We learn shortly that "He had wise blood like his daddy" (44), and it is his blood, the instinct he cannot control, that leads him to the park, to a museum, and to a "new jesus." And when he has done what he has to do, his blood leads him right out of the story, not unlike the biblical Enoch, who "walked with God, and was seen no more: because God took him" (Gen 5:24). "You may not see me again," he tells the waitress at the Paris Diner, "the way I am," and he quickly carries out his blood's plan of becoming Gonga, the fake gorilla who has long fascinated him, by commandeering a gorilla suit at the expense of its unfortunate owner in the back of a van (110–11). Before he puts the suit on, he digs a hole and buries his clothes, an act which could be read theologically as a kind of conversion in reverse. O'Connor surely knew that change of clothing is a common New Testament metaphor for conversion (see Eph 4:22, 24, Col 3:9–10), but as narrator she cautions us here that "Burying his clothers was not a symbol to him of burying his former self; he only knew he wouldn't need them any more" (111).

Finally Enoch begins to act out his new gorilla identity, and for a moment at least, "No gorilla in existence, whether in the jungles of Africa or California, or in New York City in the finest apartment in the world, was happier at that moment than this one, whose god had finally rewarded it" (112). He had anticipated that in meeting Gonga "he was going to be rewarded after all and have the supreme moment he had expected" (100), but was disappointed when the man in the Gonga suit told him, "You go to hell" (102). The theme of reward points unmistakably toward the biblical Enoch, who according to the book of Hebrews "had testimony that he pleased God. But without faith it is impossible to please God. For he that cometh to God must believe that he is; and is *a rewarder to them that seek him*" (Heb 11:5–6, emphasis added).[4] Enoch Emery is a comic parody of the biblical Enoch, who like him "was seen no more" (Gen 5:24). Our last glimpse is of a lonely gorilla sitting on a rock, staring "over the valley at the uneven skyline of the city" (112). He has just reached out his hand to a couple sitting on a bench only to see them flee in terror, confirming what he has said all along: "I ain't never been to such an unfriendly place before" (25), and "nobody here'll have anything to do with nobody else. They ain't friendly" (32). Enoch and his biblical namesake seem to move in opposite directions, the one toward God and the other toward his animal nature, yet they have one thing in common. They are not at home in the world—and neither is Hazel Motes.

The episode of the "new jesus" begins when Enoch overhears Haze, desperate to get rid of Jesus once and for all, crying out to a very small audience, "What you need is something to take the place of Jesus, something that would speak plain. The Church Without Christ don't have a Jesus but it needs one! It needs a new jesus! It needs one that's all man, without blood to waste, and it needs one that don't look like any other man so you'll look at him. Give me such a jesus, you people. Give me such

4. George Kilcourse (*Flannery O'Connor's Religious Imagination*, 60) makes a connection to a different Enoch, according to Genesis 4:17 the name both of Cain's son and the city Cain built: "St. Augustine mentions Enoch and the secular city as opposed to the heavenly city. Enoch personifies for O'Connor the genius of the secular city. It is a place composed of country boys who have come to town; she anticipates the displacement that characterizes modern American metropolises where virtually everyone has come from somewhere else." Strangely, Kilcourse does not mention the better known Enoch of Genesis 5:24.

a new jesus and you'll see how far the Church Without Christ can go!"
(80). "Take counsel from your blood," Haze continued, "and come into the
Church Without Christ and maybe somebody will bring us a new jesus
and we'll all be saved by the sight of him!" (80–81). But it is Enoch's blood
that now takes over: "Listen here," he whispers, "I got him! I mean I can
get him! You know! Him! Him I shown you to. You seen him yourself"
(81). Enoch is remembering an earlier moment when the two of them had
stared together into a glass case at a museum in the city park, at "a man in
the case. It was the man Enoch was looking for. He was about three feet
long. He was naked and a dried yellow color and his eyes were drawn almost shut as if a giant block of steel were falling down on top of him" (56).

Thrilled that he has already seen the "new jesus" that Haze wants,
Enoch prepares a kind of tabernacle in his room without quite knowing
why (74–75), and in the end steals the shrunken mummy from the museum and hides it in his room before delivering it to Haze (97–98). When
he does deliver it, he leaves it with Sabbath Lily Hawks because, as she
tells him, "My man is sick today and sleeping" (103). When she sees the
mummy, Sabbath is "held by whatever it was that was familiar about him.
She had never known anyone who looked like him before, but there was
something in him of everyone she had ever known, as if they had all been
rolled into one person and killed and shrunk and dried" (104). By this
time, Haze in the next room is awake and packing to leave for another
city. In doing so he notices but does not touch "the Bible that had sat like
a rock in the bottom of the bag for the last few years," and with it his
mother's glasses. He puts the glasses on and sees in the mirror first "his
mother's face in his," and then, before he can take the glasses off, Sabbath
Lily holding the mummy like a madonna with the Christ child, saying
"Call me Momma now." Haze is motionless at first, but then his hand
"lunged and snatched the shriveled body and threw it against the wall.
The head popped and the trash inside sprayed out in a little cloud of dust."
He snatched what was left off the floor and and hurled it away through an
outside door. So much for the "new jesus" (105–6).

Sabbath Lily knew immediately that Haze "didn't want nothing but
Jesus!" Like the taxi driver, and Leora Watts, and Asa Hawks and Enoch
Emery, and the people of Taulkinham, she understands Hazel Motes better than he understands himself. They all knew, even if he did not, that
"Jesus would have him in the end!" He asked for a "new jesus" and Enoch,
ever the literalist, found it for him. But now that he sees it, through his
mother's glasses, it repels him and he destroys it, leaving him with his

grandfather's Jesus, the Jesus who "would have him in the end!" Hazel himself, of course, does not yet see it that way. If Enoch took the new jesus literally, someone else did as well, Onnie Jay Holy (*a.k.a.* Hoover Shoats), a huckster who tried to turn the Church Without Christ into a profit-making venture. Instead of finding it for Haze, he expected Haze to produce it: "You know, friend, I certainly would like to see this new jesus," he had told Haze, "I never heard a idear before that had more in it than that one. All it would need is a little promotion." This gave Haze the chance to explain himself, as he never had a chance to do with Enoch or Sabbath Lily. "Listen here," he told Onnie Jay, "you get away from here. I've seen all of you I want to. There's no such thing as any new jesus. That ain't anything but a way to say something," adding that "there's no such thing or person," and "No such thing exists!" "That's the trouble with you innerleckchuls," Onnie Jay Holy replied, "you don't never have nothing to show for what you're saying" (90).

From the time I first read it, the narrative of the "new jesus" sounded to me like a comic parody of certain trends in academic biblical scholarship since the Enlightenment. *Wise Blood* has frequently been understood as a satire on existentialism, or, in Onnie Jay's words, on "innerleckchuls" generally. But the "new jesus" targets more specifically the pretensions of modern biblical criticism. The nineteenth century "quest of the historical Jesus" so carefully documented by Albert Schweitzer was fueled by a desire to find alternatives—almost any alternative—to the Jesus of traditional orthodoxy, Haze's grandfather's Jesus who "could walk on the waters of sin," and "would have died ten million deaths" for one lost soul (11). As we have seen, O'Connor reviewed works of biblical scholarship with respect, yet respect was by no means inconsistent with satire. She satirized that which she took seriously, whether existentialism or nihilism or academic biblical criticism—or even the Bible itself. The reader is compelled to wonder if she is suggesting here that such "quests" for a different Jesus often end up with just what Haze was asking for, "one that's all man, without blood to waste" (80), in short, a shriveled up bloodless mummy?

O'Connor could hardly have anticipated the "New Quest" of the historical Jesus that began some years after her death (Schweitzer's first Quest having come to naught), nor the famous—to some, notorious—Jesus Seminar of the 1980s and 1990s, but if she had lived long enough to read the programmatic words of the Seminar's founder, Robert W. Funk, she would have smiled. "We require a new, liberating fiction," Funk once wrote, [5] "one that squares with the best knowledge we can now accumulate and one that transcends self-serving ideologies. And we need a fiction that we recognize to be fictive," something he further characterized as "a new narrative of Jesus, a new gospel, if you will, that places Jesus differently in the grand scheme, the epic story." Even the Seminar's primary test for establishing historicity, the so-called "criterion of dissimilarity" dictating that the historical Jesus must be unique, resembling neither the Judaism of his day nor the Christianity that came into being as a result of his life and death, corresponds to Hazel's own criterion that the "new jesus" must be "one that don't look like any other man so you'll look at him" (80)! Now that Haze has looked at him, he does not like what he sees, yet he stubbornly insists, "I've seen the only truth there is!" (107). If his "new jesus" repels him, it doesn't matter because it was only a metaphor anyway, only "a way to say something" (90). Two more things must happen before he comes face to face with who he is and where he is going.

THE DOUBLE

Enoch Emery's story overlaps that of Solace Layfield, Haze's double or alter ego. Having parted company with Hoover Shoats, Haze is preaching from his car at some length to people coming out of the Odeon Theater. "Your conscience is a trick," he tells them, "it don't exist though you may think it does, and if you think it does, you had best get it out in the open and hunt it down and kill it, because it's no more than your face in the mirror is or your shadow behind you" (93–94). Just then, as if on cue, he becomes aware of "a high rat-colored car," with "a man in a glare-blue suit and white hat" sitting "up on the nose of it." It is as if Hazel Motes is looking at his own shadow sitting on his own car, or at himself as in a mirror: "He was so struck with how gaunt and thin he looked in the illusion that he stopped preaching. He had never pictured himself that way before. The man he saw was hollow-chested and carried his neck thrust forward and his arms down by his side; he looked there as if he were waiting for some signal he was afraid he might not catch" (94). By then Hoover Shoats is introducing the stranger as "the True Prophet" and giving him the signal to begin. In a "high nasal singsong voice" he repeatedly chants his fraudulent message, a cheap imitation of Haze's own: "The unredeemed are redeeming

5. I can no longer locate the original source ot Funk's words. My quote of him is taken from an article I wrote about O'Connor and the Jesus Seminar more than twenty years ago (Michaels, "Off on a New Quest," 4).

themselves and the new jesus is at hand! Watch for this miracle! Help yourselves to salvation in the Holy Church of Christ Without Christ!" ("It don't make no difference how many Christs you add to the name," Hoover Shoats had said, "if you don't add none to the meaning, friend.") A woman touches Haze's elbow and asks him, "Him and you twins?" Haze, quickly finishing up his unfinished sermon, says only, "If you don't hunt it down and kill it, it'll hunt you down and kill you," and gets in his car and drives off. "He's nuts," she tells a bystander, "I never seen no twins that hunted each other down" (94–95). Haze's theme of hunting down one's conscience and killing it has morphed into the prospect of hunting down and killing a person, a real twin.

After Enoch and the "new jesus" disappear from the story, the grim prospect becomes reality. "On his second night out," we are told, "working with his hired Prophet and the Holy Church of Christ Without Christ, Hoover Shoats made fifteen dollars and thirty-five cents clear." The Prophet is now formally introduced as "Solace Layfield; he had consumption and a wife and six childen and being a Prophet was as much work as he wanted to do." He does not know that he is being closely watched, and followed by another "high rat-colored car." Finally, "'You ain't true,' Haze said, 'What do you get up on top of a car and say you don't believe in what you do believe in for?'" and "You believe in Jesus" (113–14). The glaring irony is that Hazel Motes's words are just as true of himself as they are of the unfortunate Solace Layfield. When he proceeds to murder his fraudulent double by running over him again and again (114–15), Haze thinks he is murdering his conscience, just as he told the crowds in Taulkinham to do. But in reality he is murdering part of himself, his inauthentic self, the part of him that has been denying what his grandfather and mother knew, what the taxi driver and Leora Watts and Asa Hawks and Sabbath Lily and Enoch all knew, and what O'Connor told us in her Note to the Second Edition: that *he too* is standing on top of a car and claiming not to believe in what he does in fact believe in—his grandfather's Jesus, "the ragged figure who moves from tree to tree in the back of his mind" (1265).

In one sense, of course, Solace Layfield is a real person, a tragic character in the story, with "consumption and a wife and six children," but in another he is merely Haze's alter ego, whether (as Haze thought) the embodiment of his conscience, or (as it will turn out) the next-to-last barrier between him and Jesus. Like a priest, Haze presides over Solace Layfield's death, hearing his confession even as he tells him to shut up. His verdict on the two things he cannot stand, "a man that ain't true and one that mocks what is" (115), amounts finally to a verdict on himself. While O'Connor credited Haze with "integrity" for not being able to get rid of the "ragged figure" of Jesus, it must be acknowledged that his "integrity" is a long time in coming. For most of the book he lacks integrity, as he tries mightily to do what he is in the end unable to do, and even this late in the story he is still trying. His last refuge is his car.

THE PATROLMAN

The next morning Hazel Motes sets off in his own "high rat-colored car," the broken down Essex that has been his true home and his pulpit since early in the story, to make a new start with his Church Without Christ in a new city. He has the gas tank filled at a service station, where he learns that both the gas tank and the radiator are leaking and that the rear tire will not last. He replies that "this car is just beginning its life. A lightning bolt couldn't stop it!" and pushes on anyway. His fierce attempts at blasphemy are so informative as to what the New Testament gospel actually is that they lack credibility as blasphemy: "As for the Jesus who was reported to have been born in Bethlehem and crucified on Calvary for man's sins, Haze said, He was too foul a notion for a sane person to carry around in his head" (116; the capitalization of "He" is a particularly nice touch). On the highway stood "a sign that said, 'Jesus Died for YOU,' which he saw and deliberately did not read" (117).

Presently a black patrol car comes into view, and a patrolman with "a red pleasant face and eyes the color of clear fresh ice" motions Haze to pull over. They both agree that Haze was not speeding, nor driving on the wrong side of the road, but, "'I just don't like your face,' the patrolman said. 'Where's your license?'" Then, when Haze admits that he has no license: "'Well,' the patrolman said in a kindly voice, 'I don't reckon *you* need one.'" He then asks Haze to drive to the top of the next hill "to see the view from up there, puttiest view you ever did see" (117). Haze does so, and the patrolman asks him to get out of the car: "I think you could see better if you was out." Haze gets out and looks over a thirty-foot embankment "into a partly burnt pasture where there was one scrub cow lying near a puddle," and "in the middle distance there was a one-room shack with a buzzard standing hunch-shouldered on the roof." The patrolman then pushes the old Essex over the embankment, scaring off the cow and the buzzard, so that "The car landed on its top, with the three wheels that stayed on, spinning. The motor bounced out and rolled some distance away and various odd pieces scattered this way and that." Explaining his earlier remark that Haze did not need a license, the patrolman says, "Them that don't have a car, don't need a license" (118).

At this point the reader, and Haze too, is afforded another glimpse of "the blank grey sky that went on, depth after depth, into space," the same sky that no one in Taulkinham was looking at when Haze first arrived there (see 19). The effect on Haze is that "His knees bent under him and he sat down on the edge of the embankment with his feet hanging over." His last refuge, his last means of escape from Jesus, is gone. When the patrolman asks him, "Could I give you a lift to where you was going?" and "Where was you going?" and "Was you going anywheres?" his answer is "No." And when the patrolman puts his hand on Haze's shoulder and anxiously persists, "You hadn't planned to go anywheres?" he only "shook his head. His face didn't change and he didn't turn it toward the patrolman. It seemed to be concentrated on space" (118). All the plans for a new start in a new city with the Church Without Christ have disappeared. Without hesitation Hazel Motes walks the three hours back to town, buys a tin bucket and a sack of quicklime, and blinds himself (119).

The bizarre encounter with the patrolman prompts the question, "What just happened here?" and "Who was this patrolman?" There is, on the face of it, a certain justice in Hazel Motes getting his comeuppance after the brutal murder of Solace Layfield, but there is no causal connection between the two events. His crime goes unpunished, and he is then punished for no reason. The patrolman stops him only because he does not like his face. The destruction of the car is gratuitous, in that sense an act of "grace," but how can an officer of the law be an agent of grace, and what kind of grace is it that sends a man on his way to blindness and death? I vividly recall a conference I once attended at Conception Abbey in Missouri in 1987, at which Flannery O'Connor's friend Sally Fitzgerald gave a lecture. In the question period I asked her if perhaps the patrolman in this sequence might have been an angel. She seemed pleased, and later when I asked her to sign my copy of *Three by Flannery O'Connor*, to which she had written the introduction, she wrote in it, "For Ramsey Michaels, who knows an angel when he sees one. Sally Fitzgerald." Of course one is always pleased when others agree with one's own view, and I have since had it verified that this was indeed Sally Fitzgerald's view.

Were we right? Do the patrolman's "kindly voice," his repeated offer to take Haze where he was going, and his body language in leaning ever closer and putting his hand on Haze's shoulder add up to a beneficent, even angelic, intention, or do they simply compound his act of police brutality? One other incident in the novel invites comparison: earlier, when he was unable to get the car started after his failed seduction of Sabbath Lily, Haze walked half a mile to an old gas station, and the man who was there drove them back to the stalled Essex, where he "opened up the hood and studied the inside for a while. He was a one-armed man with two sandy-colored teeth and eyes that were slate blue and thoughtful" (71). Then he "sat down on the ground and eased under the Essex. He wore hightop shoes and gray socks. He stayed under the car a long time." Finally, "he eased himself out and wiped his face with a piece of flannel rag he had in his pocket." Haze and Sabbath got into the car and he pushed it, and "After a few hundred yards the Essex began to belch and gasp and jiggle. Haze said, "I told you, didn't I? This car'll get me anywhere I want to go," and asked, "What do I owe you?" "Nothing," the man said, "not a thing," and refused to take anything even for the gas. Haze thanked him, but told Sabbath Lily "I don't need no favors from him." Finally, as the man's pickup pulled alongside at the end of the dirt road, Haze told him again, "I told you this car would get me anywhere I wanted to go," and the man replied with his longest speech yet: "Some things . . . 'll get some folks somewheres" (71–72). Here too we are afforded a glimpse of the sky: "The blinding white cloud had turned into a bird with long thin wings and was disappearing in the opposite di-rection" (72)—this at the end of a chapter that began with an image of the same sky, "just a little lighter blue than his suit, clear and even, with only one cloud in it, a large blinding white one with curls and a beard" (66).

Mercy and judgement, both from the sky, or so it seems. The one-armed man's kindness, like the patrolman's cruelty, is gratuitous, free, an act of grace or mercy, but unlike the patrolman's cruelty, easily recogniz-able as mercy. That is not always the case, for mercy and judgment look very much alike in O'Connor's fiction. If these two cameo appearances are appearances of angels, the first allowed Hazel, mercifully, to travel a bit further in his Essex, while the second, just as mercifully, stopped him in his tracks.

"In my end is my beginning"

The "blinding" cloud in the sky is perhaps a subtle hint of how the story will end. Another, not so subtle, hint comes in the preceding chapter, where we learn of the fraudulent self-blinding of Sabbath's father, the evangelist Asa Hawks: "He had preached for an hour on the blindness of

Paul, working himself up until he saw himself struck blind by a divine flash of lightning and, with courage enough then, he had thrust his hand into the basket of wet lime and streaked them down his face; but he hadn't been able to let any of it get into his eyes" (65). In retrospect, Hawks attributed his lofty intentions to "devils," and his abject failure to follow through to Jesus, who drove the devils away: "He fancied Jesus, Who had expelled them, was standing there too, beckoning to him; and he had fled out of the tent into the alley and disappeared." Still, he claimed to have actually carried out the blinding "to justify his belief that Christ had redeemed him," and when Sabbath Lily had told Haze, "Anybody that blinded himself for justification ought to be able to save you," he had replied, "Nobody with a good car needs to be justified" (64). But now, without his "good car," he emphatically will need to be "justified," and even though he has learned in the meantime that Hawks' self-blinding was fraudulent, he will seek "justification" in the same way.

Religious readings have routinely noticed parallels between Haze's so-called "conversion" and Paul's Damascus road experience, on the ground that Asa Hawks viewed Paul as a role model ("He blinded Paul," 63). Some have gone further, to the point of comparing Haze's murder of Solace Layfield and the stoning of Stephen, or Paul's light from heaven and Haze's remark that "A lightning bolt couldn't stop" his car, or even comparing Haze's car to Paul's horse—a horse conspicuous in medieval iconography but nonexistent in the New Testament! (for example Ragen, *A Wreck on the Road to Damascus*, 148–55). None of this is convincing. Paul obviously did not blind himself, his blinding was only temporary, and his conversion is linked not to his blindness but quite explicitly to the recovery of his sight (see Acts 9:18). Here then is where *Wise Blood* becomes problematic, especially for those who want to believe with O'Connor herself that Hazel Motes is redeemed. Here if anywhere religious and secular readings part company. Secular readings tend to be "resistant" readings, on the ground that the stories themselves speak louder and clearer than anything O'Connor has to say about them. Secular readers do not, for the most part, find *Wise Blood*, and in particular its ending, either as "comic" or as "affirmative" as O'Connor claimed. Religious readings are for the most part "compliant" readings, accepting O'Connor's own interpretations of her fiction wherever these are known. Hazel Motes' self-blinding, however, puts even the distinctly religious readings to the test, and not all of them find Haze's actions redemptive, or even acceptable. Brian Ingraffia, for example, critiquing the novel from the standpoint of Reformation

Protestantism, argues that "religious readings of O'Connor do not necessarily involve accepting her own theological interpretations of her fiction, or the theology that she incarnates in her fiction" (Ingraffia, "'If Jesus Existed,'" 78). Admittedly, the book's language invites just such a critique with its references to "justification" and being "justified," for justification in both Protestant and Roman Catholic thought is, in the words of the Apostle Paul, "by faith, without the works of the law" (Rom 3:28).

Ingraffia's critique centers on two closely-related issues: first, the notion that Haze's self-blinding, compounded by acts of self-torture, including stones and broken glass in his shoes, and barbed wire around his chest (125–26), amounts to seeking redemption "through a renunciation of the world and of the body" (Ingraffia, 80); second, Haze's claim that this is how he must "pay," because, as he now insists, "I'm not clean" (127). Ingraffia finds the latter inconsistent with justification by faith, and the former directly contrary to the New Testament and Christian theology, including O'Connor's own theology, and more in line with an early heresy known as Manicheism. Regarding Manicheism, O'Connor herself once wrote, "The Manicheans separated spirit and matter. To them all material things were evil. They sought pure spirit and tried to approach the infinite directly without any mediation of matter. This is also pretty much the modern spirit, and for the sensibility infected with it, fiction is hard if not impossible to write because fiction is so very much an incarnational art" (*Mystery and Manners,* 68). It is evident from this quotation, and from her fiction generally, that O'Connor roundly rejected Manicheism, embracing instead its opposite, a Christian sacramentalism based on the Christ who became flesh. Yet Frederick Asals, long before Ingraffia's article, concluded that "*Wise Blood* is in its deepest implications a 'Manichean' book'" (*The Imagination of Extremity,* 58). Without going quite that far, Ingraffia claims that Haze himself "renounces the world and his body, acting out his Manichean theology" (Ingraffia, 80). If so, is O'Connor herself implicated? Did she or did she not approve Hazel Motes' horrific actions?

There is some evidence that she did approve, at least up to a point. In a letter to her friend John Hawkes she wrote, "everything works toward its true end, or away from it, everything is ultimately either saved or lost. Haze is saved by virtue of having wise blood; it's too wise for him ultimately to deny Christ. Wise blood has to be these people's means of grace—they have no sacraments. The religion of the South is a do-it-yourself religion, something which I as a Catholic find painful and touching and grimly comic" (*Collected Works,* 1107). If O'Connor did approve Haze's actions, even to the limited degree implied by this quotation, can they be accurately described as Manichean? She seems rather to view them as the "do-it-yourself" equivalent of sacraments. While "do-it-yourself" may sound patronizing, it is not. O'Connor is deadly serious, and quick to add that she shares "the same fundamental doctrines of sin and redemption" with the rural southern Protestants of whom she writes. Hazel Motes tortures his body not because the body is evil or because it is something that can be dispensed with, but precisely because the body matters. Haze's repentance must be not only "spiritual," written in his heart, but physical, inscribed on his very flesh. "Rend your hearts and not your garments," the prophet wrote (Joel 2:13), but Hazel Motes needs to rend his garments as well—the garments of his own flesh. His is a religion not of the Old Testament but of the New, where the Word becomes human flesh.

In short, Ingraffia is partly right. Like Enoch Emery, Hazel Motes is not at home in the world and without question *has* renounced the world, but he has *not* renounced his body. Instead, he has made it the visible sacrament of his redemption. Like Paul and the other apostles, he has become "a spectacle to the world and to angels and to men" (1 Cor 4:9), and consequently "the refuse of this world, the offscouring of all, even until now" (4:13). Admittedly it is not that simple, for as Ingraffia reminds us (83), Paul "is not referring to self-imposed suffering but rather to the suffering he has endured for the sake of the Gospel, that is, the persecutions he has suffered as a Christian witness." This is a legitimate point, and must be taken into account as well in connection with Paul's claim to be "Always bearing about in our body the mortification of Jesus, that the life also of Jesus may be made manifest in our bodies" (2 Cor 4:10), or his aspiration to "fill up those things that are wanting of the sufferings of Christ, in my flesh," sufferings which unlike Haze's are "for his body, which is the church" (Col 1:24).

Nor is Hazel Motes redeemed if redemption, or justification, depends solely on faith. While one may agree with O'Connor that Haze's blood is "too wise for him ultimately to deny Christ," one must also agree with Ingraffia that he never explicitly confesses his faith in Christ either. Does he do so implicitly? His landlady, Mrs. Flood, tells him that what he has done is "not normal. It's like one of them gory stories, it's something people have quit doing—like boiling in oil or being a saint or walling up cats." "They ain't quit doing it as long as I'm doing it," he replies, and she can only conclude, "You must believe in Jesus or you wouldn't do these foolish things"—a slightly different version of what people have been saying about him all along, except that she goes on to define his "belief in Jesus" in distinctly Catholic terms: "You must have been lying to me when you named your fine church.[6] I wouldn't be surprised if you weren't some kind of a agent of the pope or got some connection with something funny" (127). More telling, perhaps, was his comment to her earlier when she claimed to be as good "not believing in Jesus as a many a one that does." "You're better," he told her, "If you believed in Jesus, you wouldn't be so good" (125)—this coupled with his own acknowledgement that "I'm not clean." If he is not "clean" or "good," the implication is that he does believe in Jesus and is, consequently, convicted of his sin. Nevertheless, at this point Haze is not defined by "faith" in the sense of believing the doctrines he formerly denied—the Fall, Redemption, and Judgment—but rather by a series of dramatic actions. As O'Connor put it in her letter, it is not a matter of "correcting his practical heresies" but of "working them out dramatically" (*Collected Works*,1107).

In this respect Hazel Motes' "Christian experience," if we may call it that, echoes not so much the letters of Paul as a whole class of pronouncements of Jesus in the Gospels, sayings about a topsy-turvy world in which things are not what they seem: the way up is down, the poor are rich and the rich are poor, the blind are those who see, and life comes through death. They are found in each of the four Gospels, and they can be quickly sampled.

> With respect to status: "And whosoever shall exalt himself shall be humbled; and he that shall humble himself shall be exalted" (Matt 23:12).

> With respect to riches: "If thou wilt be perfect, go sell what thou hast and give to the poor and thou shalt have treasure in heaven" (Matt 19:21).

> With respect to bodily mutilation: "And if thy hand or thy foot scandalize thee, cut if off and cast it from thee. It is better for thee to go into life maimed or lame than, having two hands or two feet, to be cast into everlasting fire. And, if thy eye scandalize thee, pluck it out and cast if from thee. It is better for thee having one eye to enter into life than, having two eyes, to be cast into hell fire" (Matt 18:8–9; see also 5:29–30).

6. When he first tried to rent a room from Mrs. Flood, she had asked him about his "Church Without Christ": "'Protestant?' she asked suspiciously, 'or something foreign?' He said no mam, it was Protestant" (60).

With respect to relationships, and life itself: "If any man come to me and hate not his father and mother, and wife and childen and brethren and sisters, yea and his own life also, he cannot be my disciple" (Luke 14:26); "If any man will follow me, let him deny himself and take up his cross and follow me. For whosoever will save his life will lose it; and whosoever shall lose his life for my sake and the gospel shall save it" (Mark 8:34–35); "Unless the grain of wheat falling into the ground die, itself remaineth alone. But if it die, it bringeth forth much fruit. He that loveth his life shall lose it, and he that hateth his life in this world keepeth it unto life eternal" (John 12:25).

Finally, with respect to blindness, Hazel Motes' first step toward losing his life: "For judgment I am come into this world; that they who see not may see; and that they who see may become blind" (John 9:39).

The last of these passages deserves some elaboration. Jesus' pronouncement begins strangely, in that giving sight to the blind, as he has just done in the preceding narrative (John 9:1–38) is not, on the face of it, an act of "judgment." The accent falls rather on the second half of the saying, "that they who see may become blind." Jesus is then asked by some Pharisees, "Are we also blind?" and he replies, "If you were blind, you should not have sin; but now you say: We see. Your sin remaineth" (vv. 40–41).

Hazel Motes, near the beginning of his street preaching in Taulkinham, had shouted at the crowd, "Don't I have eyes in my head? Am I a blind man?" (31), and much later, even after the fiasco of the "new jesus," he shouts at Sabbath Lily Hawks, "I've seen the only truth there is!" (107). He too, like the Pharisees, knew that he could "see," and Jesus might well have told him that he needed to "become blind." But the difference is that now that he is literally blind, Haze does not claim the promise, "If you were blind, you should not have sin." Instead, he insists, "I'm not clean." Consequently, he must "pay." This is perhaps the most formidable challenge to the compliant Protestant reader who wants to embrace Haze's seemingly crypto-Catholic way of redemption. The heart of the Christian message for the Bible-belt Protestants with whom O'Connor felt such sympathy was that Jesus Christ paid the full penalty for our sins by his death on the cross. Nothing is left to pay. The "finished work of Christ" is indeed finished. And yet even the quintessentially old Protestant gospel song, "Jesus Paid It All" has as its next line, "all to him I owe."

Ralph Wood offers yet another Protestant interpretation, one rather more ecumenical and less critical of Haze than Ingraffia's. Wood distinguishes between "Sin," as "our unalterable alienation from God" and "sins" as the "symptoms of our dread illness." Although he does not mention it, the distinction he makes is borne out by Haze's remark early on that "If I was in sin I was in it before I ever committed any" (29). Wood concludes that Haze "is making gargantuan penitence in gargantuan gratitude for the salvation that has already overcome his Sin. He is sacramentally participating in the atoning death of his Savior" (Wood, "Flesh Mortifying Saint," 90). Still, this does not mean that O'Connor actually approved, or is implicated in, Haze's bizarre self-torture, any more than Jesus (or Matthew) would have approved of the notion of cutting off one's arm or leg or plucking out one's eye. The point is simply that these things are matters of life and death. If the gospel is that Christ was nailed to the cross for me, its corollary, which Paul (no less than the Gospel writers) realized, is that "with Christ I am nailed to the cross" (Gal 2:20). In characteristic O'Connor fashion, this comes to expression in the profanity of the youth from whom Haze first tries to buy his car: "'Jesus on the cross,' the boy said, 'Christ nailed'" (38).

Those who challenge such redemptive interpretations of the ending of *Wise Blood* are fond of pointing out the striking parallel between between Haze's acts of self-torture at the end of his life and in his childhood, after he had seen a naked woman at a carnival. "What you seen?" his mother asked him three times, and hit him across the legs, adding "Jesus died to redeem you." The next day, carrying "a nameless unplaced guilt," the boy "took his shoes in secret out into the woods," then "filled the bottoms of them with stones and small rocks and then he put them on. He laced them up tight and walked in them through the woods for what he knew to be a mile." This, he thought "ought to satisfy Him. Nothing happened." Finally "he walked a half-mile back until he took them off" (35–36). The parallel between these incidents at the beginning and at the end of Hazel Motes' life is very real, but O'Connor has left it open, deliberately it seems, to two contrasting interpretations. The one is secular and Freudian: Haze's self-blinding and self-torture is simply a reenactment of childhood guilt and fear. The other is religious, and presumably O'Connor's own: that, as Haze once put it, "There's no change come in me" (29), or as O'Connor put it, "everything works toward its true end, or away from it" (*Collected Works*, 1107), or as Eliot put it, "In my end is my beginning."

If so, *Wise Blood* is *not*, as most religious readings have it, a conversion story, but rather the story of Hazel Motes becoming in the end what he was and was meant to be from the beginning. Mrs. Flood tried to get inside his head and failed: "How would he know if time was going back-wards or forwards or if he was going with it?" she wondered. "She saw him going backwards to Bethlehem and she had to laugh" (123). At the very end, as she looks into his eye sockets in death, she shuts her own eyes and sees only a distant pinpoint of light: "She felt as if she were blocked at the entrance of something. She sat staring with her eyes shut, into his eyes, and felt as if she had finally got to the beginning of something she couldn't begin, and she saw him moving farther and farther away, farther and farther into the darkness until he was the pin point of light" (131). In Haze's end is his beginning, but the only beginning in store for Mrs. Flood, it seems, is "the beginning of something she couldn't begin."

There is more than a hint of inevitability to all this. If there is no real "conversion," no passage from darkness to light, or from death to life (as for example in John 5:24, Eph 2:1–5, Col 1:12–13, or 1 Pet 2:9–10), what has this story to do with the New Testament? The operative para-digm, both here and in much of the New Testament, is not conversion but election. Those "converted" or "saved" in the New Testament are in retrospect frequently said to have been "elect" or chosen by God from the very beginning. The recipients of the First Epistle of Peter, for example, are identified from the outset as "elect, according to the foreknowledge of God" and at the same time "strangers" in the Roman world of their day (1 Pet 1:1–2). Hazel Motes and Enoch Emery in *Wise Blood* are without ques-tion "strangers" in their world too, and it is arguable that they are in some sense "elect" as well, driven by their "wise blood," in Haze's very last words, to "go on where I'm going" (131). The Gospel of John knows of "other sheep" who are not yet in the fold but who already belong to the Good Shepherd (John 10:16), and "children of God" not yet gathered together into one (11:52). Jesus repeatedly insists, "All that the Father giveth to me shall come to me" (John 6:37), "No man can come to me unless the Father who hath sent me draw him" (John 6:44), and "I, if I be lifted up from the earth, will draw all men unto me" (12:32, KJV; the Douay has "all things" instead of "all men").

"Draw" is a strong word in Greek, implying "that the object being moved is incapable of propelling itself or in the case of persons is unwill-ing to do so voluntarily" (Danker, *A Greek-English Lexicon*, 318). It is used in John 21:6, for example, of dragging a net full of 153 fish to shore from the sea of Tiberias, and is at least consistent with Jesus' imagery in the other three Gospels of becoming "fishers of men" (see Matt 4:19, Mark 1:17). The Bible, no less than O'Connor's fiction, knows of some who are dragged kicking and screaming into the kingdom of God, from Moses and Jeremiah and Jonah in the Old Testament to Saul of Tarsus in the New. Saul, or Paul, even though "converted" on the road to Damascus, knew in retrospect that God had separated him even from his mother's womb to be what he finally became (Gal 1:15). God could have told him what he told Jeremiah, that "Before I formed thee in the bowels of thy mother, I knew thee: and before thou camest out of the womb, I sanctified thee and made thee a prophet to the nations" (Jer 1:5). While the parallels between Paul and Hazel Motes can be (and have been) exaggerated, they could both say, in unison with all the prophets, "In my end is my beginning." Haze's long refrain of "No" to God gives way finally, not to a resounding "Yes" but to a weary "No" directed now at the world, and at all that he has tried to do and failed. As O'Connor put it, his integrity lies "in what he is unable to do." His way is still the way of negation, but to O'Connor a negation that leads to life.

All of which leaves us with Enoch Emery. To virtually everyone who has written on *Wise Blood*, myself included, he remains an enigma. In one letter O'Connor dismisses him as "a moron and chiefly a comic character" (*Mystery and Manners*, 116), yet in other letters she bonded with him, speaking fondly and humorously of "Me and Enoch" (*Collected Works*, 886), and confiding to one inquirer that "I wrote the book just like Enoch would have, not knowing too well why I did what but knowing it was right" (*Collected Works*, 919). If Haze and Enoch are both "strangers" in the world, and if one of them is also in some way "elect," is the other also elect? If, as O'Connor wrote to Hawkes, "everything works toward its true end, or away from it" and is "ultimately either saved or lost" (*Collected Works*, 1107), which is it for Enoch? Most would agree that he is moving toward his "true end," not away from it. He too is becoming what he always was, and what he is meant to be. Yet few would venture to speak of him as "saved," in anything like the sense in which Hazel Motes is (or is not!) saved. If Haze is saved by his "wise blood," is Enoch's blood not wise enough to save him? He had it first, or so he thought, and he is far less resistant to it than Hazel. As O'Connor was quick to add, "Wise blood has to be these people's means of grace—they have no sacraments" (*Collected Works*, 1107).

So Enoch too is "saved," but in nothing like the sense in which Hazel Motes is saved. Salvation, in fact, has no fixed meaning in this novel. In Enoch Emery it even parodies itself. Yet whatever else it means, it involves becoming who you are, and it begins with discovering who you are. Enoch in his gorilla suit, staring "over the valley at the uneven skyline of the city" (112), evokes other images in O'Connor's fiction. Mrs. Shortley in "The Displaced Person," for example, contemplating "for the first time the tremendous frontiers of her true country" (*Collected Works*, 305), or Tarwater in *The Violent Bear It Away*, with "his face set toward the dark city, where the children of God lay sleeping" (*Collected Works*, 479). Or even Mrs. Flood staring into Haze's blind and dead eyes, blocked at the threshold of who knows what. O'Connor leaves such things to our imaginations, evoking for us all the language of Hebrews with regard to Abraham, Sarah, Isaac and Jacob: "All these died according to faith, not having received the promises, but beholding them afar off, and saluting them, and confessing that they are pilgrims and strangers on the earth. For they that say these things do signify that they seek a country . . . But now they desire a better, that is to say, a heavenly country" (Heb 11:13–16a).

O'Connor has been charged by her critics with dualism, Manicheism, Calvinism, and Jansenism (among other things), but she stops short of the view that some are eternally destined for heaven and some for hell. "This doctrine of double predestination is strictly a Protestant phenomenon," she wrote to Alfred Corn, a young inquirer. "The Catholic Church has always condemned it" (*Collected Works*, 1173). Her view was rather that we are all created for our "true end" or "true country," but some are strong enough to turn their backs on it. Some of her stories, like *Wise Blood*, will focus attention on those "elect" or chosen ones who try their hardest to do so and fail, others on those less fortunate, who succeed.

4

The Old Testament
Wedded to the New

O'CONNOR'S TWO NOVELS HAVE two conspicuous features in common, a young protagonist with a destiny staked out for him in advance and a much older prophetic figure, already dead when the story begins but a lingering presence throughout. Hazel Motes's grandfather in *Wise Blood* gives way to Francis Marion Tarwater's great uncle in *The Violent Bear It Away*, old Mason Tarwater. Old Mason is a far more developed character than the unnamed grandfather, and thanks to innumerable flashbacks a major player, who "being dead yet speaketh" (Heb 11:4). He had kidnapped the boy as an infant from his nephew George Rayber, the boy's uncle and a schoolteacher, and had brought him up and homeschooled him. His curriculum consisted of "Figures, Reading, Writing, and History beginning with Adam expelled from the Garden and going on down through the presidents to Herbert Hoover and on in speculation toward the Second Coming and the Day of Judgment" (331).

From the beginning the boy was steeped in the Bible, and loved it: "While other children his age were herded together in a room to cut out paper pumpkins under the direction of a woman, he was left free for the pursuit of wisdom, the companions of his spirit Abel and Enoch and Noah and Job, Abraham and Moses, King David and Solomon, and all the prophets, from Elijah who escaped death, to John whose severed head struck terror from a dish. The boy knew that escaping school was the surest sign of his election" (340).

As for the old man, he saw himself as a prophet and "raised the boy to expect the Lord's call himself and to be prepared for the day he would hear

44

it." He himself "had been called in his early youth and had set out for the city, to proclaim the destruction awaiting a world that had abandoned its Saviour." But unlike Haze's grandfather, he was no circuit preacher. Young Tarwater, fourteen when the story begins, remembers that he prophesied only "To me," because "Nobody else would listen to him and there wasn't anybody else for me to listen to" (381).

Nothing else is said of old Mason's audience or his reception, only of his own dealings with his God, and his frustration that his prophecies "that the world would see the sun burst in blood and fire" were not fulfilled. Instead, the sun "rose and set, rose and set on a world that turned from green to white and green to white and green to white again. It rose and set and he despaired of the Lord's listening" (332). His was the quandary that the Christian movement faced already in the New Testament and still faces to some degree today—the haunting question, "Where is his promise or his coming? For since the time that the fathers slept, all things continue as they were from the beginning of the creation" (2 Pet 3:4).[1] But like the biblical writer, old Mason held on fervently to the traditional hope that "the day of the Lord shall come as a thief, in which the heavens shall pass away with great violence and the elements shall be melted with heat and the earth and the works that are in it shall be burnt up" (2 Pet 3:10).

DUELING VISIONS

Something else happened instead. The old man was chastened, as the sun which "rose and set, rose and set" every day suddenly changed, as "one morning he saw to his joy a finger of fire coming out of it and before he could turn, before he could shout, the finger had touched him and the destruction he had been waiting for had fallen on his own brain and his own body. His own blood had been burned dry and not the blood of the world" (332). What this incident meant concretely for him we are not told. Was it a mystical experience, or an anticipation of the stroke that later killed him?[2] Whatever it was, it was "not the last time the Lord had corrected the

---

1. Amos Niven Wilder captures the dilemma, whether for Jew or Christian, in his poem, "An Old Family Argument": "The Rabbi went to the window and looked out, and demurred: 'Nothing has changed. As of old, seedtime and harvest, cold and heat, day and night: A generation goes and a generation comes but the earth remaineth the same. What is crooked is not made straight'" (Wilder, *Grace Confounding*, 4).

2. When old Mason died, "Tarwater, sitting across the table from him, saw red ropes appear in his face and a tremor pass over him. It was like the tremor of a quake that had begun at his heart and run outward and was just reaching the surface. His

old man with fire, but it had not happened since he had taken Tarwater from the schoolteacher" (332). From such experiences he learned what the author of 1 Peter already knew: the time had come "that judgment should begin at the house of God. And if first at us, what shall be the end of them that believe not the gospel of God?" (1 Pet 4:17). Peter seems to have been comparing the persecution of Christians in his day to the judgment on Jerusalem in the book of Ezekiel, "And begin ye at my sanctuary" (Ezek 9:6). By the time he kidnapped Tarwater the old man had learned a lesson, for he knew "what he was saving the boy from and it was saving and not destruction he was seeking. He had learned enough to hate the destruction that had to come and not all that was going to be destroyed" (332–33). In short, despite all appearances to the contrary, he had become a kinder, gentler prophet. His one remaining mission was to baptize Bishop, the retarded child of his nephew Rayber. "If by the time I die," he told young Tarwater, "I haven't got him baptized, it'll be up to you. It'll be the first mission the Lord sends you" (335).

The old man's prophetic legacy rubbed off on his young protégé, but the Lord's corrections did not: "The boy doubted very much that his first mission would be to baptize a dim-witted child." Instead, "he thought of Moses who struck water from a rock, of Joshua who made the sun stand still, of Daniel who stared down lions in the pit." Whenever his great uncle would go off into the woods to "thrash out his peace with the Lord" and return "bedraggled and hungry," the boy thought, he looked the way a prophet should look, "as if he had been wrestling with a wildcat, as if his head were still full of the visions he had seen in its eyes, wheels of light and strange beasts with giant wings of fire and four heads turned to the four points of the universe. These were the times that Tarwater knew that when he was called, he would say, 'Here I am, Lord, ready!'" (334). The boy's notion of prophecy was an Old Testament notion, and a romanticized one at that, nothing less than a garbled summary of Ezekiel 1:4–16. It was an expectation the old man himself had doubtless nourished from the start. It had nothing to do with baptizing a retarded child.

But there were times "when there was no fire in his uncle's eye and he spoke only of the sweat and stink of the cross, of being born again to die, and of spending eternity eating the bread of life" (334)—in short, a distinctly New Testament vision, and it repelled young Tarwater. The thought of eating the bread of life was in his eyes demeaning and something to be ashamed of, no less so than baptizing an idiot child. When his great uncle

mouth twisted down sharply on one side and he remained exactly as he was" (336).

told him, "Jesus is the bread of life," the boy knew with "certain undeniable knowledge that he was not hungry for the bread of life," and he wondered to himself, "Had the bush flamed for Moses, the sun stood still for Joshua, the lions turned aside before Daniel only to prophesy the bread of life? Jesus? He felt a terrible disappointment in that conclusion, a dread that it was true. The old man said that as soon as he died, he would hasten to the banks of the Lake of Galilee to eat the loaves and fishes that the Lord had multiplied. 'Forever?' the horrified boy asked. 'Forever,' the old man said" (342). This he decided was madness, this insatiable hunger for the bread of life, and he was afraid "that it might be passed down, might be hidden in the blood and might strike some day in him and then he would be torn by hunger like the old man, the bottom split out of his stomach so that nothing would heal or fill it but the bread of life." Instead, "When the Lord's call came, he wished it to be a voice from out of a clear and empty sky, the trumpet of the Lord God Almighty, untouched by any fleshly hand or breath. He expected to see wheels of fire in the eyes of unearthly beasts" (343).

The contrast was between the imagery of the Old Testament and that of the New. What distinguishes them is the news that "the Word was made flesh and dwelt among us" (John 1:14), and consequently, as old Mason knew, that "Jesus is the bread of life." C. S. Lewis once drew a similar distinction in a classic and often-quoted footnote in a book O'Connor knew well: "Just as God, in becoming Man, is 'emptied' of His glory, so the truth, when it comes down from the 'heaven' of myth to the 'earth' of history, undergoes a certain humiliation. Hence the New Testament is, and ought to be, more prosaic, in some ways less *splendid* than the Old; just as the Old Testament is and ought to be less rich in many kinds of imaginative beauty than the Pagan mythologies" (*Miracles*, 161). In a similar vein Lucette Carmody, the child evangelist speaking as if with the voice of old Mason, contrasts the splendor of Old Testament expectations with their mundane fulfillment even more sharply than the old man had done:

> "Listen, you people," she said and flung her arms wide, "God told the world He was going to send a king and the world waited. The world thought, a golden fleece will do for His bed. Silver and gold and peacock tails, a thousand suns in a peacock's tail will do for His sash. His mother will ride on a four-horned beast and use the sunset for a cape. She'll trail it behind her over the ground and let the world pull it to pieces, a new one every evening." (412)

The world waited, she said, and the Lord promised, "My Word is coming, my Word is coming from the house of David, the king," but when he came he was not what the world expected: "Jesus came on cold straw, Jesus was warmed with the breath of an ox. 'Who is this?' the world said, 'who is this blue-cold child and this woman, plain as the winter? Is this the Word of God, this blue-cold child? Is this His will, this plain winter-woman?'" (413). When the Word comes, not in the splendor of a thousand suns but in the trappings of cold straw, "they nailed Him to a cross," Lucette continued, "and run a spear through His side and then they said, 'now we can have some peace, now we can ease our minds.' And they hadn't but only said it when they wanted Him to come again. Their eyes were opened and they saw the glory they had killed." Yet finally the ancient promises will come true:

> "Listen world," she cried, flinging up her arms so that the cape flew out behind her, "Jesus is coming again. The mountains are going to lie down like hounds at His feet, the stars are going to perch on His shoulder and when He calls it, the sun is going to fall like a goose for His feast. Will you know the Lord Jesus then? The mountains will know Him and bound forward, the stars will light on His head, the sun will drop down at His feet, but will you know the Lord Jesus them?" (413–14)

Whether in the prophecies of old Mason or of young Lucette Carmody, the dueling visions come together in the end, but for now Tarwater must come to terms with the humbler prospect of a gnawing hunger for the bread of life. The image of Jesus as the bread of life evokes for Catholics and most Protestants the Eucharist, or Lord's Supper. The old man knew nothing of the church's Eucharist, yet as a "crypto-Catholic" (1183) he managed to find it exactly where the Gospel of John finds it, in the feeding of five thousand on "the banks of the Lake of Galilee" (see John 6:1–13). He hungered for it, and believed his hunger would be satisfied "as soon as he died" (342). Young Tarwater, by contrast, anticipated that when his great uncle died, his vision of "wheels of fire in the eyes of unearthly beasts" would come true, freeing him from his fear of such hunger and madness, and from what the narrator calls the "threatened intimacy of creation." The latter was the boy's irrational fear that "if he let his eye rest for an instant longer than was needed to place something—a spade, a hoe, the mule's hind quarters before his plow, the red furrow under him—that the thing would suddenly stand before him, strange and terrifying, demanding that he name it and name it justly and be judged for the name he gave it" (343). His fear is strikingly similar to what is said elsewhere about Rayber, his unbelieving uncle, for whom almost any object in the physical world could awaken "the horrifying love" he felt for his retarded son Bishop: "Anything he looked at too long could bring it on. Bishop did not have to be around. It could be a stick or a stone, the line of a shadow, the absurd old man's walk of a starling crossing the sidewalk. If, without thinking, he lent himself to it, he would feel suddenly a morbid surge of the love that terrified him—powerful enough to throw him to the ground in an act of idiot praise. It was completely irrational and abnormal" (401).

All this is akin to what Clark Pinnock, a Baptist, calls the sacramentality of the whole creation. O'Connor, so far as I know, never called it that, but it comes very close to what she called the "anagogical vision," (*Mystery and Manners*, 72–73). In Pinnock's words, "Just as general revelation underlies special revelation, so general sacramentality underlies Christian sacramentality and heralds it" ("The Physical Side of Being Spiritual," 11). Here if anywhere is a theological rationale—a Baptist one at that—for what O'Connor called the South's "do-it-yourself" religion (*Collected Works*, 1107). Creation is of course rooted in the Old Testament, as O'Connor reminds us in her reference to the demand of any given material object that Tarwater "name it and name it justly" (see Gen 2:19–23), yet Pinnock states, and O'Connor implies, that this creation becomes sacramental only in the wake of, and by by virtue of, the Word made flesh: "We struggle here against a matter/spirit dualism. According to scriptures, the Spirit is not a ghost but the giver of life, shaper of the material creation and the power of resurrection. He implemented the coming of the Son in flesh and bone, annointed [*sic*] him in body, mind and spirit, brought about many concrete changes in life, and will bring about a new creation" (Pinnock, 10).

Gerard Manley Hopkins, a Catholic like O'Connor, put it more eloquently: not only that "The world is charged with the grandeur of God," but that "the Holy Ghost over the bent world broods with warm breast and with ah! bright wings" (Hopkins, *Poems*, 66). And it is Hopkins whose notions of "inscape" and "instress" best describe the experiences of Tarwater and Rayber with material objects in the world, whether natural or man-made. "Inscape" has been defined as "The inward essential unique quality of an observed object," and "instress" as "The force of the individual or essential quality of an observed object on the mind of the observer."[3] This

---

3. *The New Shorter Oxford Dictionary*, 1.1377, 1383. O'Connor shows her familiarity with Hopkins' theory of "inscape" in a different connection, in a 1963 letter to Sister Mariella Gable (*Collected Works*, 1183).

is the force, or at least one expression of it, pulling at both Rayber and Tarwater, the force that each in his own way tries valiantly to resist.

TARWATER AND HIS CALL

When old Mason dies, Tarwater does not receive the prophetic call he wants and expects—no voice from the sky, no trumpet, no "wheels of fire" (343). Yet the old man's words are still ringing in his ears: "The Lord is preparing a prophet. The Lord is preparing a prophet with fire in his hand and eye and the prophet is moving toward the city with his warning. The prophet is coming with the Lord's message. 'Go warn the children of God,' saith the Lord, 'of the terrible speed of justice.' Who will be left? Who will be left when the Lord's mercy strikes?" (368). No distinction here between justice and mercy. Either one is God's intervention in a fallen world, intervention for which no one is fully prepared. "Listen boy," old Mason would say, "even the mercy of the Lord burns," grabbing the boy's overalls and shaking him, finally letting go and allowing him "to fall back into the thorn bed of that thought" (342). The call that actually comes is the one old Mason promised, a call to baptize Bishop. Tarwater resists it, but when he hears Bishop babbling into the telephone and finally lays eyes on the child, he knows that resistance is futile. Even before he enters the house where Bishop lives with his father Rayber, Tarwater's uncle, he knows instinctively what is coming. At the door, the silence around him "seemed almost to be patiently waiting patiently, biding its time until it should reveal itself and demand to be named." Hopkins' "instress" is at work again! Tarwater grabs the brass door knocker, shattering the silence "as if it were a personal enemy." When he stops, "the implacable silence descended around him, immune to his fury," and he felt hollow, "as if he had been lifted like Habakkuk by the hair of his head, borne swiftly though the night and set down in the place of his mission" (385).

The "as if" clause cannot be in Tarwater's mind, for it is no part of his Bible, nor any part of the curriculum old Mason had designed for him (see 340). It comes from "Bel and the Dragon," a story added to the book of Daniel in the Roman Catholic Bible,[4] and while it can only be the formulation of an intrusive Catholic narrator (that would be Flannery!), it conveys vividly the boy's unwillingness to fulfill his mission coupled with a sense

---

4. "And Habacuc said: 'Lord, I never saw Babylon, nor do I know the den.' And the angel of the Lord took him by the top of his head and carried him by the hair of his head and set him in Babylon over the den in the force of his spirit" (Dan 14:24–35).

of inevitability. Once he is inside the house and finally lays eyes on his re-tarded cousin, all the imagery fades away, both his own and the narrator's, and the stark mundane reality sets in: "He did not look into the eyes of any fiery beast or see a burning bush. He only knew, with a certainty sunk in despair, that he was expected to baptize the child he saw and begin the life his great-uncle had prepared him for. He knew that he was called to be a prophet and that the ways of his prophecy would not be remarkable" (388–89). The inevitability becomes explicit. Tarwater now knows that he *will* baptize Bishop. He *will* eat the bread of life. He *will* be a prophet. And the "ways of his prophecy" will *not* be remarkable. He sees himself "trudging into the distance in the bleeding, stinking mad shadow of Jesus, until at last he received his reward, a broken fish, a multiplied loaf" (389). He will be a prophet, but not of biblical proportions, a minor prophet at best, like Hazel Motes, or old Mason or Lucette Carmody, or even Buford Munson, the black neighbor who buried the old man.

What Tarwater is going through is more like a conversion than a call. Like any follower of Jesus he is called first to eternal life. Whatever else he is called to is secondary to that. He will be found at the end, just one of a multitude, "eating the bread of life." He will be a prophet only in the sense that all genuine followers of Jesus are both prophets and potential martyrs. The very word "martyr" comes from a Greek verb meaning to "testify" or "bear witness." Strictly speaking, the so-called martyrs were not martyrs because they were put to death; they were put to death because they were *already* "martyrs" in the proper sense of the word, in that they testified to their faith. In the book of Revelation, for example, saints (that is, believers), prophets and martyrs are scarcely distinguishable (see Rev 16:6, 17:6, 19:10, and 22:9). Tarwater will be all three, not a solitary prophet in the Old Testament tradition but, like his great-uncle part of a redeemed community feeding on Jesus, the "bread of life." Like Hazel Motes, he is not in the process of becoming a great prophet, but simply what he was meant to be from the start, a disciple of Jesus, and therefore in O'Connor's eyes a true Catholic. Like Hazel too, he will in the end be dragged kicking and screaming into the Kingdom of God, "by the hair of his head" like Habak-kuk of old, not from Haze's nihilism, however, but from spirit to flesh, from the splendor of the Old Testament into the shame and humiliation of the New, into "the bleeding, stinking mad shadow of Jesus."

This is *not* how we customarily view the Old and New Testaments. The Old Testament is supposed to be physical. God created the physical world and pronounced it good. The New Testament is supposed to be spiritual. The Spirit came at Pentecost, heralding the age of the Spirit. Or so we are told. But here the logic is reversed, and O'Connor's way of looking at it makes just as good sense. In the Old Testament, God is Spirit; no one can see the face of God and live (Exod 33:20). In the New Testament the Word who is God becomes flesh. Material creation becomes sacramental, and particular objects, sights, sounds, even silences, take on the look of potential sacraments. A purist might object that if everything is sacramental nothing is, and sacramentally O'Connor was a purist. When Mary McCarthy once called the Eucharist a symbol and "a pretty good one," O'Connor famously replied, "Well, if it's a symbol, to hell with it" (*Collected Works*, 977). Yet in the rural South where the very word "sacrament" was foreign, and where baptism and the Lord's Supper were understood in decidedly unsacramental ways, a sacramental creation alive with "inscape" and "instress" could and did serve her literary purposes admirably.

What Pinnock calls creation's "general sacramentality" pulls Tarwater inexorably toward the specific sacraments of baptizing Bishop and eating the bread of life. A stray loaf of bread in a bakery window (407); a marble lion in a park with water pouring from its mouth into a pool and the sun resting on Bishop's head as the child lurches into the pool (420–21, 432); a "glass-like" little lake at the Cherokee Lodge, "so unused that it might only the moment before have been set down by four strapping angels for him to baptize the child in" (434)—each of these in its own way draws Tarwater ever closer to his unwelcome destiny, and each has a biblical point of reference. The first reawakens his hunger for the bread he claims to shun (see John 6:35 and 48, "I am the bread of life"). The second evokes old Mason's warning, "Remember the Lord's lion set in the path of the false prophet!" (344), and with it a story of two prophets in 1 Kings 13—not false, but flawed prophets, like Hazel Motes, Tarwater, and old Mason himself.[5] The marble lion in Tarwater's path draws him toward the pool, uncertain whether to baptize Bishop or drown him (421). The third evokes the "sea of glass, like to crystal" in the book of Revelation (4:6) with "four living

5. In the biblical story a "man of God" from Judah prophesies against King Jeroboam of Israel, who built an idolatrous altar at Bethel. A second "old prophet" from Israel, deceives the first prophet into disobeying the Lord who sent him, but then prophesies the Lord's judgment against him, so that "a lion found him in the way and killed him" (1 Kgs 13:24). This prophet then retrieves the body, buries it in his own grave and affirms the same oracle against Jeroboam. Later, when Josiah destroys Jeroboam's altar, he spares the tombs of these two prophets (see 2 Kgs 23:16–18), so that, flawed as they are, they rest in peace, much like old Mason in O'Connor's novel. Could O'Connor have known Karl Barth's lengthy discussion of this passage in his *Church Dogmatics* (II.2., 393–409)?

creatures" around it, the same "sea of glass" the redeemed must cross to enter the throne room of God (Rev 15:2), yet in the same moment Tarwater is reminded that "water is made for more than one thing" (434). Will it be drowning or baptism? The flawed prophet is drawn toward his calling by the visible "sacraments" in the material world around him even as he resists them, almost to the very end.

IN PRAISE OF SACRAMENTS

If the sacramentality of a creation made new is at work in Tarwater's calling, what of the actual sacraments toward which he is being drawn, baptism and the Eucharist? O'Connor described the novel to her friend Ted Spivey the year before it was published as "built around a baptism," and just after it appeared as "a very minor hymn to the Eucharist" (*Habit of Being*, 341, 387). The two are not mutually exclusive, for as she went on to explain in the second letter, "There are two main symbols in the book—water and the bread that Christ is." Yet within the story a distinction must be made. Tarwater and his great uncle seem to have known nothing of the Eucharist, or even a Protestant Lord's Supper, for they lived deep in the woods, isolated from any religious community. But old Mason knew about water baptism, and believed it was efficacious, whether or not the one baptized was a believer, or even aware of what was happening. On the one hand he had kidnapped Rayber at the age of seven, "instructed him in his Redemption," and in four days "taught him what was necessary to know and baptized him" (371). But on the other he had baptized young Tarwater as an infant in Rayber's house, "pouring water over his head out of the bottle that had been on the table by the crib"—this in full knowledge that, as he told Tarwater later, "You didn't even know what was going on" (377).[6] The same would be true of Bishop. According to the old man, the Lord had preserved Bishop from corruption "in the only possible way: the child was dim-witted" (334), and yet Mason believed that baptism was still necessary for his salvation.

The old man was not a typical Baptist for whom baptism is an act of obedience, not a means of salvation, nor a kindred Campbellite for whom believers' baptism by immersion is necessary for salvation, nor even an infant-baptizing Methodist. He was far closer to the "crypto-Catholic" that O'Connor claimed he was and intended him to be (*Collected Works*,

6. "Oh yes I did," Tarwater insists, in one of his more humorous lines in the novel, "I was laying there thinking."

1183). At the same time, he understood something of what baptism meant biblically. "You were born into bondage and baptized into freedom," he told Tarwater, "into the death of the Lord, into the death of the Lord Jesus Christ" (342), echoing the Apostle Paul's words, "Know you not that all we who are baptized in Christ Jesus are baptized in his death? For we are buried together with him by baptism into death; that, as Christ is risen from the dead by the glory of the Father, so also we may walk in newness of life" (Rom 6:3–4). Old Mason seems to have understood that, at least in its origins, baptism is a violent sacrament, a "burial" with Christ signaling that one has died with Christ and will rise again with him. It is, if not a drowning a close call, a narrow escape from drowning, in waters evoking the memory of Noah's flood (see 1 Pet 3:20–21). John the Baptist baptized in water, while announcing a coming baptism "in the Holy Ghost and fire" (Matt 3:11), while Jesus himself saw a second "baptism" in his future, one that would bring fire on the earth (Luke 12:49–50), and challenged his disciples to share in it (Mark 10:38–39). O'Connor, in the same letter to Spivey in which she spoke of the twin symbols of water and bread, added, "Water is a symbol of purification and fire is another. Water, it seems to me, is a symbol of the kind of purification that God gives irrespective of our efforts or worthiness, and fire is the kind of purification we bring on ourselves—as in Purgatory. It is our evil which is naturally burnt away when it comes anywhere near God" (*Habit of Being*, 387). Yet in almost the same breath she wrote, "I believe that God's love for us is so great that He does not wait until we are purified to such a great extent before he allows us to receive Him"—presumably in the Eucharist.

Here O'Connor and her characters part company. As we have seen, there is no literal Eucharist or Lord's Supper in this "minor hymn to the Eucharist," and in order to participate in its equivalent, that is, eating "the loaves and fishes that the Lord had multiplied" (342), Tarwater and his great uncle must undergo the purification by fire of which O'Connor speaks in her letter. For old Mason it came in the "finger of fire" that had touched his brain and body and burned his blood dry (332), teaching him that "even the mercy of the Lord burns" (342). When he baptized young Tarwater as a baby, he scrawled on Rayber's journal the message, "THE PROPHET I RAISE UP OUT OF THIS BOY WILL BURN YOUR EYES CLEAN" (379). Tarwater's father, a troubled and suicidal divinity student, had (as Rayber remembered him) a face "as raw red as if a blast of fire had singed the skin off it and the eyes that had seemed burnt too." To Rayber they were "the eyes of repentance and lacked all dignity." When Tarwater first came to his house and Rayber looked at him, he saw a face that mirrored his own, "but the eyes were not his own. They were the student's eyes, singed with guilt" (392). Later, Rayber himself hears Lucette Carmody shout, "I've seen the Lord in a tree of fire! The Word of God is a burning Word to burn you clean!" (414). The old man's scrawled prophecy comes back to haunt Rayber, word for word, and he vows to resist it to the end (422).

Tarwater too resists the purification by fire and the prophetic call that goes with it, but unsuccessfully. In the end, as we will see, the mercy of the Lord burns him clean, so that his eyes "looked small and seedlike, as if while he was asleep, they had been lifted out, scorched, and dropped back into his head." Only then does he begin to exorcise his demons, and when he does, "His scorched eyes no longer looked hollow or as if they were meant only to guide him forward. They looked as if, touched with a coal like the lips of a prophet, they would never be used for ordinary sights again (472–73). The biblical reference is to Isaiah, who wrote, "one of the seraphim flew to me: and in his hand was a live coal, which he had taken with the tongs off the altar. And he touched my mouth, and said: Behold, this hath touched thy lips, and thy iniquities shall be taken away, and thy sin shall be cleansed. And I heard the voice of the Lord saying, Whom shall I send, and who shall go for us? And I said, Lo, here am I. Send me" (Isa 6:6–8). In O'Connor's fiction the eyes and not the lips are burned because her prophets are first of all "seers." Prophecy was to her, as she put it in a letter to Robert Lowell, "a matter of seeing, not saying, and is certainly the most terrible vocation. My prophet will be inarticulate and burnt by his own visions" (*Collected Works*, 1120). In her letter to Ted Spivey she called it Purgatory (*Habit of Being*, 387). The New Testament calls it a baptism in fire (Matt 3:11–12; Luke 3:16–17), or a trial by fire (1 Cor 3:13; 1 Pet 1:7, 4:12). In Catholic theology it comes after death, but in O'Connor's world (as in the New Testament) it comes before death—or in some stories at the very moment of death. That way, it has a legitimate place in the story. It is not left simply to our imaginations, as Purgatory must be if one is writing a realistic story and not a fantasy about the afterlife.

Surprisingly, though, in this "minor hymn to the Eucharist," it is the Eucharist that comes after death, like the messianic banquet in early Judaism, or the marriage supper of the Lamb in the book of Revelation (see Rev 19:9). It comes to expression within the story only in a vision, the vision Tarwater dreaded all along, old Mason's vision of eating the bread of life. In the end, in spite of himself, it is the boy's vision as well. When

Buford Munson finally tells him that he has given the old man a decent burial, Buford rides off on his mule, leaving Tarwater right by his great uncle's grave,

> standing there, his eyes still reflecting the field the Negro had crossed. It seemed no longer empty but peopled with a multitude. Everywhere, he saw dim figures seated on the slope and as he gazed he saw that from a single basket the throng was being fed. His eyes searched the crowd for a long time as if he could not find the one he was looking for. Then he saw him. The old man was lowering himself to the ground. When he was down and his bulk had settled, he leaned forward, his face turned toward the basket, impatiently following its progress toward him. The boy too leaned forward, aware at last of the object of his hunger, aware that it was the same as the old man's and that nothing on earth would fill him. His hunger was so great that he could have eaten all the loaves and fishes after they were multiplied. (477–78)

Here, in contrast to the New Testament and Roman Catholic theology alike, the Eucharist, or Lord's Supper, turns out to be a future eschatological experience, not a present one, not a way of showing "the death of the Lord until he come" (1 Cor 11:26), but itself "their reward in the end," nothing less than "the Lord Jesus Himself, the bread of life!" (369). Tarwater is given a foretaste of what it will be, but only a foretaste, as "the scene faded in the gathering darkness" (478).

A strange feature of the scene and one easily overlooked is the old man's body language in the boy's vision. Tarwater sees him "lowering himself to the ground," as he "leaned forward" toward the basket to receive the bread, and then Tarwater "leaned forward" as well. In another story, "A Temple of the Holy Ghost," O'Connor felt free to speak openly of the Eucharist because her main character was a Catholic child modeled in part after herself. In that story two convent-trained girls sing for their boyfriends a not-so-minor "hymn to the Eucharist" by Thomas Aquinas, with the opening line, "*Tantum ergo Sacramentum, Veneremur Cernui*" (*Collected Works*, 202). Sally Fitzgerald in a note supplies an English translation: "Lowly bending, deep adoring, Lo! The Sacrament we hail" (1266). "Lowly bending" is *Cernui*, defined in *Cassell's Latin Dictionary* (92) as "falling headlong, with the face toward the ground"—a fairly apt description of old Mason's posture as he waits for the bread. Instead of singing the *Tantum Ergo* he acts it out, receiving the Eucharist in an act of humble worship! Nothing in the New Testament quite prepares us for this, except perhaps the association of Jesus's last meal with the self-humiliation displayed in the washing of each other's feet (see John 13:3–5, 12–17).

MERCY AND JUDGEMENT

Along with the vision of eating the loaves, Tarwater finally receives his long-awaited and long-dreaded commission. The "dueling visions"—his own from the Old Testament and his great uncle's from the New—come together at last:

> He whirled toward the treeline. There, rising and spreading in the night, a red-gold tree of fire ascended as if it would consume the darkness in one tremendous burst of flame. The boy's breath went out to meet it. He knew that this was the fire that had encircled Daniel, that had raised Elijah from the earth, that had spoken to Moses and would in the instant speak to him. He threw himself to the ground and with his face against the dirt of the grave, he heard the command. Go warn the children of God of the terrible speed of mercy. The words were as silent as seeds opening one at a time in his blood. (478)

The Old Testament splendor of God's dealings with Moses, Elijah, and Daniel ends here in the dirt of the grave, as Tarwater once again falls headlong to the ground, not in a vision this time, but literally. When he gets up he takes a handful of dirt from the old man's grave and anoints himself for his mission by smearing it on his forehead. The boy's only living role model in the path of discipleship is Buford Munson, the faithful black neighbor who had buried old Mason, and "after a moment, without looking back he moved across the far field and off the way Buford had gone" (478). We last see him with "his face set toward the dark city, where the children of God lay sleeping" (479), like Jesus when he "set his face to go to Jerusalem" for the last time in the Gospel of Luke (9:51).

O'Connor's phrase "the children of God" reminds us that prophets are normally sent to their own people, not to foreigners, and yet "a prophet hath no honour in his own country" (John 4:44). She envisions the "dark city" as a city much like Taulkinham in *Wise Blood*, but (more to the point) like the biblical Jerusalem, a city "that killest the prophets and stonest them that are sent unto thee" (Matt 23:37). "Therefore, behold," Jesus told "the children of God" of his generation, "I send to you prophets and wise men and scribes; and some of them you will put to death and crucify; and some you will scourge in your synagogues and persecute from city to city; That upon you may come all the just blood that hath been shed upon the

earth, from the blood of Abel, the just, even unto the blood of Zacharias
... whom you killed between the temple and the altar" (Matt 23:34–35).

Tarwater, with some such prophecy in mind, felt his hunger for
the bread of life rising within him, knowing "that it rose in a line of men
whose lives were chosen to sustain it, who would wander in the world,
strangers from that violent country where the silence is never broken except to shout the truth. He felt it building from the blood of Abel to his
own, rising and engulfing him" (478). He too, no less than Hazel Motes,
is driven by "wise blood," but now with a connotation of persecution and
martyrdom, not at his own hand but at the hands of "the children of God."
The phrase "children of God" presupposes a kind of covenant between
God and fallen humanity. In her view, the "children of God" are unfaithful
and in need of pardoning grace, but because the very offer of grace brands
them as unfaithful, it is at first—and maybe forever—unwelcome.

O'Connor hinted as much in a letter to Betty Hester even before the
book was published:

> He must of course not live to realize his mission, but die to real-
> ize it. The children of God I daresay will despatch him pretty
> quick. Nor am I saying that he has a great mission or that God's
> solution for the problems of our particular world are prophets
> like Tarwater. Tarwater's mission might only be to baptize a few
> more idiots. The prophets in the Bible are only the great ones
> but there is doubtless unwritten sacred history like uncanonized
> saints. Someday if I get up enough courage I may write a story
> or a novella about Tarwater in the city. (*Collected Works*, 1101;
> 25 July 1959)

And less than a week before the novel appeared (on February 8, 1960), she
wrote to Robert Lowell, "I think the next one will be about how the children of God finish off Tarwater in the city; and that one may finish me off.
(*Collected Works*, 1120; 2 February 1960). Yet two days later she floated a
very different scenario in a letter to her friend Andrew Lytle:

> I have got to the point now where I keep thinking more and
> more about the presentation of love and charity, or better call it
> grace, as love suggests tenderness, whereas grace can be violent
> or would have to be to compete with the kind of evil I can make
> concrete. At the same time, I keep seeing Elias in that cave, wait-
> ing to hear the voice of the Lord in the thunder and lightning
> and wind, and only hearing it finally in the gentle breeze,[7] and I

7. See 1 Kings 19:11–12. The "still small voice" of the King James version appears in

feel I'll have to be able to do that sooner or later, or anyway keep
trying. (*Collected Works,* 1121; 4 February 1960)

O'Connor did not live long enough to realize either of these competing aspirations, but together they raise the question of her understanding of the
grace, or mercy of God. A sacrament, as Catholics and Protestants both
know, is a "means of grace," but what is grace? In her own Catholic piety,
grace is linked not only to baptism and the Eucharist but to Purgatory,
which she called "the kind of purification we bring on ourselves" (*Habit
of Being,* 387). And in her fiction as in the Bible, grace is seldom linked
to any ritual act. The southern, mostly Protestant setting of her fiction
made it necessary for her to focus not on the sacrament itself, but on the
grace it mediated. Grace in her stories is more like Purgatory than like
the sacraments, for it is unbridled, reckless, beyond our control, and, in
a world she once called "territory held largely by the devil" (*Mystery and
Manners,* 118), generally unwelcome. In contrast to the standard Protestant view which sees grace as "free," that is, simply a judicial declaration
of innocence, O'Connor sees it as something that purifies, transforms, or
as old Mason would say, "burns" (342), and to that extent, though she
never quite says it, rather like Purgatory. In her words, "All human nature vigorously resists grace because grace changes us and the change is
painful," and "Human nature is so faulty that it can resist any amount of
grace and most of the time it does" (*Collected Works,* 1084). Hence, "the
terrible speed of mercy," a phrase calculated to shock her religious readers
no less than her secular ones. How can the mercy of God, or the speed
of it, be seen as something "terrible"? The answer leads us to the heart of
O'Connor's vision of a fallen world where any abrupt invasion or visitation
of the good can be as grotesque and terrifying as an incursion of evil, and
our corrupted human nature is ill-equipped to tell the difference. Charles
Williams made the point well in his 1949 novel, *Descent into Hell* (11–12),
in an exchange between Mr. Stanhope and Miss Fox over her offhand use
of the phrase "terribly good." Mr. Stanhope replied that "when I say 'terribly' I think I mean 'full of terror'. A dreadful goodness." "I don't see how
goodness can be dreadful," she objected, "If things are good they're not
terrifying, are they?" and he concluded, "Yes, surely," leaving her with the
unanswered question, "Are our tremors to measure the Omnipotence?"

Like Purgatory too, grace is eschatological. While it can and does
make its appearance in this life, whether in the Bible or in O'Connor's
stories, it belongs properly to "the End," whether understood as the Old

O'Connor's Douay Bible as "a whistling of a gentle air" (3 Kgs 19:12).

Testament "Day of the Lord," the New Testament *Parousia*, or Second Coming of Christ, or (like Purgatory in Catholic thought) the death of an individual. It is a kind of reckoning, involving forgiveness but also purification, and to that extent not altogether distinct from judgement. In the New Testament, the brief letter of Jude urges its readers to "Keep yourselves in the love of God, waiting for the mercy of our Lord Jesus Christ, unto life everlasting" (Jude 21), but with the stipulation that it will not be an easy or pleasant moment for all concerned: "And some indeed reprove, being judged: But others save, pulling them out of the fire. And on others have mercy, in fear, hating also the spotted garment which is carnal (Jude 22–23). The phrase, "the terrible speed of mercy," evokes some such expectation as this, one that could be ambiguous even to the biblical "children of God." In the classic words of the prophet Amos, "Woe to them that desire the day of the Lord! To what end is it for you? The day of the Lord is darkness and not light. As if a man should flee from the face of a lion, and a bear should meet him: or enter into the house and lean with his hand upon the wall, and a serpent should bite him. Shall not the day of the Lord be darkness and not light: and obscurity, and no brightness in it?" (Amos 5:18–20).

In the New Testament, where the "day of the Lord" has been redefined as the "coming of the Lord Jesus Christ" (1 Thess 3:13; also 4:13–17), the Apostle Paul can describe it in much the same way: "For you yourselves know perfectly that the day of the Lord shall so come as a thief in the night. For when they shall say: Peace and safety; then shall sudden destruction come upon them, as the pains upon her that is with child. And they shall not escape" (1 Thess 5:2–3), even while reassuring his Christian readers that "you, brethren, are not in darkness that that day should overtake you as a thief. For all you are the children of light and of the day; we are not of the night nor of darkness. Therefore, let us not sleep, as others do; but let us watch, and be sober" (1 Thess 5:4–6). Surely there is irony in the last sentence of the novel, with its vision of "the dark city, where the children of God lay sleeping" (*Collected Works*, 479). For those who sleep, "the terrible speed of mercy" is a wake up call they do not want to hear. The "terrible" ambiguity in O'Connor's fiction between mercy and judgement points finally toward an even deeper and more terrible ambiguity between good and evil, God and the Devil.

5

The Devil and His Legions

O'CONNOR'S STORIES ABOUT "THE action of grace in territory held largely by the devil" (*Mystery and Manners,* 118) are, in that respect, not unlike the stories about Jesus in the Gospels. Yet the differences are huge. In the Gospels, the signs of grace, or of the kingdom of God, are that "the blind see, the lame walk, the lepers are cleansed, the deaf hear, the dead rise again, the poor have the gospel preached to them" (Matt 11:5). In O'Connor's world, as we have seen, none of those things happen. The devil holds on to his territory far more tenaciously than in the world of the New Testament.

How then does she show "the action of grace"? Her much-quoted answer was that "you have to make your vision apparent by shock—to the hard of hearing you shout, and for the almost blind you draw large and startling figures" (*Collected Works,* 805–6). The irony was that her "large and startling figures" were so large and so startling as to give the impression that she herself was, as her friend John Hawkes put it, "on the devil's side" (Hawkes, "Flannery O'Connor's Devil," 399). As a rule, O'Connor had little patience with those whose interpretations of her work contradicted her own. But her dialogue with Hawkes was an exception. She took him seriously from the beginning, even acknowledging that "your vision, though it doesn't come by way of theology, is the same as mine" (*Collected Works,* 1109; 6 October 1959). Certainly the devil is alive and well in O'Connor's fiction, and she was proud of it. As she freely admitted to Hawkes, "the Devil can always be the subject for my kind of comedy one way or another. I suppose this is because he is always accomplishing ends other than his own" (*Collected Works,* 1118–19; 26 December 1959). And yet she was careful to set firm boundaries between Hawkes' devil and hers:

"My devil has a name, a history and a definite plan. His name is Lucifer, he's a fallen angel, his sin is pride, and his aim is the destruction of the Divine plan. Now I judge that your devil is co-equal with God, not his creature; that pride is his virtue, not his sin; and that his aim is not to destroy the Divine plan because there isn't any Divine plan to destroy. My devil is objective and yours is subjective" (*Collected Works,* 1156; 28 November 1961). While O'Connor's devil may owe as much to John Milton as to the Bible, he is recognizably the devil of the New Testament as well, who (in her words and Peter's) "goes about like a roaring lion seeking whom he may devour" (*Collected Works,* 1151; see 1 Pet 5:8).

Stranger, Friend, and Adversary

O'Connor's devil is undeniably a conspicuous presence in *The Violent Bear It Away*, in a way in which he was not in *Wise Blood*. Even in the dark world of Taulkinham, the devil was conspicuously absent in the earlier novel. God was present at least in the sky and in Haze's blasphemies, but the devil was nowhere to be found. Not so in the later one: "I certainly do mean Tarwater's friend to be the Devil," O'Connor told Hawkes (*Collected Works,* 1118), referring to the voice that began to speak to Tarwater and through him the moment his great uncle died.

At issue is the old man's burial, and Tarwater blurts out to the corpse, "Just hold your horses. I already told you I would do it right." But he notices that his voice sounded "like a stranger's voice, as if the death had changed him instead of his great-uncle" (336). His spoken words are in quotation marks in O'Connor's text, but inside Tarwater's head the voice continues to speak, and those words are not in quotes. Inside his head or not, the voice is "loud and strange and disagreeable" (337). O'Connor continues throughout the practice of using quotation marks to distinguish what Tarwater says out loud, whether in the stranger's voice or his own, from the stranger's words inside his head. Notice, for example in the following paragraph both the quotation marks and the absence thereof where we might have expected them:

> "The dead are poor," he said in the voice of the stranger. You can't be any poorer than dead. He'll have to take what he gets. Nobody to bother me, he thought. Ever. No hand uplifted to hinder me from anything; except the Lord's and He ain't said anything. He ain't even noticed me yet.

Both the words in quotation marks and the unspoken words that Tarwater merely "thought" are words of the "loud" and "disagreeable" stranger. The dialogue that follows between Tarwater and the stranger at the half dug grave has to do with the fate of the old man in particular and of the dead in general, with Tarwater "softening the stranger's voice so that he could stand it" (345). In the course of it, the stranger reminds Tarwater that "In the rest of the world they do things different than what you been taught" (345; the quotation marks are mine, not O'Connor's). To Tarwater "the rest of the world" means the city, and he replies, "I been there once," promptly introducing a flashback about his visit to the city with his great uncle (346–51).

The stranger makes no appearance in the flashback, for O'Connor carries through consistently the notion that the stranger came into his life only when the old man died. But the flashback, long as it is, is merely an interruption in the dialogue, and as soon as it is over, his attitude toward the stranger changes:

> He didn't search out the stranger's face, but he knew by now that it was sharp and friendly and wise, shadowed under a stiff broad-brimmed panama hat that obscured the color of his eyes. He had lost his dislike for the thought of the voice. Only every now and then it sounded like a stranger's voice to him. He began to feel that he was only just now meeting himself, as if as long as his uncle had lived, he had been deprived of his own acquaintance. (352)

Tarwater is now in some sense "possessed," in that the stranger is part of his very being. Such terms as "the stranger" and "his new friend" (352) occur interchangeably, and he offers only token resistance to the stranger's insistence that the old man was crazy and his repeated denial of the resurrection of the dead. When Tarwater poses the alternatives, "Jesus or the devil," his "new friend" corrects him: "No, no, no, the stranger said, there ain't no such thing as a devil. I can tell you from my own self-experience. I know that for a fact. It ain't Jesus or the devil. It's Jesus or *you*." "Jesus or me," Tarwater repeated (354). If the devil is indeed "a liar, and the father thereof" (John 8:44), his greatest lie is that "there ain't no such thing as a devil." In that sense Tarwater's "new friend" is lying, yet from his "own self-experience" he is not, because if you *are* the devil, then it *is* a question of "Jesus or you." And to the extent that Tarwater is possessed by the devil, it is true of him as well.

The dialogue ends in a drunken stupor, as "A burning arm slid down Tarwater's throat as if the devil were already reaching inside him to finger his soul" (358). The stranger, having counseled "moderation" at first, now leaves with a final blasphemy: "You might as well drink all that liquor since you've already drunk so much. Once you pass the moderation mark you've passed it, and that gyration you feel working down from the top of your brain, he said, that's the Hand of God laying a blessing on you. He has given you your release. That old man was the stone before your door and the Lord has rolled it away. He ain't rolled it quite far enough, of course. You got to finish up yourself but He's done the main part. Praise Him" (359). With this, the voice goes silent for a time, only because it has done its work so well. Tarwater is fully under the stranger's control. When Buford Munson, the old man's black neighbor, grips Tarwater's arm and warns him that the old man "deserves to lie in a grave that fits him" and "needs to be rested," he replies, "Nigger . . . take your hand off me," and "He'll be rested all right when I get through with him" (360)—arguably the voice of the stranger speaking through him. And when he sets fire to the home he had shared with his great uncle at Powderhead (361) it is unmistakably the stranger's work.

The "stranger" is Tarwater's own devil, no one else's. O'Connor wrote, "Most of us have learned to be dispassionate about evil, to look it in the face and find, as often as not, our own grinning reflections with which we do not argue" (*Collected Works*, 830). In a letter to Hawkes she imagines a "Devil who prompts Rayber" as well, but who "speaks a language I can't get down, an idiom I just can't reproduce—maybe because it's so dull I can't sustain any interest in it" (*Collected Works*, 1118). Only once does she even try, when Rayber stumbles over a garbage can and hears "his own curses like the voice of a stranger broadcast through his hearing aid" (407). What haunts Rayber is not the devil but God, or what he calls the "horrifying love" he feels for Bishop, the love he can barely control, that "began with Bishop and then like an avalanche covered everything his reason hated" (401):

> He could control his terrifying love as long as it had its focus on Bishop, but if anything happened to the child, he would have to face it in itself. Then the whole world would become his idiot child. He had thought what he would have to do if anything happened to Bishop. He would have with one supreme effort to resist the recognition; with every nerve and muscle and thought, he would have to resist feeling anything at all, thinking anything at all. He would have to anesthetize his life. (442)

In the end, when Bishop drowns, Rayber finds that there is nothing to resist, for he felt nothing, and "it was not until he realized that there would be no pain that he collapsed" (456).

If Rayber resists God and falls into the devil's trap, Tarwater resists his private devil and in the end falls into the arms of God. Yet Tarwater's devil is open to conflicting interpretations. Is he the boy's *doppelgänger* or alter ego, or is he the literal devil of Milton and the Bible, who "goes about like a roaring lion seeking whom he may devour"? In biblical terms, it looks like a borderline case of demon possession, keeping in mind that O'Connor's Douay Bible makes no distinction in its vocabulary between "the devil" (that is, Satan) and the many "devils" (elsewhere translated as "demons" or "unclean spirits") that Jesus confronted in his ministry. The reader's interpretation of such phenomena, whether as a multiple personality disorder or as literal demonic possession, will be shaped by the reader's own presuppositions, and for the time being O'Connor leaves the question open.

After Tarwater sets fire to Powderhead he catches a ride with Meeks, a salesman "selling copper flues throughout the Southeast" (361), and it is as if the now absent stranger has taken on flesh. Meeks is even called "the stranger" (362), and further identified as Tarwater's "new friend" (364). Even as he rides with him, Tarwater remembers in another flashback his great uncle's warning: "'You are the kind of boy,' the old man said, 'that the devil is always going to be offering to assist, to give you a smoke or a drink or a ride, and to ask you your bidnis. You had better mind how you take up with strangers. And keep your bidnis to yourself'" (367). Meeks plays the part, asking him his business not once but repeatedly: "What line you going to get into?" (367); "What line you gonna get into, boy?" and "What you going to do? What kind of *work*?" (380). Tarwater's answer is guarded: "I ain't said what I'm going to do" (381). His involvement with Meeks goes on at some length (361–84), punctuated with flashbacks of his life with the old man, but Meeks finally takes him to a telephone, where he hears on the other end the voice of his retarded cousin Bishop, "the schoolteacher's child" he is called to baptize—a "bubbling noise, the kind of noise someone would make who was struggling to breathe in water" (383). It draws him relentlessly to itself, as if it were the voice of the old man. Meeks drops him at the schoolteacher's house, and the encounter with this "stranger" ends, as Tarwater "gave him one white-faced outraged look and flung himself from the car" (384). In a letter to Hawkes, O'Connor describes Meeks as a "comic" character who is "of the Devil because nothing in him resists the Devil. There's not much use to distinguish between them" (*Collected*

Passing by the Dragon

Works, 1119). Still, Meeks is not quite an embodiment of the devil, only his surrogate, and Tarwater survives the encounter.

The stranger's voice is silent for the next five chapters, as Tarwater is involved with Rayber and Bishop, first in the city and then at the Cherokee Lodge. Rayber is no devil, only a nihilist, and like Tarwater a candidate for grace, a failed one as we have seen. All the while a "strange waiting silence" surrounds Tarwater, demanding that he "baptize the child and begin at once the life the old man had prepared him for" (429). When he is finally reintroduced as "the wise voice that sustained him—the stranger who had kept him company while he dug his uncle's grave" (429–30), his "friend— no longer a stranger" speaks at considerable length. "What you want is a sign, a real sign, suitable to a prophet," he tells the boy. Not some "waiting silence," not the "peculiar hunger" he kept feeling for the bread of life, but a visible sign worthy of a Jonah or an Elijah or any true prophet (430–31).

The devil's strategy is two-pronged: to urge Tarwater either to wait for the unmistakable "sign" that will never come, and so do nothing to fulfill his calling, or else do "one thing to prove you ain't going to do another"—that is, drown Bishop in the lake instead of baptizing him. The second strategy plays out, yet misfires, as Tarwater tries to drown Bishop, but in the process blurts out the words of baptism (which O'Connor never quotes verbatim). The act is described twice: first through Rayber's hearing aid, as the quiet of the lake was broken "by an unmistakable bellow" (455) and Rayber knew instinctively that Tarwater "had baptized the child even as he drowned him" (456), and then in retrospect, as Tarwater, in the truck where he has hitched a ride, remembers Bishop's eyes on him in the boat, "fish-colored and fixed," and

> By his side, standing like a guide in the boat, was his faithful friend, lean, shadow-like, who had counseled him in both country and city. Make haste, he said. Time is like money and money is like blood and time turns blood to dust. The boy looked up into his friend's eyes, bent upon him, and was startled to see that in the peculiar darkness, they were violet-colored, very close and intense, and fixed on him with a peculiar look of hunger and attraction. He turned his head away, unsettled by their attention. (461)

And then the voice again: "Be a man, his friend counseled, be a man. It's only one dimwit you have to drown," and "This is no time to dwaddle, his mentor said. Once it's done, it's done forever" (462).

Finally, as daylight dawns in the cab of the truck, Tarwater relives the deed itself: "Suddenly in a high raw voice the defeated boy cried out the words of baptism, shuddered, and opened his eyes. He heard the sibilant oaths of his friend fading away in the darkness" (463). It is as if the "words of baptism" now repeated in the truck have become words of exorcism, dismissing Tarwater's Satanic "friend," at least momentarily. But it is not to be. Tarwater remains unchanged, "tried in the fire of his refusal, with all the old man's fancies burnt out of him, with all the old man's madness smothered for good" (464). Nowhere is this more evident than in Tarwater's startling vision of himself, as the sun of a new day rises, changing from a "ball of glare" to "something distinct like a large pearl."

Without warning, the point of view changes, so that we are now looking at Tarwater through "the stranger's" eyes: "Beyond the glare, he was aware of another figure, a gaunt stranger, the ghost who had been born in a wreck and who had fancied himself destined at that moment to the torture of prophecy. It was apparent to the boy that this person, who paid him no attention, was mad" (465). "The boy" is now the stranger—the devil himself—and "the gaunt stranger" in the vision none other than Tarwater, "the ghost who had been born in a wreck," and is "mad," even as old Mason was mad. It is a moment unique in the novel. The tables are turned, as if the reader is drawn into Tarwater's divided personality, forced to look at him through the devil's eyes as "the other," and in that sense demon possessed along with him.

The abrupt reversal is momentary. It would have been difficult to sustain for very long, and O'Connor does not try. Nor is the devil as fully in control as he seems. If he were, he would not have perceived young Tarwater as "mad." Instead, the battle for the boy's soul goes on. The devil makes his last and decisive move in the person of a young man driving "a lavender and cream-colored car" and dressed in "a lavender shirt and a thin black suit and a panama hat," with eyes "the same color as his shirt" (469). Like the salesman Meeks, he gives Tarwater a ride, but unlike Meeks he is no mere surrogate but the very embodiment of Tarwater's "friend" and "mentor." All the earlier hints, the imagined "stiff broad-brimmed panama hat that obscured the color of his eyes" (352), and the eyes themselves, "violet-colored, very close and intense" (461), now fall into place. Just as we were about to conclude that Tarwater's "stranger" was a merely psychological phenomenon, a kind of multiple personality disorder, O'Connor's literalism reasserts itself, as her devil takes on flesh in the person of a sexual predator who gets Tarwater drunk, rapes him and leaves him unconscious

(469–72). Here if anywhere in the novel, "the kingdom of God suffereth violence." Even though she knew that the faces of evil were "as often as not, our own grinning reflections" (830), O'Connor also knew that the devil is literally "out there" as well. Tarwater does not rape himself, and it is no hallucination, for the act is described from the rapist's own viewpoint as Tarwater sleeps (471). Once again, Tarwater is seen as "the other," through the eyes of the devil himself.

In this act of violence and violation O'Connor's very literal devil, like the devil of the Bible, overreaches. All the destructive intentions of Tarwater's "friend" and "mentor" are unmasked. Tarwater, on waking up, seizes the initiative with a violence of his own, as he "tore off a pine branch and set it on fire, and began to fire all the bushes around the spot until the fire was eating greedily at the evil ground, burning every spot the stranger could have touched" (472). He has finally begun to exorcise his demon. He returns to Powderhead, "ground that had been familiar to him since his infancy but now it looked like strange and alien country" (473). The devil is again a disembodied voice, yet "as pervasive as an odor," a kind of "violet shadow" around the boy's shoulders: "Go down and take it, his friend whispered. It's ours. We've won it. Ever since you first begun to dig the grave, I've stood by you, never left your side, and now we can take it over together, just you and me. You're not ever going to be alone again." It is an empty threat, and it goes unheeded as Tarwater fiercely shook himself free, started another fire, then "glared through the flames and his spirits rose as he saw that his adversary would soon be consumed in a roaring blaze. He turned and moved on with the burning brand tightly clenched in his fist" (475). The "stranger"—the "wise voice," "kind friend," and "mentor"—is now at last called by his right name, "adversary," the English translation of "Satan." The exorcism is complete. Tarwater is now free to become that "gaunt stranger" in the devil's vision, born in a wreck and "destined at that moment to the torture of prophecy" (465). We know the rest of his story, at least up to a point.

As for Rayber, he too has carried out an exorcism of sorts, having ridden himself once and for all of the "horrifying" divine love that has pursued him, and with it of any capability of feeling pain at the death of his son. Yet in one of her letters O'Connor holds out even for Rayber a shadow of hope: "He makes the Satanic choice, and the inability to feel the pain of his loss is the immediate result. His collapse then may indicate that he is not going to sustain his choice—but that is another book maybe" (*Collected Works*, 1170).

"Even if I didn't believe it, it would still be true"

In the same letter to John Hawkes in which she contrasted her devil and his, Flannery O'Connor spoke of a short story she had written "about one of Tarwater's terrible cousins, a lad named Rufus Johnson, and it will add fuel to your theory though not legitimately" (*Collected Works*, 1156). Two months earlier she had written to Betty Hester, "The thing I am writing now is surely going to convince Jack [that is, Hawkes] that I am of the Devil's party" (*Habit of Being*, 449). The story is "The Lame Shall Enter First," and indeed Tarwater and Rufus Johnson were "cousins" of sorts, in that the two of them were joint protégés of Rayber in the early drafts of *The Violent Bear It Away*. Published two years after the novel, it first appeared, ironically, in the same issue of the *Sewanee Review* (Summer 1962) in which Hawkes' published his article, "Flannery O'Connor's Devil."

"The Lame Shall Enter First" is a kind of spinoff of *The Violent Bear It Away*, with a widower named Sheppard corresponding to Rayber, his son Norton corresponding (more loosely) to Bishop, and Rufus Johnson corresponding (more loosely still) to Tarwater. He and Tarwater are both fourteen, and he has a fundamentalist grandfather reminiscent of old Mason. Rufus is a juvenile delinquent with a grossly deformed foot and an I.Q. of 140, a repeat offender whom Sheppard has befriended to the neglect of his own son. At the risk of oversimplification, Rufus Johnson could be described as an odd combination of Tarwater himself and his Satanic "friend" or "stranger." Yet Rufus has no divided personality, no inner torment to his soul. In sharp contrast to her treatment of Tarwater, O'Connor never tries to get inside his head to explore his inner thoughts. She looks at him only from the outside, and pictures him as someone who knows exactly who he is. He knows that Satan "has me in his power" (600), and that "when I die, I'm going to hell." Yet Rufus is a Bible believer, no less a fundamentalist than his grandfather.[1] When Sheppard objects that "Nobody has given any reliable evidence there's a hell," he answers, "The Bible has give the evidence," adding "if you die and go there you burn forever." "Whoever says it ain't a hell," he continued, "is contradicting Jesus. The

---

1. It is hard not to think that Rufus is modeled just a little after Willie, described by Rose Hawthorne Lathrop (Nathaniel Hawthorne's daughter and founder of The Dominican Congregation), as "a flourishing slip from criminal roots," whose "eyes had the sturdy gaze of satanic vigor" (quoted by O'Connor in her "Introduction to *A Memoir of Mary Ann*," *Collected Works*, 826–27). Willie was a Roman Catholic with a devout grandmother, not a Protestant fundamentalist with a devout grandfather, but otherwise the similarities are impressive.

dead are judged and the wicked are damned. They weep and gnash their teeth while they burn," and concluded, "Satan runs it" (611).

Here Rufus Johnson, in stark contrast to Tarwater's devil, speaks for O'Connor herself. As she confided to Hawkes, "In this one, I'll admit that the devil's voice is my own" (*Collected Works*, 1157). Rufus is without doubt a devilish figure, yet she wrote to her friend, Sister Mariella Gable, "In the gospels it was the devils who first recognized Christ and the evangelists didn't censor this information. They apparently thought it was pretty good witness" (*Collected Works*, 1184). In contrast to Satan, who demands that Jesus prove himself the Son of God (see Matt 4:3, 6; Luke 4:3, 9), the demons immediately acknowledged him as such. Their voices were the first—after God's voice at the baptism—to cry out publicly who he was. A "man with an unclean spirit" in the synagogue at Capernaum cried out, "What have we to do with thee, Jesus of Nazareth? Art thou come to destroy us? I know who thou art, the Holy One of God" (Mark 1:24). Not until much later in the Gospel story, and in a different Gospel, did Jesus's own disciples make such an acknowledgment, when the Apostle Peter in the same Capernaum synagogue confessed, "You are the Holy One of God" (John 6:69, New International Version; the Douay has it differently). The demons knew what the apostles know, only sooner. Jesus in fact is said to have "suffered them not to speak, because they knew him" (Mark 1:34).

Rufus Johnson too knows and speaks the truth about himself ("Satan has me in his power"), and about Sheppard ("He thinks he's Jesus Christ!" [609]). In terms of the distinction O'Connor once drew for Hawkes, Rufus is one of those devils who "go about piercing pretensions," *not* the one "who goes about like a roaring lion seeking whom he may devour" (*Collected Works*, 1151). He is both devil and Bible believer—*and* a reliable narrative voice! His theology clashes with Sheppard's at every point. When Norton asks if his mother who has died is in hell, Sheppard is horrified: "'No, no,' he said, 'of course she isn't. Rufus is mistaken. Your mother isn't anywhere. She's not unhappy. She just isn't,'" and "'your mother's spirit lives on in other people and it'll live on in you if you're good and generous'" (611–12). But Norton persists: "Is she there, Rufus," he asks, "Is she there, burning up?" Rufus asks him, "Did she believe in Jesus?" and when Norton desperately insists that she did, replies "She's saved," and "On high." "It's in the sky somewhere," he explains, "but you got to be dead to get there. You can't go in no space ship" (612).

As for the Bible, Rufus cares enough about it to steal one from a ten cent store, and when Sheppard finds the two boys reading it, admits "I was the one lifted it. He only watched. He can't sully himself. It don't make any difference about me. I'm going to hell anyway." "Unless" he is quick to add, "I repent," and "If I do repent, I'll be a preacher," because "If you're going to do it, it's no sense doing it half way" (626–27). Norton, still thinking of his mother "On high," wants to be "A space man!"but Rufus warns him, "Those space ships ain't going to do you any good unless you believe in Jesus," leafing through the Bible's pages to find the text that says so. Rufus's search triggers a confrontation, one that he seems to relish, for when Sheppard shouts "Put that Bible up!" Rufus "stopped and looked up. His expression was startled but pleased." Sheppard calls the Bible something "for cowards, people who are afraid to stand on their own feet and figure things out for themselves," provoking Rufus' sudden revelation: "'Satan has you in his power,' he said. 'Not only me. You too'" (627). The Bible as a physical object now becomes the center of attention as Sheppard tries to grab it and Rufus hides it in his lap. Sheppard laughs and tells him, "You don't believe in that book and you know you don't believe in it," and "You don't believe it. You're too intelligent," and yet again, "You don't believe it!" Rufus fires back, "You don't know what I believe and what I don't." "I ain't too intelligent," he adds. "You don't know nothing about me. Even if I didn't believe it, it would still be true," and finally, "I'll show you I believe it!" as he "opened the book in his lap and tore out a page and thrust it into his mouth" (627).

This is vintage O'Connor. The line, "Even if I didn't believe it, it would still be true," echoes her own sentiment, expressed to Betty Hester, that "The truth does not change according to our ability to stomach it emotionally" (*Collected Works,* 952). She and Rufus Johnson agree that truth, including the truth of the Bible, is absolute, not subjective. As for Rufus, after chewing up and swallowing two pages, "His eyes widened as if a vision of splendor were opening up before him. 'I've eaten it!' he breathed. 'I've eaten it like Ezekiel and it was honey to my mouth!'" (628). Rufus Johnson knows his Bible well enough to know what he is doing. Ezekiel was shown a book "written within and without: and there were written in it lamentations and canticles and woes," and was told to "eat this book and go speak to the children of Israel." He testifies that "I did eat it: and it was sweet as honey in my mouth. And he said to me: Son of man, go to the house of Israel, and thou shalt speak my words to them" (see Ezek 2:9—3:4). John too, in the book of Revelation, "took the book from the hand of the angel and ate it up; and it was in my mouth sweet as honey; but when I had eaten it my belly was bitter. And he said to me: Thou must prophesy again to many nations and peoples and tongues and kings" (Rev 10:10–11).

In similar fashion, it appears that the pages of the Bible that Rufus Johnson eats represent nothing less than a prophetic call, not unlike Tarwater's call to "Go warn the children of God of the terrible speed of mercy." Can it be that Rufus, like Ezekiel, John and Francis Marion Tarwater, is called to be a prophet? Well, yes and no. What kind of prophet claims that "Satan has me in his power," and "when I die, I'm going to hell"? Yet within the story he does have a prophecy, just one, directed at Sheppard and no one else. When he had eaten the two pages, "The boy rose and picked up the Bible and started toward the hall with it. At the door he paused, a small black figure on the threshold of some dark apocalypse. 'The devil has you in his power,' he said in a jubilant voice and disappeared" (628). In the end his prophecy turns out to be true, as Sheppard finally sees "the clear-eyed Devil, the sounder of hearts, leering at him from the eyes of Johnson" (632). He is overcome with "a rush of agonizing love" for his son Norton, closely akin to the "horrifying love" that Rayber desperately feared in *The Violent Bear It Away* (401). He promises to make everything up to Norton, but it is too late, as he finds the boy's body hanging "in the jungle of shadows, just below the beam from which he had launched his flight into space" in search of the mother he had lost (632).

As for Rufus, if his prophecy to Sheppard that "The devil has you in his power" was true, his knowledge that "Satan has me in his power" was just as true. The reader is left wondering whether he is an altogether false prophet like Tarwater's devil, or simply a flawed one like Hazel Motes, or the Tarwaters, or the ill-fated prophets from Judah and Israel in 1 Kings 13. He lies when he charges Sheppard with making "Immor'l suggestions," adding sanctimoniously that "I ain't having none of it, I'm a Christian," yet almost in the same breath, when Sheppard assures him that "You're not evil, you're morally confused. You don't have to make up for that foot," he shouts back, "I lie and steal because I'm good at it! My foot don't have a thing to do with it! The lame shall enter first! The halt'll be gathered together. When I get ready to be saved, Jesus'll save me," and "The lame'll carry off the prey!" (630–31). Once again, O'Connor herself is a kindred spirit. Just months after the story first appeared in print, she wrote to John Hawkes, "The more I see of students the vaguer my answers get. One of them in Texas fixed me with a seedy eye and said, 'Miss O'Connor, what is your motivation in writing?' 'Because I'm good at it,' says I" (November 4, 1962; *Habit of Being,* 500–501).

Even Rufus's garbled quotations of Scripture make a kind of sense in light of promises in Isaiah that "The Lord is our judge, the Lord is our lawgiver, the Lord is our king: he will save us," and "Then shall the spoils of much prey be divided: the lame shall take the spoil" (Isa 33:22–23), or that "God himself will come and save you. Then shall the eyes of the blind be opened: and the ears of the deaf shall be unstopped. Then shall the lame man leap as a hart, and the tongue of the dumb shall be free" (Isa 35:4–6). Or in Jeremiah: "Behold I will bring them from the north country and will gather them from the ends of the earth: and among them shall be the blind and the lame" (Jer 31:8). Or on the lips of Jesus, that "it is better for thee to enter lame into life everlasting than having two feet to be cast into the hell of unquenchable fire" (Mark 9:44; also Matt 18:8). Will Jesus in fact save Rufus Johnson when he is ready to be saved? His final words offer a glimpse of redemption, but only a glimpse. Even though the story's title echoes his frantic insistence that "The lame shall enter first!" his future remains murky, and O'Connor, in characteristic fashion, leaves it that way.

A GOSPEL STORY, TWICE RETOLD

Rufus Johnson is not the only demonic figure in O'Connor's fiction. Her familiarity with the New Testament accounts of demon possession surfaces in other stories as well. As we have seen, she knew that "it was the devils who first recognized Christ" (*Collected Works*, 1184), and in particular she knows of the remarkable account of "a man with an unclean spirit" (Mark 5:2), who when he saw Jesus at the lake of Galilee ran and fell at his feet:

> And, crying with a loud voice, he said: What have I to do with thee, Jesus the Son of the Most High God? I adjure thee by God that thou torment me not. For he said unto him: Go out of the man, thou unclean spirit. And he asked him: What is thy name? And he saith unto him: My name is Legion, for we are many. And he besought him much that he would not drive him away out of the country. And there was there near the mountain a great herd of swine, feeding. And the spirits besought him, saying: Send us into the swine, that we may enter into them. And Jesus immediately gave them leave. And the unclean spirits, going out, entered into the swine. And the herd with great violence was carried headlong into the sea, being about two thousand, and were stifled in the sea. (Mark 5:7–13)

The passage bristles with difficulties, even beyond the demoniac's startling knowledge of Jesus's divinity. How can one man be possessed by demons equal in number to a Roman legion? And what have demons to do with pigs? And who drowned in the sea, the pigs only or the demons as well? And if the demons did not drown, where did they go? This strange narrative is at work in one story from O'Connor's first collection ("The River"), and one from her second ("Revelation").

In "The River," young Harry Ashfield learns from his babysitter, Mrs. Connin, "that he had been made by a carpenter named Jesus Christ. Before that he had thought it had been a doctor named Sladewall, a fat man with a yellow mustache who gave him shots and thought his name was Herbert, but this must have been a joke. They joked a lot where he lived." Mrs. Connin reads to him out of an antique book (from 1832) entitled, "The Life of Jesus Christ for Readers Under Twelve," and he sees a picture of "the carpenter driving a crowd of pigs out of a man. They were real pigs, gray and sour-looking, and Mrs. Connin said Jesus had driven them out of this one man" (160). Harry, who was only "four or five" (155), was so fascinated by the picture that he hid the book in the lining of his coat. Harry had just learned that pigs were not, as he thought, "small fat pink animals with curly tails and grinning faces and bow ties," for he had just encountered in the Connin's backyard a "real pig," with a face "gray, wet and sour" right in his face, chasing him off in terror (158–59).

The illustration in the "small book, pale brown on the outside with gold edges and a smell like old putty," was extraordinary: instead of driving gargoyle-like demons out of the man into a nearby herd of pigs, Jesus was bringing literal pigs right out of the man's body! Such volumes were common enough around 1832, but the story of the demoniac was not exactly a favorite subject of Victorian illustrators. And does such a literalistic portrait actually exist anywhere, or is it a product of O'Connor's imagination, dramatizing the close biblical connection between "unclean spirits" and animals judged to be unclean by ancient Jewish law? In any event, the picture's stark literalism is thoroughly characteristic of O'Connor, a "literalist of the imagination" (Trowbridge, "Comic Sense," 77). The pig that had terrorized young Harry at the hog pen behind Mrs. Connin's house was quite in keeping with the pigs in the picture book, for it was "long-legged and hump-backed and part of one of his ears had been bitten off." Mrs. Connin's comment was that it "favors Mr. Paradise that has the gas station," with "the cancer over his ear," who always showed up at the healing services "to show he ain't been healed" (159). Mr. Paradise is later seen through the little boy's eyes sitting "like a humped stone on the bumper of a long ancient gray automobile," with "a gray hat that was turned down over one ear and up and over the other to expose a purple bulge on his left temple" (163), confirming in a moment Mrs. Connin's comparison of him to the pig. The parallels are unmistakable: the "hump-backed" pig and the "humped stone" on which the old man sat; the pig's "gray" face and the old man's "gray" hat and automobile; the pig's ear bitten off," and Mr. Paradise's "cancer over his ear" (see 159, 163).

If there is a devil in this story, it is Mr. Paradise, who is both comic and sinister in his resemblance to the pig that had so frightened Harry earlier in the day. And yet he has one thing in common with Bevel Summers, the young preacher and healer leading the service: Mr. Paradise comes regularly to show that he had not been healed, and for his part the healer tells the crowd, "This old red river is good to Baptize in, good to lay your faith in, good to lay your pain in, but it ain't this muddy water here that saves you. I been all up and down this river this week," adding that "Them people didn't see no healing, and "I never said they would" (163). In "territory held largely by the devil," where in Hazel Motes's words, "the blind don't see and the lame don't walk and what's dead stays that way," Bevel Summers' message is one of redemption, not necessarily physical healing: "There ain't but one river and that's the River of Life made out of Jesus' Blood. That's the river you have to lay your pain in, in the River of Faith, in the River of Life, in the River of Love, in the rich red river of Jesus' Blood, you people!" He cites the healings in the Bible, but keeps them in perspective:

> "Listen," he sang, "I read in Mark about an unclean man, I read in Luke about a blind man, I read in John about a dead man! Oh you people hear! The same blood that makes this River red, made that leper clean, made that blind man stare, made that dead man leap! You people with trouble," he cried, "lay it in that River of Blood, lay it in that River of Pain, and watch it move away toward the Kingdom of Christ, to be washed away, slow, you people, slow as this here old red water river round my feet."
> (162)

The young evangelist knows what O'Connor knew from her own illness, that healing is not guaranteed in this life, but only in Christ's kingdom, which for him as for O'Connor—and, arguably, the New Testament itself—is still future.

Young Harry is not there for healing, but he lays his pain in the river anyway. Bevel Summers baptizes him, and he cannot forget his abrupt baptism, nor the words of the young healer. "If I Baptize you," Bevel had said, "you'll be able to go to the Kingdom of Christ. You'll be washed in the river of suffering, son, and you'll go by the deep river of life." "You count now," he had told the boy, "You didn't even count before" (165). In his own way Harry had anticipated this moment, for as soon as he heard that the preacher's name was "The Reverend Bevel Summers" (155), he had decided that his own name was Bevel, even though it was really "Harry Ashfield and he had never thought at any time before of changing it" (156). That night, at home in bed after his baptism, he remembers it all. When his mother came and asked him repeatedly, "What did that dolt of a preacher say about me?" he heard her voice "from a long way away, as if he were under the river and she on top of it," and when she pulled him upright "he felt as if he had been drawn up from under the river," as if it had all been a dream or a joke. But he knew it was no joke, for he told her what the other Bevel had said: that "I'm not the same now," and that "I count" (168). His mother, having lowered him back onto the pillow, "brushed her lips against his forehead"—and promptly disappears from the story.

In the final scene, Harry wakes up early in the morning, and "all of a sudden he knew what he wanted to do" (169). Returning to the river, he "intended not to fool with preachers any more but to Baptize himself and to keep on going this time until he found the Kingdom of Christ in the river" (170). This time he does not see Mr. Paradise, who watched him from his shack at the gas station, "picked out a peppermint stick, a foot long and two inches thick, from the candy shelf, and stuck it in his hip pocket," then followed the boy first in his car and then on foot toward the river. Harry bounded into the river, "put his head under the water at once and pushed forward." At first, "The river wouldn't have him. He tried again and came up, choking." Finally, "he heard a shout and turned his head and saw something like a giant pig, bounding after him, shaking a red and white club and shouting. He plunged under once and this time, the waiting current caught him like a long gentle hand and pulled him swiftly forward and down. For an instant he was overcome with surprise; then since he was moving quickly and knew that he was getting somewhere, all his fury and his fear left him" (170–71).

From the world's standpoint the story's ending is pure tragedy, but from O'Connor's perspective it resembles nothing so much as a comic inversion or parody of the Gospel of Mark. Even though young Harry's intent was to "Baptize himself" (170), his death in the river is as much an exorcism, a self-exorcism at that, as a second baptism. To that extent, discussions of whether or not Harry was baptized twice are beside the point. Exorcism is, after all, an accompaniment of baptism in Roman Catholic ritual. Harry's self-exorcism turns the story in Mark on its head. Harry is drowning in the river like the pigs in the Gospel story, while the "pig" (Mr. Paradise) is on the shore desperately trying to "save" him from his watery journey to the kingdom of Christ! This is recognizably the same O'Connor who in an early college cartoon depicted one fish saying to another, "You can go jump out of the lake"! (see Trowbridge, "Comic Sense," 77–78).

To Harry's parents, "everything was a joke," and Mr. Paradise's "loud laugh" or "loud guffaw" when Harry was baptized sent the same message (164–65), but now the joke is on him. In the end God has the last laugh, as "the old man rose like some ancient water monster and stood empty-handed, staring with dull eyes as far down the river line as he could see" (171). His "red and white club" was the absurdly large peppermint stick he was carrying, suggesting that his first intent may have been to molest the boy, but in the end he is "empty-handed," implying that he has dropped it and now thinks only of the more immediate need to rescue young Harry, a "rescue" that would have restored Harry to the world and thwarted his salvation. The empty-handed "water monster" is robbed of his prey, in much the same way that Jesus claimed to have bound "the strong man" and robbed him of his goods (see Mark 3:27). Regardless of what her critics have thought, from O'Connor's perspective the story has a happy ending. It is comedy, not tragedy, but very serious comedy, for its ending evokes O'Connor's quotation from Cyril of Jerusalem about passing by the Dragon. The Dragon, identified in the book of Revelation as "that old serpent, who is called the devil and Satan" (Rev 12:9) makes an appearance here both as pig and water monster, in the person of Mr. Paradise.

While it may sound irreverent to speak of a "comic parody" of the Markan story about Jesus and the "Legion" of pigs, the parody is in its own way quite true to the biblical story itself, which has comic elements of its own. Jesus first commands the demon, "Go out of the man, thou unclean spirit" (Mark 5:8), but leaves room for some negotiation, as the unclean spirit first "besought him much that he would not drive him away out of the country" (v. 10), and then "the spirits besought him, saying: Send us into the swine, that we may enter into them" (v. 12). Jesus shrewdly agrees to the compromise, but whatever the Legion of demons may have had in mind backfires, as the herd of pigs, galvanized into self-destruction, drowns in the lake. Whether the demons are drowned with them or simply "go back to hell where they came from" is unclear, but in any event the joke is on them, just as the joke is on Mr. Paradise and on Harry's parents in "The River." The demons may know who Jesus is, but they cannot predict the behavior of a herd of pigs! O'Connor has paid tribute to the comic elements in the Gospel story, and thus to the story itself, in her quirky and poignant retelling of it.

If Harry Ashfield's redemptive exorcism was of his own making, the same cannot be said of Ruby Turpin's in one of O'Connor's last stories, "Revelation." But when the exorcism comes one day in a doctor's waiting room it is unmistakable, and Ruby knows it. "Go back to hell where you came from, you old wart hog," whispers the overweight unattractive Mary Grace—aptly named, for she is an agent of grace—to Ruby after "throwing the book at her" (O'Connor's literalism at work again!), hitting her just above the left eye with a substantial volume on *Human Development* (646). As in "The River," the echoes of the Gospel story of Jesus and the pigs are striking, amounting to conscious parody. Here, Ruby herself is cast in the role of the pig-like demon. Mary Grace is the exorcist, sending Ruby "back to hell where you came from"—an unmistakable formula of exorcism—yet Mary Grace herself exhibits the classic signs of someone demon possessed. She "made a loud ugly noise through her teeth"; her "raw face came crashing across the table toward her, howling," and her "fingers sank like clamps into the soft flesh of her neck" (643–44). This is not as odd as it seems, for even in the Gospel, the Greek verb from which the words "exorcize" and "exorcism" are derived comes not on the lips of Jesus but in the cry of the demoniac himself, "I *adjure* [Gr. *orkizō*] thee by God that thou torment me not" (Mark 5:7, the compound verb *exorkizō*, lit. "exorcize," is virtually synonymous). Above all, Mary Grace is demonic in that she knows the truth about Ruby, just as the demons in the Gospel knew the truth about Jesus: "There was no doubt in her mind that the girl did know her, knew here in some intense and personal way, beyond time and place and condition" (645–46). Consequently Ruby takes the girl's message as something Walker Percy might have called a "message in a bottle,"[2] in this instance nothing less than a prophecy of sorts, a message from God.

All along, Ruby has been protective of the pigs she and her husband Claude raised on their farm. Like O'Connor herself,[3] her life, or at least

2. See Percy's *The Message in the Bottle*, in particular chapter 6, and still more particularly 125–39, "The Difference between a Piece of Knowledge and a Piece of News."

3. In her battle with lupus, O'Connor wrote to her friend Maryat Lee in 1958: "I owe my existence and cheerful countenance to the pituitary glands of thousands

her livelihood, depended on them. She had boasted to the other people in the waiting room: "'Our hogs are not dirty and they don't stink,' she said. 'They're cleaner than some children I've seen. Their feet never touch the ground.'" But now, as Mary Grace's words echo in her ears, they mingle with the words of the white trash woman in the same waiting room, "Hogs. Nasty stinking things, a-gruntin and a-rootin and a-groanin" (638), and she begins to see them in the same light (651). As she angrily hoses them down in her outdoor pig parlor, Ruby turns her fury against God. "What do you send me a message like that for?" she asks in a voice strangely like that of Mary Grace herself, "a low fierce voice, barely above a whisper but with the force of a shout in its concentrated fury." Relentlessly, she presses her case: "How am I a hog and me both? How am I saved and from hell too?" (652), and finally:

> "Go on," she yelled, "call me a hog! Call me a hog again. From hell. Call me a wart hog from hell. Put that bottom rail on top. There'll still be a top and bottom!" A garbled echo returned to her. A final surge of fury shook her and she roared, "Who do you think you are?" The color of everything, field and crimson sky, burned for a moment with a transparent intensity. The question carried over the pasture and across the highway and the cotton field and returned to her clearly like an answer from beyond the wood. (653)

The echo comes back at her—"Who do you think you are?"—and at last Ruby is silent. She fixes her gaze first on the highway where her husband Claud is driving the hired help home, then, "as if through the very heart of mystery, down into the pig parlor at the hogs," with "her gaze bent to them as if she were absorbing some abysmal life-giving knowledge" (653). The words "abysmal" and "life-giving" are carefully chosen. In her pig parlor, Ruby is looking into the "abyss," or "bottomless pit," from which, according to the book of Revelation, all demons come (see Rev 9:1–2, 11; 11:7; 17:8), and yet there she finds the "life-giving knowledge" which turns out to be nothing more than simple self-knowledge. In looking, Ruby finally sees herself as demon and victim alike, in her own words "a hog and me both," someone "saved and from hell too." Just as Mary Grace knew her "beyond time and place and condition" (646), now at last Ruby knows herself. The back-handed exorcism, "Go back to hell where you came from,

---

of pigs butchered daily in Chicago Illinois at the Armour packing plant. If pigs wore garments I wouldn't be worthy to kiss the hems of them. They have been supporting my presence in the world for the last seven years" (*Collected Works*, 1063).

you old wart hog," has found its target: self-knowledge first of all, and in the end Ruby's redemption.

O'Connor, less than three months before her death, wrote to Maryat Lee, "You got to be a very big woman to shout at the Lord across a hog pen. She's a country female Jacob. And that vision is purgatorial" (*Collected Works*, 1207). One might as easily invoke Job, or perhaps Habakkuk on his watchtower (Hab 2:1), but Jacob is just as appropriate, for he was "strong against God" (Gen 32:28), and, in a passage O'Connor marked in her Bible, Jacob "saw in his sleep a ladder standing upon the earth, and the top thereof touching heaven; the angels of God also ascending and descending on it" (Gen 28:12). When he awoke, he trembled and said, "How terrible is this place! This is no other than the house of God, and the gate of heaven" (28:17). Something of the kind happens to Ruby as well. She "lifted her head" and saw "a purple streak in the sky," and she heralds a vision of her own with a "gesture hieratic and profound," as a "visionary light settled in her eyes" (653). And before her eyes the purple streak in the sky becomes

> a vast swinging bridge extending upward from the earth through a field of living fire. Upon it a vast horde of souls were rumbling toward heaven. There were whole companies of white-trash, clean for the first time in their lives, and bands of black niggers in white robes, and battalions of freaks and lunatics shouting and clapping and leaping like frogs. And bringing up the end of the procession was a tribe of people whom she recognized at once as those who, like herself and Claud, had always had a little of everything and the God-given wit to use it right ... They were marching behind the others with great dignity, accountable as they had always been for good order and common sense and respectable behavior. They alone were on key. Yet she could see by their shocked and altered faces that even their virtues were being burned away. (654)

While Ruby, not being Catholic, would not have called her vision purgatorial, she learns at last what old Mason Tarwater knew: that "even the mercy of the Lord burns" (342). She and Claud and the "tribe of people" like them, with their "good order and common sense and respectable behavior," are more like Presbyterians who want everything "done decently and according to order" (as in 1 Cor 14:40). In the same letter to Maryat Lee in which she called Ruby's vision "purgatorial," O'Connor added "I don't reckon Deanies [i.e., Maryat's niece's] Presbyterian instincts operate on middling planes of glory" (*Collected Works*, 1207), implying that

"Purrrgatory" (as she humorously spells it) might come as a shock to such "respectable" Protestants. Even in this most profoundly redemptive scene in all of her fiction, humor dances just below the surface, in the "battalions of freaks and lunatics shouting and clapping and leaping like frogs." Frogs in the Bible are at best a plague (Exod 8:1–14), and at worst, like pigs, demonic (Rev 16:13–14), but in Ruby's vision they are just part of the hilarity of the scene. The devil and all his hosts are vanquished. Ruby Turpin, the "wart hog from hell" is now "rumbling toward heaven," behind all the trashy people she once despised.

Still, the apparent universalism of the scene should not be pressed too far. The stories we have looked at so far offer little hope that, say, Harry Ashfield's parents or Mr. Paradise will find their way to God, even by way of purgatory, and if perchance Rayber or Sheppard or Rufus Johnson find it in the end, it is no part of the story proper, but something way beyond the story. Those who do find their way, from Hazel Motes to Francis Marion Tarwater to Norton to Harry Ashfield to Ruby Turpin, are apt to do so with a bit of help from the kind of devil who, as O'Connor told Hawkes, "is always accomplishing ends other than his own" (*Collected Works,* 1119). The devil is very real to her, but far from being "on the devil's side," she exorcises the devil by viewing reality through many eyes, including the devil's own and those of his victims, inviting us to do the same. She once wrote that the Christian novelist must "do the best he can with the world he has," so that "instead of reflecting the image at the heart of things, he has only reflected our broken condition and, through it, the face of the devil we are possessed by. This is a modest achievement, but perhaps a necessary one" (*Mystery and Manners,* 168).

In fact she has done more, for in reading to the end of these stories, we are drawn under the water with young Harry on his way to the Kingdom of Christ, and we look down with Ruby into the abyss that is her pig parlor before looking up through her eyes at the "vast swinging bridge extending upward from the earth through a field of living fire" (653–54). "Go up to Zion": Amos Wilder once wrote, "hear the angels sing and look through the trapdoor into Abaddon," and "Go not to be tranquilized but to be exorcised" (Wilder, *Grace Confounding,* 11–12). In much the same vein O'Connor evokes for us, not once but twice, the story of Jesus and a herd of pigs in the Gospel of Mark, offering us her own kind of exorcism.

6

The Good, the Bad,
and the Compassionate

THE TITLE OF FLANNERY O'Connor's best known short story, "A Good Man Is Hard to Find," finds unexpected confirmation in the Gospel of Mark, when a man comes and kneels before Jesus, asking him "Good Master, what shall I do that I may receive life everlasting?" and Jesus replies, "Why callest thou me good? None is good but one, that is God" (Mark 10:17–18). If even Jesus, the Son of God, is not "good," then a good man is indeed hard to find! Even the Gospel of Matthew found it necessary to record the exchange differently, as Jesus replies instead, "Why askest thou me concerning good? One is good, God" (Matt 19:16–17). Years ago, when I first encountered this strange disclaimer, it raised questions for me. How could the Son of God deny that he was "good"? Someone wiser than I suggested that I read it not as "Why do you call *me* good?" but as "*Why* do you call me good?" That is, what Jesus meant was that we should not view him as a "good teacher" or a "good man" unless we were prepared to confess him at the same time as God, for only God is truly "good." Not altogether conclusive, but as plausible a solution as any for those who—with the Gospel of Mark itself—believe that Jesus was in fact the Son of God (see for example Mark 1:1, 11; 3:11–12; 15:39). And both Gospels agree that, strictly speaking, the adjective "good" belongs to God alone, so that "A good man is hard to find" is, if anything, an understatement!

"Strictly speaking," yes, but we do not always speak strictly. Most of the time we do not, in fact, as O'Connor seems to have understood in her Introduction to *A Memoir of Mary Ann*, a book about a saintly little girl with a disfigured face: "Most of us have learned to be dispassionate about evil, to look it in the face and find, as often as not, our own grinning reflections with which we do not argue, but good is another matter. Few have stared at that long enough to accept the fact that its face too is grotesque, that in us the good is something under construction" (*Collected Works*, 830). In a number of her short stories, O'Connor explores the "good under construction" that we encounter in this fallen world. "A Good Man Is Hard to Find" is the most widely read of O'Connor's stories, the one she herself commented on most frequently, and the one she felt most compelled to "rescue" from bizarre interpretations and wrong-headed interpreters.

Good Blood

The story is about an unnamed grandmother from Atlanta who tags along with her son Bailey and his family on a trip to Florida, unnamed perhaps because she could be anyone's grandmother. The old lady values her blood relations and her memories. She would have preferred "to visit some of her connections in east Tennessee," and she even has a strategy to steer them away from Florida, pointing out a newspaper article about someone else who is unnamed, but has named himself. "Here this fellow that calls himself The Misfit is aloose from the Federal Pen and headed toward Florida," she told her son. "I wouldn't take my children in any direction with a criminal like that aloose in it. I couldn't answer to my conscience if I did." The strategy does not work. They are headed to Florida. "She wouldn't stay at home for a million bucks," her granddaughter June Star said. "Afraid she'd miss something. She has to go everywhere we go" (137).

Sure enough, the grandmother is the first one in the car next morning, with Pitty Sing, the cat, carefully hidden in a basket under her black valise. She is wearing white gloves, "a navy blue dress" with collars and cuffs of "white organdy trimmed with lace," so that if she were killed in an accident everyone "would know at once that she was a lady." She is a lady of manners, manners not shared by Bailey or the children, or by "the children's mother" with her slacks and "her head tied up in a green kerchief" (138). The generational divide is evident. The children read comics and the mother sleeps, as the old lady cautions Bailey about speed limits and points out "interesting details of the scenery." She bores the family but charms the reader, allowing us to see though her eyes "the brilliant red clay banks slightly streaked with purple; and the various crops that made rows of green lace-work on the ground. The trees were full of silver-white sunlight and the meanest of them sparkled" (138–39). When the eight-year-old grandson John Wesley scorns her beloved Tennessee as "just a hillbilly dumping ground" and his native Georgia as "a lousy state too" and June Star agrees, the grandmother drops the first hint that quite possibly a good man might indeed be hard to find. "In my time" she replies, "children were more respectful of their native states and their parents and everything else. People did right then." Her nostalgia tempered with humor continues. First, when she spots a small graveyard in the middle of a cotton field, she explains to the children, "That belonged to the plantation," and when John Wesley asks where the plantation was, "'Gone With the Wind,' said the grandmother, 'Ha, Ha.'" (139). Later, she regales the children with a funny story about "once when she was a maiden lady," courted by "a very good-looking man and a gentleman" named Edgar Atkins Teagarden (140).

Only when they stop for barbecued sandwiches at a place called The Tower, run by "a fat man named Red Sammy Butts" does the grandmother encounter a kindred spirit. Red Sammy is first seen with his head under a truck outside the place. His wife, an unnamed "tall burnt-brown woman with hair and eyes lighter than her skin," takes their order, and Sammy comes in telling her to hurry up with it. Then he sits down at a nearby table, and with "a combination sigh and yodel" exclaims repeatedly, "You can't win," as he "wiped his sweating red face off with a gray handkerchief," adding "These days you don't know who to trust," and "Ain't that the truth?"

So far as manners are concerned, Red Sammy and the grandmother could not be more different. She, as we know, is dressed like a lady, while Sammy's "khaki trousers reached just to his hip bones and his stomach hung over them like a sack of meal swaying under his shirt." Yet they see things eye to eye right from the start. She immediately agrees with him that "People are certainly not nice like they used to be" (141). Red Sammy offers a case in point, telling how he allowed two customers to "charge the gas they bought. Now why did I do that?" "Because you're a good man!" she is quick to reply. "'Yes'm, I suppose so,' Red Sam said as if he were struck with this answer." But his wife, just now bringing in the orders, is not so sure: "'It isn't a soul in this green world of God's that you can trust,' she said. 'And I don't count nobody out of that, not nobody,' she repeated, looking at Red Sammy." The grandmother brings up The Misfit again, and Sammy's wife continues, "I wouldn't be a bit surprised if he didn't attact this place right here," and "If he hears it's two cent in the cash register, I wouldn't be a tall surprised if he . . ." But Red Sammy cuts her off, sending her off for the "Co'-Colas" and resuming an amiable conversation with the grandmother: "'A good man is hard to find,' Red Sammy said. 'Everything is getting terrible. I remember the day you could go off and leave your screen door unlatched. Not no more.' He and the grandmother discussed better times. The old lady said that in her opinion Europe was entirely to blame for the way things were now. She said the way Europe acted you would think we were made of money and Red Sam said it was no use talking about it, she was exactly right" (142). The grandmother and Red Sammy are soulmates in their conviction that "Everything is getting terrible," and their nostalgia for "better times," and yet it is Sammy's wife, with her unwillingness to make any exceptions at all, who comes the closest to the biblical principle that "None is good but one, that is God."

Soon they are back on the road, and just outside of Toombsboro the grandmother, still in the nostalgia mode, remembers another "old plantation that she had visited in this neighborhood once when she was a young lady," a "house with six white columns across the front" and "an avenue of oaks leading up to it and two little wooden trellis arbors on either side in front where you sat down with your suitor after a stroll in the garden. She recalled exactly which road to turn off to get to it" (142–43). She has deceived the family once, by hiding Pitty Sing in the car knowing full well that Bailey "didn't like to arrive at a motel with a cat" (138), and now she does it again: "'There was a secret panel in this house,' she said craftily, not telling the truth but wishing that she were, 'and the story went that all the family silver was hidden in it when Sherman came through but it was never found ...'" (143). This triggers a demand from John Wesley and June Star that the mansion be found and thoroughly searched. Bailey, who did not have the grandmother's "naturally sunny disposition," is not pleased, but cannot withstand the pressure of the children's yelling and screaming, quietly abetted by the grandmother ("It will be very educational for them"). So they turn around, looking for the dirt road that she remembered, but when they find it and have been on it for awhile, "a horrible thought occurred to her," setting off a chain reaction: "The thought was so embarrassing that she turned red in the face and her eyes dilated and her feet jumped up, upsetting her valise in the corner. The instant the valise moved, the newspaper top she had over the basket under it rose with a snarl and Pitty Sing, the cat, sprang onto Bailey's shoulder" (144).

And so, the ACCIDENT! (144–46). The grandmother's two deceits, hiding the cat and then lying about the secret panel in her beloved old plantation house, come back to haunt her in a moment, as "the car turned over once and landed right-side-up in a gulch off the side of the road" (144). To make it worse, we learn belatedly that "The horrible thought she had had before the accident was that the house she had remembered so vividly was not in Georgia but in Tennessee." Where else? That, we learned from the start, was where she had "connections" (137). After the accident the grandmother decides that "she would not mention that the house was in Tennessee" (145). So much for nostalgia, and "better times."

So far, "A Good Man Is Hard to Find" could be just a comic story about a scheming but muddle-headed grandmother and a vacation gone sour. But it is not over. Manners are about to collide with mystery. While the family licks its wounds in a gulch ten feet below the road, "a big battered hearse-like automobile" comes into view, with three occupants all carrying guns, "a fat boy in black trousers and a red sweat shirt with a silver stallion embossed on the front of it," another boy with "khaki pants and a blue striped coat and a gray hat" and an older man with "silver-rimmed spectacles that gave him a scholarly look," no shirt or undershirt, and "blue jeans that were too tight for him" (145–46). The older man is in charge, for he calls the other two by name (Bobby Lee and Hiram) and tells them what to do. He is seen through the grandmother's eyes, for she "had the peculiar feeling that the bespectacled man was someone she knew. His face was as familiar to her as if she had known him all her life but she could not recall who he was" (146).

Her "peculiar feeling" is confirmed a few moments later when she "scrambled to her feet and stood staring. 'You're The Misfit!' she said. 'I recognized you at once.'" Not a wise thing to say. The Misfit says, "Yes'm," but adds ominously, "it would have been better for all of you if you hadn't of reckernized me." Bailey then "said something to his mother that shocked even the children," and The Misfit gallantly apologizes for Bailey. The grandmother pleads, "You wouldn't shoot a lady, would you?" and almost screams, "I know you're a good man. You don't look a bit like you have common blood. I know you must come from nice people" (147). And again: "you shouldn't call yourself The Misfit because I know you're a good man at heart. I can just look at you and tell." The first time she says it, The Misfit agrees that he did come from nice people: "'Yes, mam,' he said, 'finest people in the world,'" and he added, "God never made a finer woman than my mother and my daddy's heart was pure gold." The second time she says it, The Misfit and Bailey are both squatting on the ground in front of her. Bailey interrupts her and tries to take charge, but The Misfit ignores him: "I pre-chate that, lady," he replies, and orders Hiram and Bobby Lee to take Bailey and John Wesley off into the woods. The grandmother shouts, "Come back this instant!" and when she saw that it was too late, just "Bailey Boy!" Instead of Bailey she sees The Misfit alone, "squatting on the ground in front of her," and "I just know you're a good man," she says again, now for the third time, "You're not a bit common!" (147–48)

The Misfit finally "considered her statement carefully," and in contrast to Red Sammy's smug "Yes'm, I suppose so" (142), his answer is "Nome, I ain't a good man," adding "but I ain't the worst in the world neither. My daddy said I was a different breed of dog from my brothers and sisters," and with this he begins to reflect on his past (148–49). He is not far into it when two shots ring out, and again the grandmother calls out, "Bailey Boy!" But The Misfit continues, recalling that he has been, among other things, a gospel singer, "in the arm service," "twict married," "an undertaker," "with the railroads," and "somewheres along the line I done something wrong and got sent to the penitentiary. I was buried alive" (149). "Pray, pray," the old lady tells him, "pray, pray," and that if he would pray, "Jesus would help you" (149–50). The Misfit knows it. "That's right," he replies, but adds, "I don't want no hep," and "I'm doing all right by myself." Just then Bobby Lee and Hiram come back from the woods dragging Bailey's shirt, a shirt that could not be missed, yellow with bright blue parrots. The Misfit puts it on, and "The grandmother couldn't name what the shirt reminded her of" (150). Another example, perhaps, of what Gerard Manley Hopkins called "instress," recalling Rayber's reaction to anything that reminded him of Bishop (401), or Tarwater's, to any observed object that "would suddenly stand before him, strange and terrifying, demanding that he name it and name it justly" (343). In Rayber it triggered a "horrifying love" for Bishop, as we have seen, and one suspects that it is much the same with the grandmother in her love for "her only boy" (137), a love that so far as we can tell was neither deserved nor reciprocated, and that she cannot yet name.

Next, the children's mother and June Star and the baby are taken away, and the grandmother is alone with The Misfit. "Jesus, Jesus," she kept saying, meaning that, as she had said before, "Jesus will help you, but the way she was saying it, it sounded as if she might be cursing." "Yes'm." he replies, just as he had said before, "That's right," and this time it sets him to thinking about Jesus: "Jesus thown everything off balance. It was the same case with Him[1] as with me except He hadn't committed any crime and they could prove I had committed one because they had the papers on

1. The consistent capitalization of pronouns referring to Jesus on the lips of The Misfit is striking. Capitalization obviously belongs to writing and not to speech, and yet by using capital letters in the written story O'Connor is signaling at the very least The Misfit's immersion in the Christian culture of the South, and perhaps beyond that a kind of reverence that is by no means contradicted by what he actually says about Jesus.

me" (151). He sounds a little like the thief on the cross in Luke, who acknowledged that he and his companion were there "justly; for we receive the due reward of our deeds: but this man hath done no evil." Yet he is not about to say anything remotely like "Lord, remember me when thou shalt come into thy kingdom" (Luke 23:41, 42). While he admits that "they had the papers on me," he is also convinced that the punishment did not fit the crime: "'I call myself The Misfit,' he said, 'because I can't make what all I done wrong fit what all I gone through in punishment.'"

A scream and a pistol shot are heard from the woods, but the grandmother only says to The Misfit, in an effort to save her own life, "'Jesus!' the old lady cried, 'You've got good blood! I know you wouldn't shoot a lady! I know you come from nice people! Pray! Jesus, you ought not to shoot a lady. I'll give you all the money I've got'" (151–52). Two more pistol shots signal the deaths of the children's mother and June Star and the baby, and the grandmother "raised her head like a parched old turkey hen crying for water and called 'Bailey Boy, Bailey Boy!'"—now for the third and fourth time—"as if her heart would break." What is conspicuous in her outcry is that her only thought is for Bailey, her son, not for "the children's mother" or even the children. As for The Misfit, he ignores the grandmother and goes on with his soliloquy:

> "Jesus was the only One that ever raised the dead," The Misfit continued, "and He shouldn't have done it. He thown everything off balance. If He did what He said, then it's nothing for you to do but thow away everything and follow Him, and if He didn't, then it's nothing for you to do but enjoy the few minutes you got left the best way you can—by killing somebody or burning down his house or doing some other meanness to him. No pleasure but meanness," he said and his voice had become almost a snarl. (152)

All this is closely akin to C. S. Lewis' well-known assessment of the claim of Jesus to be the Son of God, a claim so shocking "that only two views of this man are possible. Either he was a raving lunatic of an unusually abominable type, or else He was, and is, precisely what He said.[2] There is no middle way" (*The Problem of Pain*, 11–12). Or, in O'Connor's own words to Betty Hester, "As for Jesus being a realist: if He was not God, He was no realist, only a liar, and the crucifixtion [*sic*] an act of justice" (*Collected Works*, 943). Lewis, O'Connor, and The Misfit are in agreement on one thing: whatever else he was, Jesus of Nazareth—in keeping with his

2. Notice again Lewis' capitalization of "He" in the second clause, in contrast to lower case "he" in the first.

disclaimer, "Why callest thou me good?"—was *not* simply a "good man," or a "good" teacher of moral principles. As O'Connor once wrote to Cecil Dawkins, "It's not a matter in these stories of Do Unto Others. That can be found in any ethical culture series. It is the fact of the Word made flesh. As The Misfit said, 'He thrown everything off balance and it's nothing for you to do but follow Him or find some meanness'" (*Collected Works*, 1035).

Still, O'Connor is no mere ventriloquist putting her own words into the mouth of a serial killer, for The Misfit's way of stating his dilemma is different. Why for example does he say Jesus "raised the dead" instead of "rose from the dead"? Clearly, Jesus' claim to be the Son of God rests on his own resurrection, not on raising three people from the dead (i.e., Jairus' daughter in Matt 9:18–26, Mark 5:21–43, and Luke 8:40–56, the widow's son at Nain in Luke 7:11–17, and Lazarus in John 11:1–44), all of whom eventually died again. Unlike Hazel Motes, who preached that "what's dead stays that way" (59), The Misfit is a believer of sorts, more like Rufus Johnson. He has no doubt that Jesus raised the dead, "the only One," in fact, who ever did. His complaint is that "He shouldn't have done it," and he adds (now for the second time) that Jesus "thown everything off balance." Why the interest in the Gospel claims that Jesus raised the dead? Is it because The Misfit himself remembered being "buried alive" in prison? "Turn to the right, it was a wall," he had said. "Turn to the left, it was a wall. Look up it was a ceiling, look down it was a floor" (149–50). Is he asking why Jesus did not raise *him* from the dead? It is difficult to say, and it is unfair to expect him to state the alternatives quite as precisely as C. S. Lewis, or O'Connor herself. Their way of putting it was "If He was who He said He was," but The Misfit's words instead are "If He did what He said." What is it that Jesus either "did" or "didn't" do that creates the dilemma? Is it raising the dead? The Misfit claimed to have no doubt about that. Or is it that he either died for sinners and rose again, as he said he would, or he did not? One suspects that this is the unspoken issue at the heart of The Misfit's inner torment.

The Misfit's soliloquy ends with talk of "killing somebody or burning down their house or doing some other meanness to him. No pleasure but meanness"—this with a "snarl"—and the grandmother is more frightened than ever. In her best self-preservation mode, she tries to dissolve (not resolve) The Misfit's dilemma: "'Maybe He didn't raise the dead,' the old lady mumbled." Whatever her motives or state of mind, her comment brings The Misfit's torment into the open: "'I wasn't there so I can't say He didn't,' The Misfit said. 'I wisht I had of been there,' he said, hitting the ground with his fist. 'It ain't right I wasn't there because if I had of been there, I would of known. Listen lady,' he said in a high voice, 'if I had of been there I would of known and I wouldn't be like I am now.'" At this "her head cleared for an instant," and the grandmother "murmured, 'Why you're one of my babies. You're one of my own children!' She reached out and touched him on the shoulder" (152). No longer just "good blood" or "not a bit common," or "nice people." It is not a matter of "good blood," but of *her own* flesh and blood, her own "connections." The scene as O'Connor develops it is just the opposite of what we might have expected. When the grandmother said, "Maybe he didn't raise the dead," it sounded like a calculated ploy to save her own life, yet we were told that she said it "not knowing what she was saying." Now when she says, "you're one of my babies. You're one of my own children!" it sounds like a fantasy, something delusional, yet this time we are told that she said it the very moment her "head cleared for an instant." It is no delusion, but exactly the right move. Belatedly she grasps the true import of her "peculiar feeling that the be-spectacled man was someone she knew," with a face "as familiar to her as if she had known him all her life" (146).

The grandmother's remark is best seen in relation to Rayber's feeling in *The Violent Bear It Away* that if anything happened to his only son Bish-op "the whole world would become his idiot child" (442). O'Connor once comments in a letter to Alfred Corn that Rayber "had this idea that his love could be contained in Bishop but that if Bishop were gone, then there would be nothing to contain it and he would then love everything and specifically Christ" (*Collected Works*, 1170). This obviously did not happen to Rayber, for when Bishop drowned, as we have seen, Rayber simply col-lapsed (456). But in "A Good Man Is Hard to Find" it does happen. Bailey, the grandmother's "only boy," is now gone. He was far from retarded, but also far from perfect. To say that he lacked a "sunny disposition" (141) was an understatement. But the old lady loved him, and she mourned her loss by crying out "Bailey Boy!" four times. When his shirt was thrown back and The Misfit put it on she "couldn't name what the shirt reminded her of," but now at last she names the love that it represented, and in her moment of grace she reaches out in a gesture that Jonathan Edwards might have called "benevolence to Being in general," in the person of The Misfit.[3]

3. It is unclear whether or not O'Connor was familiar with Edwards' classic defini-tion in his *Dissertation on the Nature of True Virtue*: "True virtue most essentially consists in benevolence to Being in general. Or perhaps to speak more accurately, it is that consent, propensity and union of heart to Being in general, that is immediately exercised in a general good will" (Edwards, 2.262). From this Edwards concluded that "true virtue must chiefly consist in love to God; the Being of Beings, infinitely the

It is worth noticing that she does not say "my baby" or "my own child," but "one of my babies" and "one of my own children." Her "babies" are not just The Misfit, or Bailey, but "the children's mother" and John Wesley and June Star, and Bobby Lee and Hiram, and Red Sammy and his wife—and the whole world! Such love, the kind that Rayber called "horrifying," is as close as human beings can come to the love God has for them, yet it can never be quite the same. The Christian gospel is not that the death of God's only Son triggered his love for the whole world, but that because God *already* loved the whole world he gave up his only Son to die on the cross (John 3:16). That is, the Father's love for the world trumps even his love for the Son! The difference between God's love and human love is that while humans, at least in their catastrophic moments of grace, are *capable* of love, God *is* love (1 John 4:16).

In the end the grandmother is not only a recipient of grace, but the channel of grace to The Misfit. As O'Connor wrote to John Hawkes, "The Misfit is touched by the Grace that comes through the old lady when she recognizes him as her child, as she has been touched by the Grace that comes through him in his particular suffering" (*Collected Works*, 1125). Yet as soon as she touched him, "The Misfit sprang back as if a snake had bitten him and shot her three times through the chest. Then he put his gun down on the ground and took off his glasses and began to clean them" (152). O'Connor explained to Andrew Lytle that "This moment of grace excites the devil to frenzy" (*Collected Works*, 1121), and although The Misfit is not the devil, he sees the grandmother through the devil's eye. We have learned by this time to look for the Dragon, or "the old serpent," in O'Connor's stories. In "The River," he found embodiment in Mr. Paradise, staring downstream "like some ancient water monster," and he makes an appearance here in The Misfit's image of "a snake" threatening him in the grandmother's touch—a typically O'Connoresque reversal of expectations. It is not a matter of the grandmother confronting the Dragon in the person of The Misfit. On the contrary, he is one of her "own children." Instead, The Misfit confronts a gesture of grace that is to him the Dragon or "snake" that he fears most. "Grace is never received warmly," O'Connor wrote to Hawkes. "Always a recoil, or so I think" (*Collected Works*, 1150).

So while the grandmother is changed, even at the moment of death, The Misfit is not, at least not yet. As in the case of Tarwater, and Rayber, and Rufus Johnson, what happens *after* the story ends is another matter, and O'Connor always leaves that open-ended. Still, she cannot resist

greatest and best of Beings" (2.266).

imagining: "I don't want to equate the Misfit with the devil," she once wrote, "I prefer to think that, however unlikely this may seem, the old lady's gesture, like the mustard-seed, will grow to be a great crow-filled tree in the Misfit's heart,[4] and will be enough of a pain to him there to turn him into the prophet he was meant to become. But that's another story" (*Mystery and Manners*, 112–13). Within the story O'Connor actually wrote, The Misfit is indeed unchanged, at least on the surface. At the moment the grandmother reached out to him, he looked "as if he were going to cry." Now she lies in a puddle of blood with "her face smiling up at the cloudless sky," and The Misfit's eyes, without his glasses, are still "red-rimmed and pale and defenseless-looking" (152–53). Does he see more clearly without them? Perhaps, for in the end when Bobby Lee sums up the day as "Some fun!"[5] he tells Bobby Lee to "Shut up," because "It's no real pleasure in life."

In contrast to what he said earlier, no pleasure even in meanness. And while nothing like the prophetic calling that O'Connor imagined for him is anywhere on the horizon, The Misfit does see the grandmother more clearly, no longer through the devil's eye but through God's, or at least O'Connor's. "She would of been a good woman," he tells Bobby Lee, "if it had been somebody there to shoot her every minute of her life" (153). His verdict on the old lady, reminiscent of Samuel Johnson's famous remark that "when a man knows he is to be hanged in a fortnight, it concentrates his mind wonderfully,"[6] is fully in keeping with the consistent presupposition of the New Testament that "the kingdom of God is at hand" (Mark 1:15), "the coming of the Lord is at hand" (Jas 5:8), "the end of all is at hand" (1 Pet 4:7), and "the time is at hand" (Rev 1:3). A constant sense of accountability and the nearness of final judgement is a powerful incentive to a "good" life. In the end, "a good woman" is as hard to find as "a good man," and the price to be paid just as great.

4. The biblical reference is unmistakable (see Luke 13:19, where the Kingdom of God is "like a grain of mustard seed, which a man took and cast into his garden, and it grew and became a great tree, and the birds of the air lodged in the branches thereof"; also Matt 13:31–32).

5. Remembering that Nathaniel Hawthorne was one of O'Connor's models, it is worth noticing that Bobby Lee sounds a bit like the withered old crone who said, "Here has been a sweet hour's sport!" at the end of Hawthorne's tale of evil, "The Hollow of the Three Hills" (Hawthorne, *Tales and Sketches*, 11).

6. *Boswell's Life of Johnson*, 2.127.

What is the effect of this story on the reader? "Compassion" above all, or so it would seem—surely for the majority of readers, who are on the look-out for "the dead bodies," but even for those who know what O'Connor is up to and are fully aware of the "action of grace in the Grandmother's soul" (*Mystery and Manners*, 113). Who can read it and not feel compassion for Bailey Boy, June Star, and John Wesley, despite their less than endearing qualities, not to mention "the children's mother" and the baby, the old lady herself, and even The Misfit and his companions? All but the cat, perhaps, who is safe in The Misfit's arms when the story ends.

And yet O'Connor herself was ambivalent at best about compassion: "It's considered an absolute necessity these days for writers to have compassion. Compassion is a word that sounds good in anyone's mouth and which no book jacket can do without. It is a quality which no one can put his finger on in any exact critical sense, so it is always safe for anyone to use" (*Mystery and Manners*, 43). She put it far more strongly in her Introduction to *A Memoir of Mary Ann*:

> Ivan Karamazov cannot believe, as long as one child is in tor-
> ment; Camus' hero cannot accept the divinity of Christ, because
> of the massacre of the innocents. In this popular pity, we mark
> our gain in sensibility and our loss in vision. If other ages felt
> less, they saw more, even though they saw with the blind, pro-
> phetical, unsentimental eye of acceptance, which is to say, of
> faith. In the absence of this faith now, we govern by tenderness.
> It is a tenderness which, long since cut off from the person of
> Christ, is wrapped in theory. When tenderness is detached from
> the source of tenderness, its logical outcome is terror. It ends in
> forced labor camps and in the fumes of the gas chamber. (*Col-
> lected Works*, 830–31)

Twenty-six years later, her words came to life again in the sermon of the crazed yet very wise Father Smith in Walker Percy's *The Thanatos Syndrome*:

> "But beware tender hearts! Don't you know where tenderness
> leads?" Silence. "To the gas chambers. Never in the history of
> the world have there been so many civilized tenderhearted souls
> as have lived in this century. Never in the history of the world
> have so many people been killed. More people have been killed
> in this century by tenderhearted souls than by the cruel barbar-
> ians in all other centuries put together." Pause. "My brothers, let

me tell you where tenderness leads." A longer pause. "To the gas chambers! On with the jets!" (361)

So far as I know, Percy never explicitly acknowledged O'Connor as the source of those remarks, but the two of them clearly shared a common distaste for the kind of tenderness or compassion that values quality of life over life itself. O'Connor, for her part, never made misplaced compassion a major theme in her stories to quite the same degree. Her portrait of Rayber comes close, perhaps, for he is torn between his "horrifying love" for Bishop and its polar opposite, the wrong-headed compassion that tempts him to drown the child. And he exemplified the same wrong-headed compassion when Bishop was born, and the doctor told him, "You should be grateful that his health is good. In addition to this, I've seen them born blind as well, some without arms and legs, and one with a heart outside." As if channeling Ivan Karamazov, Rayber asked, "How can I be grateful . . . when one—just one—is born with a heart outside?" and the unsentimental doctor told him, "You'd better try" (416). And it is the compassionate Rayber as well who envisions himself (like Holden Caulfield in J. D. Salinger's *Catcher in the Rye*) "moving like an avenging angel through the world, gathering up all the children that the Lord, not Herod, had slain" (413), "the exploited children of the world," so as to "let the sunshine flood their minds" (414). Not at all the "horrifying love" for the whole world that he feared would engulf him if he lost Bishop, but a sentimental and self-absorbed parody of that love.

"Compassion," of course, is not a bad word so far as the Bible is concerned, perhaps because in the Bible it is not, as O'Connor feared, "cut off from the person of Christ." Example can be piled upon example. The "good" Samaritan in Jesus' parable, though never explicitly called "good," was said to have been "moved with compassion" at the sight of the man in the ditch (Luke 10:33), and so too was the father of the prodigal son, when he saw his son "yet a great way off" and "running to him fell upon his neck and kissed him" (Luke 15:20). So was Jesus himself, when he saw the multitudes "distressed and lying like sheep that have no shepherd" (Matt 9:36), and again when he saw a widow who had lost her only son (Luke 7:13). In most of O'Connor's stories as well, compassion comes to more benign expression than in Father Smith's sermon, or even her own remarks in *A Memoir of Mary Ann*. Sometimes it is "good," and sometimes not. Ruby Turpin in "Revelation," for example, aspired to be what the grandmother in "A Good Man Is Hard to Find" might have been, "a good woman," and to her "good" meant compassionate, although she did not use the word:

> To help anybody out that needed it was her philosophy of life.
> She never spared herself when she found somebody in need,
> whether they were white or black, trash or decent. And of all she
> had to be thankful for, she was most thankful that this was so. If
> Jesus had said, "You can be high society and have all the money
> you want and be thin and svelte-like, but you can't be a good
> woman with it," she would have had to say, "Well don't make me
> that then. Make me a good woman and it don't matter what else,
> how fat or how ugly or how poor!" (642)

As we have seen, Ruby is finally moving in that direction at the end of the story, but not without cost.

Two other stories standing side by side in O'Connor's second collection, "The Lame Shall Enter First" and "The Comforts of Home," and are not usually thought of as a matched pair, yet together they illustrate O'Connor's ambivalence about compassion, or what it means to be "good." "The Lame Shall Enter First" is, as we have seen, among the most tragic of O'Connor's stories. Like "A Good Man Is Hard to Find," it evokes compassion from the reader, yet within the story itself compassion is the culprit. Sheppard, the widower in this story, did not have high expectations for Norton, his ten-year-old son: "All he wanted for the child was that he be good and unselfish and neither seemed likely." Sheppard himself had the look of a good and unselfish man, with his prematurely white hair that "stood up like a narrow brush halo over his pink sensitive face." Norton's selfishness frustrated him. He "tried to pierce the child's conscience with his gaze," and to teach him "what it means to share," but without noticeable success (595). The child missed his mother, and Sheppard told him, "Don't you think I'm lonely without her too? . . . but I'm not sitting around moping. I'm busy helping other people" (597–98). He was City Recreational Director, but also volunteered at the reformatory, "receiving nothing but the satisfaction of knowing he was helping boys no one else cared about" (596–97). That was how he met Rufus Johnson, and he was quick to remind Norton of everything Norton had that Rufus did not. As Sheppard saw it, Rufus Johnson "had a capacity for real response and had been deprived of everything from birth," while "Norton was average or below and had had every advantage." Consequently, Rufus "was worth any amount of effort because he had the potential" (599). What was "wasted" on Norton would cause Rufus Johnson to flourish (602).

We have already seen how it turns out. Norton, loyal to his father, tells Rufus Johnson, "He's good," because "He helps people," but Rufus knows better, and he speaks for O'Connor herself: "'Good!' Johnson said savagely. He thrust his head forward. 'Listen here,' he hissed, 'I don't care if he's good or not. He ain't *right*!'" (604). His further verdict on Sheppard is "He thinks he's Jesus Christ!" (609), or "He thinks he's God" (630). Sheppard himself confirms this judgement when, finally disillusioned with Rufus, he tells him, "I'm stronger than you are and I'm going to save you. The good will triumph." "Not when it ain't true," Rufus replies, "Not when it ain't right." Twice more Sheppard insists, "I'm going to save you," but again "Johnson thrust his head forward. 'Save yourself,' he hissed. 'Nobody can save me but Jesus'" (624). Defeated, Sheppard "wished he had never laid eyes on the boy. The failure of his compassion numbed him" (625). Still, he "knew without conceit that he was a good man, that he had nothing to reproach himself with" (626). The last phrase, interwoven with its companion refrain, "I did more for him than I did for my own child" (630–31), is one that he will repeat three more times before the story ends. In the end, his own words condemn him, and again it turns out that "a good man" is hard, if not impossible, to find.

Still, Sheppard's demonic "compassion" toward Rufus Johnson does not rise to the level of "forced labor camps," or "the fumes of the gas chamber." And in the story just preceding "The Lame Shall Enter First" in O'Connor's posthumous collection, *Everything That Rises Must Converge*, we encounter another kind of compassion that looks the same but in subtle ways is very different indeed. "The Comforts of Home" is also about a parent-child relationship, but in this instance, the "child" is thirty-five years old, not ten, the parent is a widow, not a widower, and the story is told from the viewpoint of the son, not the mother. Thomas's mother, unnamed like the grandmother in "A Good Man Is Hard to Find," is the kind of "good woman" that the grandmother might have been and that Ruby Turpin aspired to be: "Taking a box of candy was her favorite nice thing to do. When anyone within her social station moved to town, she called and took a box of candy; when any of her friend's children had babies or won a scholarship, she called and took a box of candy; when an old person broke his hip, she was at his bedside with a box of candy" (576). So when she saw in the paper a picture of a young girl in jail on a bad check charge, Thomas's mother said, "I'll take her a little box of candy."

That was how it began. The girl, Sarah Ham, a.k.a. Star Drake, plays the Rufus Johnson role in this story, but she is neither a demonic nor a prophetic figure like Rufus, but (as O'Connor put it in a letter to John Hawkes), more "like Enoch and Bishop—the innocent character, always unpredictable and for whom the intelligent characters are in some measure responsible for." She is just the "sort of innocent person who sets the havoc in motion" (*Collected Works*, 1147). Thomas, who lives with his mother, is amused at first, but in retrospect he "cursed his amusement" when he learned that the girl was addicted to alcohol and criminal behavior, and something else as well: "'That's just another way she's unfortunate,' his mother said. 'So awful, so awful. She told me the name of it but I forget what it is but it's something she can't help. Something she was born with. Thomas,' she said and put her hand to her jaw, 'suppose it were you?'" "Nimpermaniac," she finally remembers. "Nymphomaniac," Thomas corrects her (574–75). Thomas already knows of her tendencies: "She had invaded his room," and Thomas "had sprung out of his bed and snatched a straight chair and then he had backed her out the door, holding the chair in front of him like an animal trainer driving out a dangerous cat" (573–74).[7]

Later Thomas' mother lectures him on compassion. "Think of all you have," she reminds him. "All the comforts of home. And morals, Thomas. No bad inclinations, nothing bad you were born with" (582). Her admonition is eerily similar to Sheppard's lecture to ten-year-old Norton about Rufus Johnson in the other story: "Suppose you had to root in garbage cans for food? Suppose you had a huge swollen foot and one side of you dropped lower than the other when you walked?" "You have a healthy body," he told him, "a good home. You've never been taught anything but the truth. Your daddy gives you everything you need and want" (597). But Thomas, unlike Norton, does not take it lying down. So far as he is concerned, what his mother was about to do would "wreck the peace of the house" (573). She had a tendency, he thought, "with the best intentions in the world, to make a mockery of virtue, to pursue it with such a mindless intensity that everyone involved was made a fool of and virtue itself became ridiculous" (574). He loved his mother "because it was his nature to do so, but there were times when he could not endure her love for him. There were times when it became nothing but pure idiot mystery and he sensed about him forces, invisible currents entirely out of his control. She proceeded always from the tritest of considerations—it was the *nice thing to do*—into the most foolhardy engagements with the devil, whom, of course, she never recognized." Thomas was a historian, for whom the devil "was only a manner of speaking," but he believed that if his mother

7. This amusing scene evokes a story O'Connor once recounted to Betty Hester about Thomas's namesake, Thomas Aquinas, who, when his brothers (who did not want him to waste his life as a Dominican) "locked him up in a tower and introduced a prostitute into his apartment," drove her out with a red hot poker. "It would be fashionable today to be in sympathy with the woman," O'Connor commented, "but I am in sympathy with St. Thomas" (*Habit of Being*, 94).

had been "in any degree intellectual, he could have proved to her from early Christian history that no excess of virtue is justified, that a moderation of good produces likewise a moderation in evil, that if Antony of Egypt had stayed at home and attended to his sister, no devils would have plagued him" (575). He appreciated his mother's "saner virtues," above all the "well-regulated house she kept and the excellent meals she served. But when virtue got out of hand with her, as now, a sense of devils grew upon him, and these were not mental quirks in himself or the old lady, they were denizens with personalities, present though not visible, who might any moment be expected to shriek or rattle a pot" (576).

In short, Thomas allowed himself to view his mother's compassion for the wayward Sarah Ham as devilish, even though he himself did not believe in the devil. But in the course of the story he encounters his own devil in the person of his deceased father. He knew that "The old man would have had none of this foolishness. Untouched by useless compassion, he would (behind her back) have pulled the necessary strings with his crony, the sheriff, and the girl would have been packed off to the state penitentiary to serve her time." For his part, "Thomas had inherited his father's reason without his ruthlessness and his mother's love of good without her tendency to pursue it. His plan for all practical action was to wait and see what developed" (577). What developed was that Thomas's father "took up a squatting position in his mind" (583). His father, not his mother, becomes the truly Satanic presence in the story, a presence every bit as palpable as Tarwater's devil in *The Violent Bear It Away*: "The old man—small, wasp-like, in his yellowed panama hat, his seersucker suit, his pink, carefully-soiled shirt, his small string tie—appeared to have taken up his station in Thomas' mind and from there, usually squatting, he shot out the same rasping suggestion every time the boy paused from his forced studies. Put your foot down. Go to see the sheriff" (585). It is Tarwater's "friend" all over again, right down to the "yellowed panama hat" and the "pink, carefully-soiled shirt."

From here on the story moves inevitably to its tragic yet oddly farcical conclusion, orchestrated all the way by the same insistent voice: "The criminal slut stole your gun! See the sheriff! See the sheriff!" (589), "Go plant it in her pocketbook! (592), "You *found* it in her bag, you dimwit!" and in the end, "Fire!" (593). Thomas's mother, having thrown herself in front of the gun to protect the girl, is dead. The sheriff bursts in the door and draws the conclusion that "the killer and the slut were about to collapse into each other's arms" (594). There is no one to tell Thomas what Rufus Johnson told Sheppard, that "The devil has you in his power"

(628), but it is just as true. The irony is that Sheppard, "a good man" who had "nothing to reproach himself with" (626), became the devil's victim because of his misplaced and self-absorbed "compassion," while Thomas, who preferred "a moderation of good" to an "excess of virtue" (575), fell victim because he failed to recognize genuine compassion when he saw it, in his mother's treatment of "the little slut," Sarah Ham.

O'Connor in these two stories dramatizes "good" compassion first, in "The Comforts of Home," and then in "The Lame Shall Enter First" its Satanic counterfeit. If we go back to her remarks in her Introduction to "A Memoir of Mary Ann," we can infer that the issue is whether or not the compassion—or tenderness—is cut off from its source, "the person of Christ" (*Collected Works*, 830). Compassion in the New Testament, for example in the parable of the "good" Samaritan (Luke 10:33), obviously is not, for it is introduced as an example of love, the love of neighbor that for Jesus was the inevitable corollary of loving God "with thy whole heart and with thy whole soul and with all thy strength and with all thy mind" (Luke 10:27). Sheppard's compassion, by contrast, has nothing to do with love of God, for he has neither respect for the Bible, nor hope of heaven nor fear of hell. His is the compassion of a rationalist, directed solely at someone with "a capacity for real response," someone with "potential" (599). And what of Thomas's mother? Nothing in the text suggests that she, any more than Sheppard, does what she does out of any kind of explicitly Christian conviction. In her letter to Hawkes, O'Connor acknowledged that in this story, "nobody is 'redeemed'" yet almost in the same breath she added (*Collected Works*, 1146–47): "To me, the old lady is the character whose position is right and the one who is right is usually the victim. If there is any question of a symbolic redemption, it would be through the old lady, who brings Thomas face to face with his own evil—which is that of putting his own comfort before charity (however foolish)."

"Charity," she calls it, not "compassion," or "tenderness," and she freely acknowledges it as "foolish." Thomas too spoke of his mother's "daredevil charity" (573), and even dreaded the "pure idiot mystery" of her love for him (575). He hated her efforts to rehabilitate Sarah Ham, especially when, "To his annoyance, she appeared to look on *him* with compassion, as if her hazy charity no longer made distinctions" (578). Yet this was inevitable because he was, after all, like Bailey in "A Good Man Is Hard to Find," his mother's "only boy" (137). In contrast to Rayber, who feared his own "horrifying love" for his only son Bishop, Thomas hated being on the receiving end of a mother's love that was almost as frightening to him, and just as "idiotic" as the "irrational and abnormal" love that repelled Rayber

(401). Like that love too, it was a love that threatened to spill over into a "general sorrow that would have found another object," in this instance not if she should lose either her son or her erratic protegé, but "no matter what good fortune came to either of them"—in that case rendering her compassion for them no longer necessary. In short, "The experience of Sarah Ham had plunged the old lady into mourning for the world" (587). While nothing is known of her religious faith, Thomas's mother is apparently subject to some form of Christian love, the same sort of "intimacy of creation" or "benevolence to Being in general" that haunted Tarwater (343) and threatened Rayber, and to which the grandmother in "A Good Man Is Hard to Find" at last succumbed. Her compassion, unlike Sheppard's, does not calculate the "potential" or "capacity for response" of its object, but is, as Thomas saw clearly, a kind of "daredevil" charity, "foolish" even in O'Connor's eyes, much like the charity of the "good" Samaritan in Jesus' parable. Thomas's mother is perhaps the closest we have come yet to a "good" person, even though O'Connor preferred to characterize her simply as "right" (*Collected Works*, 1147).

In the three stories we have looked at in this chapter, "the good" is every bit as problematic as in the New Testament, for it is, as O'Connor recognized, a "terrible" goodness, terrible at least to those who live in "territory held largely by the devil." If God alone is truly good, then the relative "goodness" we encounter in this world and recognize as such is not the mysterious goodness of God, but something less than that, something still, as she put it, "under construction" (*Collected Works*, 830).

7

Creator, Host, and Holy Ghost

I F "NONE IS GOOD but one, that is God" (Mark 10:18), it is fair to ask where God is to be found in O'Connor's fiction. Most often God is present in the sky, whether as "some vast construction work" over Taulkinham, as Ruby Turpin's "purple streak in the sky," as a cloud formation, or simply as the sun. Once when she was asked, "The sun is a common image in your stories. Why?" Flannery replied, "It's there. It's so obvious. And from time immemorial it's been a god" (*Conversations*, 59). But in certain stories God is present as well in other, more distinctly "religious" ways, particularly in communities where some semblance of traditional manners is still at work, in sharp contrast to Taulkinham, or the city that "rose like a cluster of warts on the side of the mountain" in "The River" (162), or "the dark city, where the children of God lay sleeping" in *The Violent Bear It Away* (479). O'Connor recognized that even though "good and evil appear to be joined in every culture at the spine," it is still the case that "traditional manners, however unbalanced, are better than no manners at all" (*Collected Works*, 856). And traditional manners are visible in most of her short stories, where more often than not they collide in some way with "mystery," as the manners of the grandmother and her kin collided with The Misfit, with lethal results. These collisions are not always lethal, but they are always transformative.

COMING OF AGE IN THE BODY

How does one become part of a community in O'Connor's world, and subject to its manners? By being born into it, obviously, but in one story at least, "A Temple of the Holy Ghost," O'Connor looks at the process of coming of age in such a community. To some degree the story is untypical, because the community in question is not only Southern but Roman Catholic, just the sort of community in which O'Connor herself came of age. It is arguably the nearest thing we have to autobiography in O'Connor's fiction. The "child" through whose eyes and thoughts the story unfolds is twelve years old. She is always "the child," never a "girl," while her cousins visiting for the weekend from the Mount St. Scholastica convent—fourteen and boy-crazy—are introduced right away as "the two girls," and even have names, Susan and Joanne. By birth, the child is part of a community not unlike the O'Connor household in Savannah in the 1930s, and she looks at her community and its manners with a jaundiced eye, much as O'Connor seems to have done in her own childhood. O'Connor's remarks in a 1956 letter to Betty Hester are revealing:

> When I was twelve I made up my mind absolutely that I would not get any older. I don't remember how I meant to stop it. There was something about "teen" attached to anything that was repulsive to me. I certainly didn't approve of what I saw of people of that age. I was a very ancient twelve; my views at that age would have done credit to a Civil War veteran. Anyway, I went through the years 13 to 20 in a very surly way ... I am much younger now than I was at twelve or anyway, less burdened. The weight of centuries lies on children, I'm sure of it. (*Collected Works*, 985)

In much the same vein, the child in the story saw her two older cousins as "practically morons and she was glad to think that they were only second cousins and she couldn't have inherited any of their stupidity." As the story begins, she observes the two of them "calling each other Temple One and Temple Two, shaking with laughter and getting so red and hot that they were positively ugly, particularly Joanne who had spots on her face anyway" (197).

In due course, amid "gales of giggles," the girls let the child's mother in on their little joke. "Sister Perpetua, the oldest nun at the Sisters of Mercy in Mayville," they told her, "had given them a lecture on what to do if a young man should," in her very words, "behave in an ungentlemanly manner with them in the back of an automobile." The remedy was to say, "Stop, sir! I am a Temple of the Holy Ghost!" and that, the Sister assured them, "would put an end to it." The story's title has already given it away, for it is taken from 1 Corinthians 6:19, "Or know you not that your members are the temple of the Holy Ghost, who is in you, whom you have from God, and you are not your own?" The two cousins found it so hilarious they could hardly finish recounting it, but the child didn't see anything so funny and neither did her mother. "I think you girls are pretty silly," her mother said. "After all, that's what you are—Temples of the Holy Ghost." This convinced the cousins that the child's mother was "made of the same stuff as Sister Perpetua," but the child, for her part, was not, nor was she lacking a sense of humor. She was at least as full of mischief as they were, and was even then plotting to fix them up with improbable or disastrous boyfriends: "What was really funny was the idea of Mr. Cheatam or Alonzo Myers beauing them around. That killed her." Yet the nun's words struck home: "I am a Temple of the Holy Ghost, she said to herself, and was pleased with the phrase." To that extent, she and her mother were on the same page, yet the phrase that to her mother was little more than a cliché, was to her something altogether unexpected that "made her feel as if somebody had given her a present" (199). She had no idea that it was Holy Scripture. It came to her simply as hearsay, a piece of news, a "message in the bottle," but unlike Ruby Turpin's in the waiting room, a welcome one, nothing less than a precious piece of ancient wisdom from "Sister Perpetua, the oldest nun at the Sisters of Mercy."

The name Perpetua appears to have been carefully chosen. In itself, it suggests great age, or agelessness, and O'Connor must have known who Perpetua was in history and early Christian tradition. One of the earliest of the Christian Acts of the Martyrs is *The Martyrdom of Perpetua and Felicitas*, which probably originated in North Africa in the late second century. Perpetua, "a newly married woman of good family and upbringing," said to be "about twenty-two years old," with "an infant son at the breast" (*Martyrdom* 2.1, in Musurillo, *Acts of the Christian Martyrs*, 109) is represented as giving a first-person account of events leading up to her martyrdom, including a series of visions. In the first of her visions, "I saw a ladder," she testifies, "of tremendous height made of bronze, reaching all the way to the heavens, but it was so narrow that only one person could climb up at a time." The ladder was surrounded with "all sorts of metal weapons: there were swords, spears, hooks, daggers, and spikes," and at the foot of it "lay a dragon of enormous size, and it would attack those who tried to climb up and try to terrify them from doing so." Perpetua's companion Saturus was the first to ascend, and she testifies that "he looked back and said to me, 'Perpetua, I am waiting for you. But take care; do not let the dragon bite you.' 'He will not harm me,' I said, 'in the name of the Lord Jesus Christ.' Shortly, as though he were afraid of me, the dragon stuck his head out from underneath the ladder. Then, using it as my first step, I trod on his head and went up" (*Martyrdom* 4.3–7, in Musurillo, 111). In the last of her visions, "on the day before we were to fight with the beasts," Perpetua is summoned to the arena and is "surprised that no beasts were let loose on me; for I knew that I was condemned to die by the beasts. Then out came an Egyptian against me, of vicious appearance." She is prepared for combat, "and suddenly I was a man." As a man, she is given a man's strength and vanquishes her evil foe: "We drew close to one another and began to let our fists fly. My opponent tried to get hold of my feet, but I kept striking him in the face with the heels of my feet. Then I was raised up into the air and I began to pummel him without as it were touching the ground." Then, she reports, "I put my two hands together linking the fingers of one hand with those of the other and thus I got hold of his head. He fell flat on his face and I stepped on his head" (*Martyrdom* 10.6–11, in Musurillo, 119).

So much for the historical Perpetua. I have found no mention of her in O'Connor's writings, but O'Connor's favorite citation from Cyril of Jerusalem surely reminds us of Perpetua's world: "The dragon is by the side of the road, watching those who pass. Beware lest he devour you. We go to the father of souls, but it is necessary to pass by the dragon." While the dragon in some form can be traced in each of the stories we have looked at so far, he is hardly visible in "A Temple of the Holy Ghost"—unless we focus on "Perpetua," and what her name evokes. It seems a bit of a stretch until we discover that the child in our story, like Perpetua of old, had "visions" (in her case, more like fantasies!) of becoming a martyr. A fair had come to town, and her two cousins were off at the fair with Wendell and Corey, the two boys she had talked her mother into fixing them up with. The child in her bedroom remembers what she had seen there last year, including tents that were closed to her "because they contained things that would be known only to grown people," tents with "faded-looking pictures on the canvas of people in tights, with stiff stretched composed faces like the faces of the martyrs waiting to have their tongues cut out by the Roman soldier" (203–4). Now, "as she looked out the window and followed the revolving searchlight" from the fair, she thought about becoming a saint, "because that was the occupation that included everything you could know; and yet she knew she would never be a saint. She did not steal or murder, but she was a born liar and slothful and she sassed her mother and was deliberately ugly to almost everybody. She was eaten up with the sin of Pride, the worst one."

Still, although she could never be a saint, "she thought she could be a martyr if they killed her quick":

She could stand to be shot but not to be burned in oil. She didn't know if she could stand to be torn to pieces by lions or not. She began to prepare her martyrdom, seeing herself in a pair of tights in a great arena, lit by the early Christians hanging in cages of fire, making a gold dusty light that fell on her and the lions. The first lion charged forward and fell at her feet, converted. A whole series of lions did the same. The lions liked her so much she even slept with them and finally the Romans were obliged to burn her but to their astonishment she would not burn down and finding she was so hard to kill, they finally cut off her head very quickly with a sword and she went immediately to heaven. She rehearsed this several times, returning each time at the entrance of Paradise to the lions. (204)

The child obviously knows (because O'Connor knows) something of the early accounts of Christian martyrdom, though not necessarily the story of Perpetua. O'Connor may have purposely avoided alluding directly to that narrative lest it confuse or compete with her own story. The child's fantasies seem based on other apocryphal accounts, in particular the third-century *Acts of Paul*, in which the Apostle Paul's female companion, Thecla, is bound to a fierce lioness, and "the lioness, when Thecla was set upon her, licked her feet, and all the people marveled." Later, "a fierce lioness running to her lay down at her feet, and the press of women cried aloud" (*Acts of Paul* 28 and 33; in James, *Apocryphal New Testament*, 278–79).

The feminist overtones of these ancient accounts are visible in the child's fantasies as well. She does not, like Perpetua, turn into a man, but she longs to be a doctor or an engineer (still predominantly male professions in the 1950s), and in yet another overheated fantasy envisions herself as a military commander, female nonetheless, in charge of her cousins' two young suitors, Wendell and Corey: "We fought in the world war together. They were under me and I saved them five times from Japanese suicide divers and Wendell said I am going to marry that kid and the other said oh no you ain't I am and I said neither one of you is because I will court marshall you all before you can bat an eye" (200–201). In some ways a robustly male vision, despite the offer of marriage! As we have seen, only the feminine pronouns identify the "child" as a girl. There is something vaguely indeterminate about her gender, in contrast to the boy-crazy adolescent cousins, and this indeterminacy becomes a major theme in the story when the girls return from the fair.

Susan and Joanne arrive back just before midnight with news from one of those tents containing "things that would be known only to grown people" (203). The freak they had seen "was a man and a woman both," a hermaphrodite (although the term is not used) who went first to the men on one side of the tent, saying in a flat country voice, "I'm going to show you this and if you laugh, God may strike you the same way," and then, "God made me thisaway and if you laugh He may strike you the same way. This is the way He wanted me to be and I ain't disputing His way. I'm showing you this because I got to make the best of it. I expect you to act like ladies and gentlemen. I never done it to myself nor had a thing to do with it but I'm making the best of it. I don't dispute hit." Then "the freak came over to the women's side and said exactly the same thing" (206). Like the news that "I am a Temple of the Holy Ghost," the report comes to the child as hearsay, the latest news, yet another "message in the bottle." Lying in bed she processes the news, remembering at the same time something else that came to her firsthand at supper in the kitchen, when "the thin blue-gummed cook" had said to her, "How come you be so ugly sometime?" and "God could strike you deaf dumb and blind" (202–3).

From such tattered threads of the day, the child weaves in her mind a litany or choral response between the freak and the people looking on in the carnival tent:

> God done this to me and I praise Him.
>
> Amen. Amen.
>
> He could strike you thisaway.
>
> Amen. Amen.
>
> But he has not.
>
> Amen.
>
> Raise yourself up. A temple of the Holy Ghost. You! You are God's temple, don't you know? Don't you know? God's Spirit has a dwelling in you, don't you know?
>
> Amen. Amen.
>
> If anybody desecrates the temple of God, God will bring him to ruin and if you laugh, He may strike you thisaway. A temple of God is a holy thing. Amen. Amen
>
> I am a temple of the Holy Ghost.
>
> Amen.

Finally, "The people began to slap their hands without making a loud noise and with a regular beat between the Amens, more and more softly, as if they knew there was a child near, half asleep" (207).

The imagined litany is remarkable in that it draws not only on the "master text" behind the story, "know you not that your members are the temple of the Holy Ghost" (1 Cor 6:19), but also on its companion text three chapters earlier (1 Cor 3:16). This text comes to expression in the litany in words directed not to an individual but to a "congregation" in a circus tent: "God's Spirit has a dwelling in you, don't you know?" and "If anybody desecrates the temple of God, God will bring him to ruin," and "A temple of God is a holy thing." The wording is neither that of the Douay Bible nor of the King James, but of another Roman Catholic translation, by Ronald A. Knox: "Do you not understand that you are God's temple, and that *God's Spirit has* his *dwelling in you? If anybody desecrates the temple of God, God will bring him to ruin.* It is *a holy thing*, this *temple of God*, which is nothing other than yourselves" (1 Cor 3:16–17; my italics call attention to the verbatim agreements between Knox's text and the litany in the carnival tent).[1] O'Connor is drawing together two closely related texts from 1 Corinthians in a fairly sophisticated manner, surely too sophisticated for the child in the story. The two texts come at different points in Paul's argument in 1 Corinthians. In simplest terms, the difference between them is that the text in chapter 6 has to do with the individual, with the body, and specifically with sexuality, while in chapter 3 it has to do with the believing community, the corporate body as it were, and with the responsibility of individuals to the community to which they belong. O'Connor is concerned with both things in this story: a "child" coming of age in her own female body, with the assurance that she is a "temple of the Holy Ghost," and at the same time coming of age (as O'Connor herself did) in a community both Southern and Catholic, a community of "manners," evident even in the carnival freak's warning not to "laugh," but to "act like ladies and gentlemen" (206).

"A Temple of the Holy Ghost," is a story unique in the O'Connor canon, in that mystery and manners are for once *not* on a collision course. The child in the story is, as the cook in the kitchen knew, something of a brat. If traditional manners are indeed "better than no manners at all" (*Collected Works*, 856), when the story begins she is counted among those

1. At the O'Connor archives in Milledgeville in 2007 I discovered that O'Connor had marked this very passage in her personal copy of Knox's translation. On 1 Corinthians 6:19, however, Knox does not have "the temple of the Holy Ghost," but has substituted "the shrines of the Holy Spirit."

with no manners. Mystery is what draws her into the world of manners, first in the good news that "I am a temple of the Holy Ghost," then in the musings of a freak in a carnival tent, and finally in a bloodless Benediction of the Blessed Sacrament at Mount St. Scholastica, when she and her mother take the two girls back to the convent after the weekend visit. There, as is customary, they listen to the *Tantum Ergo*, a hymn to the Eucharist that was quoted in full in an earlier scene when the two cousins sang it in chorus to their country boyfriends on the porch, evoking from one of the boys the response, "That must be Jew singing," and in turn from the child standing on a barrel beside the porch, the outburst: "You big dumb ox!" and again, "You big dumb Church of God ox!" (202).[2] But now, on hearing it again, "her ugly thoughts stopped and she began to realize that she was in the presence of God. Hep me not to be so mean, she began mechanically. Hep me not to give her so much sass. Hep me not to talk like I do" (208). When the priest "raised the monstrance with the Host shining ivory-colored in the center of it," it brought to her mind another "monstrance," or demonstration, when the freak at the fair showed itself, first to the men and then to the women, with the words "I don't dispute hit. This is the way He wanted me to be" (208–9).

The juxtaposition of Christ with the hermaphrodite is striking and, to some, shocking. John Sykes ("Two Natures," 89) comments that "The hermaphrodite embodies two 'natures,' as does Christ," and calls it a "seemingly blasphemous analogy" by which "O'Connor pushes to its extreme limit her steady insistence that fallen humanity continues to display the divine image." But the freak's "two natures" are male and female, not divine and human. The analogy is not with the issues raised at the Council of Chalcedon but with Galatians 3:28, "There is neither Jew nor Greek; there is neither bond nor free; there is neither male nor female. For you are all one in Christ Jesus." Those three distinctions, the Apostle Paul claimed, are broken down in Christ. The distinction between divine and human is not. The Galatians text, unlike 1 Corinthians 6:19, is never cited in the story, but the two are closely related. Male, female, or indeterminate—like the hermaphrodite, or like a "child" not yet come of age—all are "one in Christ Jesus," or to put it another way, "a temple of the Holy Ghost." God

2. O'Connor's little joke is that the original "dumb ox" was Thomas Aquinas, who is said to have composed the *Tantum Ergo* (see Sally Fitzgerald's note, *Collected Works*, 1266: "Dumb [mute] ox, the nickname of St. Thomas Aquinas as a seminarian"). This, along with the name of the convent, "Mount St. Scholastica," and probably "Sister Perpetua" as well, provides the story with more than its share of Catholic inside jokes.

comes to expression in the story as Creator—"God made me thisaway"— whether in the old Creation or the new.

With this, yet another biblical text comes into play, the Apostle Paul's rhetorical question, "O man, who art thou that repliest against God? Shall the thing formed say to him that formed it: Why hast thou made me thus?" (Rom 9:20). The hermaphrodite had said "I don't dispute hit," and by now the child has learned not to dispute it either. The hermaphrodite's words seem to echo even the editorial note on this text in O'Connor's Douay Bible: "This similitude is used only to shew *that we are not to dispute with our Maker*, nor to reason with him why he does not give as much grace to one as to another" (emphasis added).[3] Once again, self-knowledge is the prelude to redemption. As soon as she acknowledges her "ugly thoughts" and her meanness, two signs are given in answer to her prayer. First, as she and her mother are leaving the convent, the "big moon-faced nun" who had greeted them when they came in "swooped down on her mis- chievously and nearly smothered her in the black habit, mashing the side of her face into the crucifix hitched onto her belt." Yet despite her fervent prayers, she is not noticeably changed. On the way home she still looks at Alonzo Myers, their unattractive and overweight eighteen-year-old chauf- feur, with mischievous scorn, noticing "three folds of fat in the back of his neck," and "that his ears were pointed almost like a pig's." But when she learns that the fair has been shut down for good, and looks out the car window, the sunset over the dark woods becomes for her a second sign: the Benediction of the Blessed Sacrament reenacted in the sky: "The sun was a huge red ball like an elevated Host drenched in blood and when it sank out of sight, it left a line in the sky like a red clay road hanging over the trees" (209). The Host in the sky, no longer "ivory-colored" but now "drenched in blood," announces the "child's" coming of age physically as a "girl," soon to be a woman, and at the same time heralds her redemp- tion. Mystery ushers her into a community both Southern and Catholic, a world of manners, but beyond that, who knows where? On a perilous journey past the dragon, perhaps, with Perpetua of old, or Hazel Motes or

---

3. O'Connor's interest in this passage in Romans is evident in a letter to Alfred Corn, who had asked her about predestination and free will. "Romans IX, is held by the church to refer not to eternal reward or punishment but to our actual lives on earth, where one is given talent, wealth, education, made a 'vessel of honor,' and another is given the short end of the horn, so to speak—the 'vessel of wrath.'" She deferred to the church's teaching because, she said, "If left to myself, I certainly wouldn't know how to interpret Romans IX. I don't believe Christ left us to chaos" (*Collected Works*, 1173).

Tarwater? A journey down that red clay Georgia road that will be the way of the cross?

O'Connor hints as much, commenting in a letter to Betty Hester that "the martyrdom that she had thought about in a childish way (which turned into a happy sleeping with the lions) is shown in the final way that it has to be for us all—an acceptance of the Crucifixtion [*sic*], Christ's and our own" (*Collected Works*, 976). O'Connor repeatedly wrote to at least two of her correspondents that this most Catholic of all her stories was about purity, "the most mysterious of the virtues" (*Collected Works*, 925, 953, 970)—purity not simply as chastity but as an affirmation of God as both Creator and Redeemer, in O'Connor's words "an acceptance of what God wills for us, an acceptance of our individual circumstances" (*Collected Works*, 976). Surely the best preparation of all for meeting the dragon!

Coming of Age in the Spirit

If "A Temple of the Holy Ghost" is the most explicitly Catholic of O'Connor's stories, "The Enduring Chill" comes in at least a distant second. Asbury Fox is a failed poet and novelist returning home by train, deathly sick, from New York city to his mother's farm outside Timberboro (Tennessee? Georgia? it matters not). "He was puffy and pale and his hair had receded tragically for a boy of twenty-five." Before he even gets off the train, Asbury sees his mother waiting for him with a look of shock on her face, signaling that "he must look as ill as he was." She "looked aghast," and Asbury is "pleased that she should see death in his face at once." As he steps off the train under a "chill gray" sky, he sees that "a startling white-gold sun, like some strange potentate from the east was rising beyond the black woods that surrounded Timberboro," threatening to transform the flat roofs of the shabby town into "the mounting turrets of some exotic temple for a god he didn't know" (547). Once again the sun is a stand-in for God, not "an elevated Host drenched in blood" this time, but in Asbury's eyes a "strange potentate from the east"— emphatically "a god he didn't know." The momentary illusion irks him, above all in a dreary place like this, where he had grown up: "He had become entirely accustomed to the thought of death, but he had not become accustomed to the thought of death *here*" (548). His sister Mary George, eight years his senior, is asleep in his mother's car, "packed into a black suit" with "a white rag around her head with metal curlers sticking out from under the edges" (548–49). In the car, his mother promises to take him that very afternoon to Doctor

Block, who would "take a personal interest in you," but Asbury insists that this will not happen, that afternoon or ever, because "What's wrong with me is way beyond Block."

On the ride home, Asbury's mind wanders back to New York and a friend named Goetz who, enthralled with Buddhism and "certain that death was nothing at all," had taken "the news of Asbury's approaching end with calm indifference" (549). In a small group in Goetz's flat after a boring lecture on Vedanta, Asbury was told by a girl in a sari that "self-fulfillment was out of the question since it meant salvation and the word was meaningless," and Goetz had added that "no one is saved." But Asbury had spotted in the group "a lean, spectacled figure in black, a priest," whose "taciturn superior expression" seemed to express perfectly Asbury's own feelings. Seizing the occasion, he had asked the priest, "And what do you think of that?" The priest said, "'There is a real probability of the New Man, assisted, of course,' he added brittlely, 'by the Third Person of the Trinity'" This with a smile that "seemed to touch on some icy clarity." Another oracle, a "message in the bottle" that he could not forget, comparable to "I am a Temple of the Holy Ghost," or "God made me thisaway." The girl in the sari called it "Ridiculous!" but Asbury had been duly impressed, not because he was ready to embrace either salvation or "the Third Person of the Trinity," but because he thought he had encountered "someone who would have understood the unique tragedy of his death, a death whose meaning had been far beyond the twittering group around them" (550). Bringing himself suddenly back to the present, Asbury again muses, "And how much more beyond Block." The priest had quietly given him his card, "Ignatius Vogle, S.J.," and Asbury now regrets that he had not followed up the contact.

Asbury's Jesuit, with his "real probability of the New Man," is a thinly-disguised stand-in for the French Jesuit paleontologist and theologian Pierre Teilhard de Chardin, whose work O'Connor admired and whose evolutionary theology supplied her with the title of the short story collection, *Everything That Rises Must Converge*, in which "The Enduring Chill" can be found. "Remain true to yourselves," Teilhard wrote, "but move ever upward toward greater consciousness and greater love! At the summit you will find yourself united with all those who, from every direction, have made the same ascent. *For everything that rises must converge*" (quoted in Wood, "Heterodoxy," 26). Like Aquinas, and like O'Connor herself, Teilhard envisioned grace working through nature, not against it, and he attempted to combine Christian thought with the scientific and philosophical fashions of his day. Specifically, he sought to merge evolutionary theory with Christian theology into a vision of the cosmos moving both materially and spiritually toward an "omega point" that could be understood in Christian terms as "the New Man," or even as "a culminating Body of Christ."[4] Ralph Wood has shown that O'Connor's admiration for Teilhard centered more on the spirit than on the substance of his work, and so far as the latter is concerned was neither uncritical nor unqualified.[5] This is consistent with her fictional portrayal of "Ignatius Vogle, S.J.," who reappears later in one of Asbury's fevered dreams as a "lean dark figure in a Roman collar" with "a mysteriously saturnine face in which there was a subtle blend of asceticism and corruption" (564).

While Asbury's Jesuit was the messenger testifying to the "probability of the New Man," one suspects that the real source of the message, for both Teilhard and O'Connor, is the New Testament, in particular the Apostle Paul's admonition to "put on the new man, who according to God is created in justice and holiness of truth" (Eph 4:24). Earlier in the chapter, Paul speaks of the work of building up "the body of Christ; until we all meet into the unity of faith and of the knowledge of the Son of God, unto a perfect man, unto the measure of the age of the fulness of Christ" (Eph 4:12–13), and in another letter, of "stripping yourselves of the old man and his deeds, and putting on the new, him who is renewed unto knowledge, according to the image of him who created him" (Col 3:9–10).[6] If there is anything like Teilhard's "omega point" in the New Testament, it comes to expression in passages like these. Robert Fitzgerald once wrote that Teilhard's notion of an omega point "has appealed to people to whom it may seem to offer one more path past the Crucifixion," a path that "could be corrected by no sense of life better than by O'Connor's" ("Introduction," xxx). By contrast, Paul's vision of the "New Man" rests precisely on the Crucifixion, for in Ephesians he also wrote that Christ has broken down

4. The latter term is Brad Gooch's (*Flannery*, 322). I have not documented it in Teilhard's own writings.

5. Wood, "Heterodoxy," 21–27. He finds in O'Connor's work something "very much like a parody of the cosmic optimism" of that quotation. In much the same vein, Robert Fitzgerald writes in his "Introduction" to the first edition of *Everything That Rises Must Converge* that "It is a title taken in full respect and with profound and necessary irony" (xxx).

6. It is worth noticing that while the "new man" in Ephesians 4:24 and Colossians 3:10 is not specific as to gender (i.e. *ton kainon anthrōpon*, the new person), the "perfect man" in Ephesians 4:13 is specifically male (*eis andra teleion*), possibly because he is viewed as synonymous with "the fullness of Christ" (Christ being understood as male).

the wall between Jew and Gentile, "that he might make the two in himself into one new man, making peace, and might reconcile both to God in one body by the cross" (Eph 2:14–15), with the result that "by him we have access both in one Spirit to the Father" (2:18). Nothing other than Father Vogle's "Third Person of the Trinity"!

None of this is on Asbury's radar screen. His fascination with the Jesuit's "icy clarity" has everything to do with style and nothing to do with substance. While still in New York, he had made up his mind he was going to die, and, frustrated that he had accomplished nothing, had written a long letter to his mother to be read only after his death. In the letter he compared his blunted imagination to a bird unable to fly. He had come home, he wrote, "to find freedom, to liberate my imagination, to take it like a hawk from its cage and set it 'whirling off into the widening gyre' (Yeats) and what did I find? It was incapable of flight. It was some bird you had domesticated, sitting huffy in its pen, refusing to come out!" "Woman, why did you pinion me?" the letter concluded (554). Asbury wanted to leave his mother "with an enduring chill and perhaps in time lead her to see herself as she was" (555).

In the end, the "chill" of self-knowledge will be his, not his mother's. The "enduring chill" he anticipates for himself is something altogether different, the chill of death, displayed for him in "the water stains on the gray walls" of his bedroom now that he is home and has put himself straight to bed:

> Descending from the top molding, long icicle shapes had been etched by leaks and, directly over his bed on the ceiling, another leak had made a fierce bird with spread wings. It had an icicle crosswise in its beak and there were smaller icicles depending from its wings and tail. It had been there since his childhood and had always irritated him and sometimes had frightened him. He had often had the illusion that it was in motion and about to descend mysteriously and set the icicle on his head. He closed his eyes and thought: I won't have to look at it for many more days. And presently he went to sleep. (555–56)

He wakes up in the afternoon with a stethoscope in his face. "Here's Doctor Block!" his mother is saying "as if she had captured this angel on the rooftop and brought him in for her little boy" (556). "Get him out of here," Asbury tells her, and to the doctor (twice), "What's wrong with me is way beyond you," but it is all in vain. Block, one of the few "normal" people in all of O'Connor's fiction, acknowledges that "Most things are beyond me," adding "I ain't found anything yet that I thoroughly understood" and calmly finishing what he came to do (557).

Asbury's condition does not improve, and as he sits idly on the porch staring at the sky, the lawn, and the pastures of his mother's farm, he again remembers his last visit home a year ago. He had been working on a play about "Negroes" and had cultivated the friendship of the hired help, Morgan and Randall, by smoking with them in the milking barn. Randall, the older one, had protested, "She don't 'low no smoking in here," but Asbury had prevailed, resulting in something he now remembered as "one of those moments of communion when the difference between black and white is absorbed into nothing" (558). This had "so exhilarated him that he had been determined to repeat it in some other way." The next day, as they were pouring fresh milk into the cans, he had "picked up the jelly glass the Negroes drank out of and, inspired, had poured himself a glass-ful of the warm milk and drained it down"—this even though he hated milk. "She don't 'low that," Randall had said, "That's *the* thing she don't 'low." "Listen," he had told them, "the world is changing. There's no reason I shouldn't drink after you or you after me!" (559). This time there was no magic "moment of communion," for he could not get either of them to drink the milk. Frustrated in his gestures toward racial reconciliation, Asbury had returned to New York two days early.

Now that he is back in Timberboro, his mother realizes that Asbury needs "someone intellectual to talk to," and it occurs to him that she is right. "I want a priest," he announces, "Preferably a Jesuit." His mother, humoring him, calls for a priest, who agrees to come the next day. In the night, he dreams of Art and Death, and his own funeral procession shad-owed by "a lean dark figure in a Roman collar" who might have been ei-ther Ignatius Vogle, S.J. or the priest he was expecting in the morning. He wakes up in a cold sweat and waits all morning for the priest, while on the ceiling "the bird with the icicle in its beak seemed poised and waiting too" (564). The priest arrives in the late afternoon, blind in one eye and with a grease spot on his shirt, introducing himself in a hearty voice as "Fahther Finn—from Purrgatory."[7] Asbury "had not expected a priest like this one,"

7. This appears to have been the Father's (and O'Connor's) little joke. In a 1956 letter to Betty Hester, O'Connor told of her encounter with a deaf priest named Fa-ther Murphy at a luncheon of the National Association of Catholic Women (*Collected Works*, 995). Their conversation as she recounts it was as follows: "And wharre are you from? Milledgeville, Georgia, Father. Eh? Milledgeville, Georgia. I didn't get that. MILLEDGEVILLE GEORGIA. What city is that near? M A C O N (great volume). Mi-kun? I never heard of that. Where are you from, Father? (Pause—waiting to get the ladies' attention.) Purrrgatory. (Laughter)."

who looks nothing like a Jesuit, knows nothing of James Joyce ("Joyce? Joyce who?" he had asked), and begins the conversation with "Do you say your morning and night prayers?" Then three questions from the old Baltimore Catechism: "Who made you?" and "Who is God?" and "Why did God make you?" Asbury's only answers are "Different people believe different things about that," and "God is an idea created by man." The priest calls him "a very ignorant boy," and answers all three questions for him right from the catechism: "God made you," "God is a spirit infinitely perfect," and "God made you to know Him, to love Him, to serve Him in this world and to be happy with Him in the next!" When Asbury protests that "I'm not a Roman," the old priest calls it "A poor excuse for not saying your prayers!" and "How do you expect to get what you don't ask for? God does not send the Holy Ghost to those who don't ask for Him. Ask Him to send the Holy Ghost" (565–66).

One thing at least in common with Father Vogle, S.J.—"the Third Person of the Trinity." When Asbury protests that "the Holy Ghost is the last thing I'm looking for!" the priest, now with "his one fierce eye inflamed," replies, "And He may be the last thing you get!" Yet as he leaves, the old priest lapses back into the ritual of a routine, even pleasant, pastoral call: "He turned back to the bed and said affably, 'I'll give you my blessing and after this you must say your daily prayers without fail,'" whereupon he put his hand on Asbury's head and rumbled something in Latin. "Call me any time," he said, "and we can have another little chat." And to Asbury's mother: "He's a good lad at heart but very ignorant" (567).

Father Finn's words and his "one fierce eye" have their effect. Like Gregor Samsa, the hero of Franz Kafka's *The Metamorphosis*,[8] Asbury "moved his arms and legs helplessly as if he were pinned to the bed by the terrible eye," and when his mother comes back upstairs she finds him "sitting up in his bed, staring in front of him with large childish shocked eyes" (567). Shocked eyes, not unlike Tarwater's "scorched eyes" (473), or the "shocked and altered faces" of Ruby Turpin and Claud (654). Asbury's "metamorphosis," it seems, has begun. The next morning he looks again at "the fierce bird with the icicle in its beak and felt that it was there for some purpose that he could not divine" (567–68). Yet still searching for

8. O'Connor once wrote to Sally and Robert Fitzgerald, "Regina [Flannery's mother] is getting very literary. 'Who is this Kafka?' she says. 'People ask me.' A German Jew, I says, I think. He wrote a book about a man that turns into a roach. 'Well I can't tell people *that*,' she says" (*Collected Works*, 896). Again, there is T. S. Eliot's Prufrock: "The eyes that fix you in a formulated phrase, and when I am formulated, sprawling on a pin. When I am pinned and wriggling on the wall . . ." (Eliot, 5).

"some last culminating experience that he must make for himself before he died," he persuades his mother to summon Randall and Morgan to "smoke together one last time," just as in the dairy a year ago (568). But the "experience of communion" he hopes for is a fiasco. The two keep telling him how well he looks, and when he absent-mindedly hands each of them a package of cigarettes instead of just one, they accept it as something to take home and enjoy at their leisure. As they "filed out agreeing with each other how well he looked," Asbury knows that "now there would be no significant experience before he died" (569–70). He falls asleep, again to a fevered dream, only to be awakened by his mother and Dr. Block with the "good news" that what he had was undulant fever. "It'll keep coming back but it won't kill you," his mother told him. Dr. Block confirmed that "You ain't going to die," adding, "Undulant fever ain't so bad, Azzberry," and "It's the same as Bang's in a cow." His mother guessed that "He must have drunk some unpasteurized milk up there" (571–72).

If Asbury's first "message in the bottle" was Ignatius Vogle, S.J.'s pronouncement of "a real probability of the New Man," assisted by "the Third Person of the Trinity" (550), this is now the occasion for his second, delivered with the same "icy" clarity. His eyes "looked shocked clean as if they had been prepared for some awful vision about to come down on him." Two visions actually, one through the window and one on the ceiling of his room. Outside, "A blinding red-gold sun moved serenely from under a purple cloud. Below it the treeline was black against the crimson sky. It formed a brittle wall, standing as if it were the frail defense he had set up in his mind to protect him from what was coming." God in the sky once again, but this time coming right down through the waterstained ceiling into Asbury's room, and he knows it: "The old life in him was exhausted. He awaited the coming of the new." And it is not long in coming:

> The fierce bird which through the years of his childhood and the days of his illness had been poised over his head, waiting mysteriously, appeared all at once to be in motion. Asbury blanched and the last film of illusion was torn as if by a whirlwind from his eyes. He saw that for the rest of his days, frail, racked, but enduring, he would live in the face of a purifying terror. A feeble cry, a last impossible protest escaped him. But the Holy Ghost, emblazoned in ice instead of fire, continued, implacable, to descend. (572)

The biblical dimensions of the story come to a head in these final sentences. The image of the Holy Ghost as an innocent or harmless dove, as in the New Testament accounts of Jesus' baptism (Matt 3:16, Mark 1:10, Luke 3:22, John 1:32), gives way here to that of a fierce predator, an image the New Testament only hints at with its baptism "in the Holy Ghost and fire" (Matt 3:11).

O'Connor knows and uses effectively the imagery of purgatorial "fire," but here she quite deliberately replaces it with "ice instead of fire," not the "ice" of hatred, as in Robert Frost's poem, "Fire and Ice," but rather the terrible "clarity" of divine mercy. Like Gerard Manley Hopkins, who wrote, "the Holy Ghost over the bent World broods with warm breast & with ah! bright wings," O'Connor knew that she lived in a "bent World," but her "Holy Ghost" looks quite different. Asbury feels no warmth of a breast but at most "the beginning of a chill, a chill so peculiar, so light, that it was like a warm ripple across a deeper sea of cold." He is sentenced to live and not die. The chill he feels is the chill not of death but of life, unwelcome as it might be, an "enduring" chill and one to be endured "for the rest of his days." Not the unfettered bird of his imagination, "whirling off into the widening gyre" at last (554), but a lifelong Companion, "the Third Person of the Trinity." As almost always in O'Connor, the end of the story told is the beginning of a story left untold.

8

Two Gentleman Callers

IN ONE OF HER papers in the O'Connor Special Collection at Georgia College and State University in Milledgeville, Flannery described the "modern hero," or "outsider" in modern fiction as "the new man for the new world—the one who belongs everywhere and nowhere. His baggage is light; he takes little with him but spirit. If you see him coming, retreat, and don't attempt to rebuild until he is gone. He soon will be; then you can take stock of what is left" (*File 281c* in the O'Connor Special Collection).[1] This "new man" is not to be confused with Asbury Fox's "New Man" brought to realization by "the Third Person of the Trinity." He is if anything a parody or counterfeit of the "new man" of which the Apostle Paul speaks in Ephesians and Colossians, a parody all the more apparent by virtue of the mention of "spirit." Even in the Bible, the "Holy Ghost" or "Third Person of the Trinity" has his imitators. The author of First John claims that believers can know that Christ dwells in them "by the Spirit which he hath given us" (1 John 3:24), but quickly adds, "Dearly beloved, believe not every spirit, but try the spirits if they be of God: because many false prophets are gone out into the world"(1 John 4:1).

O'Connor herself put it this way in the very first letter she wrote to her friend and admirer Betty Hester: "I believe that there are many rough beasts now slouching toward Bethlehem to be born and that I have

---

1. A shortened version can be found in her lecture on "The Catholic Novelist in the Protestant South": "The modern hero is the outsider. His experience is rootless. He can go anywhere. He belongs nowhere. Being alien to nothing, he ends up being alienated from any kind of community based on common tastes and interests" (*Collected Works*, 856).

reported the progress of a few of them" (*Collected Works*, 942). This was in July 1955, the same year her first collection of short stories, *A Good Man is Hard to Find*, was published, and that collection is rich indeed in just such rogue "spirits" or "rough beasts." Two of these come in stories about courtship, surely a conspicuous feature of the world of Southern manners, and something that in O'Connor's hands could trigger either comedy or mystery, or both. There are comic glimpses of courtship in the title story in the grandmother's tale about "Mr. Edgar Atkins Teagarden" who had once courted her by bringing her "a watermelon every Saturday afternoon with the initials cut in it, E.A.T." (140), and in "A Temple of the Holy Ghost," when the child arranged dates for her two cousins with "those two Wilkinses, Wendell and Cory," who were "both going to be Church of God preachers because you don't have to know nothing to be one" (200). In both instances, O'Connor exploited to the full the comic possibilities of the "gentleman caller." But in "The Life You Save May Be Your Own" and "Good Country People" (in some respects a matched pair) the gentleman callers become agents of mystery.

He Who Saves His Life

In the first of these, a drifter named Tom T. Shiftlet shows up one evening while Lucynell Crater is sitting on her porch watching the sunset with her deaf mute daughter, who bears the same name. The sun, almost always in O'Connor carrying a hint of the divine, is no Benediction of the Blessed Sacrament here, for they are unlikely to be Catholics, but it captures Shiftlet's attention. Because he has only one good arm, Shiftlet's "gaunt figure listed slightly to the side," and when he turns to face the sun, he strikes a pose that forms a "crooked cross" in front it. "Lady," he opines, "I'd give a fortune to live where I could see me a sun do that every evening," and the old woman replies matter-of-factly, "Does it every evening" (172–73). And so the courtship, or rather the negotiation, begins.

Mr. Shiftlet, it turns out, is courting neither mother nor daughter, but a car, "a 1928 or '29 Ford," sitting in a shed in the backyard (173). As for the mother, "She was ravenous for a son-in-law" (177), and so the negotiations center on the "afflicted" Lucynell the younger, "a large girl in a short blue organdy dress" who, when she first saw Shiftlet "jumped up and began to stamp and point and make excited speechless sounds" (172). "My only," her mother told him, "and she's the sweetest girl in the world. I wouldn't give her up for nothing on earth. She's smart too. She can sweep the floor, cook, wash, feed the chickens, and hoe. I wouldn't give her up for a casket of jewels," but adding that any man who wanted her would "have to stay around the place" (176). The next day she told Shiftlet again, "If it was ever a man wanted to take her away, I would say, 'No man on earth is going to take that sweet girl of mine away from me!' but if he was to say, 'Lady, I don't want to take her away, I want her right here,' I would say, 'Mister, I don't blame you none. I wouldn't pass up a chance to live in a permanent place and get the sweetest girl in the world myself. You ain't no fool,' I would say." When Shiftlet asked how old she was, "'Fifteen, sixteen,' the old woman said. The girl was nearly thirty but because of her innocence it was impossible to guess" (178).

Shiftlet resurrects the old car with the help of a new fan belt, and the old woman makes her move. "Listen here, Mr. Shiftlet," she told him, "you'd be getting a permanent house and a deep well and the most innocent girl in the world. You don't need no money. Lemme tell you something: there ain't any place in the world for a poor disabled friendless drifting man." His reply is guarded, and not altogether compliant: "Lady, a man is divided into two parts, body and spirit," and again, "A body and a spirit," adding "The body, lady, is like a house: it don't go anywhere; but the spirit, lady, is like a automobile: always on the move, always . . ." With this he becomes the best spokesman yet for O'Connor's "modern hero" or "outsider," who "belongs everywhere and nowhere," whose "baggage is light" and who "takes little with him but spirit." As if she had not heard, the old woman "laid the bait carefully," offering Shiftlet *both* body and spirit, *both* a house and an automobile. "Listen, Mr. Shiftlet," she tells him "my well never goes dry and my house is always warm in the winter and there's no mortgage on a thing about this place," adding in the car as a bonus. "And yonder under that shed is a fine automobile," she tells him "You can have it painted by Saturday. I'll pay for the paint" (179). Yet spirit is what Shiftlet wants, not "a permanent house and a deep well" and by no means a wife, but the car and that alone. His crafty answer is the story's turning point: "In the darkness, Mr. Shiftlet's smile stretched like a weary snake waking up by a fire. After a second he recalled himself and said, 'I'm only saying a man's spirit means more to him than anything else. I would have to take my wife off for the week end without no regards at all for cost. I got to follow where my spirit says to go'" (179–80). The image of a snake who "recalled himself" (i.e., "recoiled" with a Georgia accent!) underscores Shiftlet's use of deception and half-truths, a technique as old as the Garden of Eden. Without quite saying so, he has given Mrs. Crater the impression that he accepts her proposal and is merely negotiating enough money up front for a weekend honeymoon. So far as she is concerned, she has not lost a daughter but gained a son-in-law and a reliable hired hand. She offers him fifteen dollars, then "Seventeen-fifty," and finally he says, "I'll make that do." But he has no intention of returning, and he has just said as much: "I got to follow where my spirit says to go."

Shiftlet's scheme is successful. He and young Lucynell are married in town with her mother as witness. "You got a prize!" the mother tells him, but Shiftlet is not pleased. He looks "morose and bitter," for the car is the prize he wants, not Lucynell (180). Once on the road, he enjoys the car so much that he "forgot his morning bitterness. He had always wanted an automobile but he had never been able to afford one before. He drove very fast because he wanted to reach Mobile by nightfall." Yet when he looks at Lucynell beside him he is again "depressed in spite of the car." After about a hundred miles he stops at a diner and orders a plate of ham and grits for his young bride. She rests her head on the counter and falls asleep. "Give it to her when she wakes up," he tells the boy behind the counter and, like a not-so-good Samaritan, adds, "I'll pay for it now."[2] The boy bends over, staring at her "long, pink-gold hair and the half-shut sleeping eyes," and murmurs, "She looks like an angel of Gawd." "Hitch-hiker," Shiftlet explains. "I can't wait. I got to make Tuscaloosa." Two lies in one breath, one necessary and one not, for he was actually headed for Mobile. The boy then "very carefully touched his finger to a strand of the golden hair and Mr. Shiftlet left" (181–82).

On the road again, Tom T. Shiftlet is "more depressed than ever." There were times when he "preferred not to be alone," and, lying even to himself, he "felt too that a man with a car had a responsibility to others and he kept his eye out for a hitch-hiker"—a real one this time. Doubtless he would have attributed his motivation to the "moral intelligence" he had claimed for himself to Lucynell's mother (176), but just at this point we are told that "Occasionally he saw a sign that warned: 'Drive carefully. The life you save may be your own'" (182). While by no means a biblical text, this safety slogan from the 1950s sounds like a public relations version of Mark 8:35: "For whosoever will save his life shall lose it; and whosoever shall lose his life for my sake and the gospel shall save it." For Shiftlet, it is a warning, his own "message in the bottle." His goal all along has been

---

2. The biblical "good Samaritan" paid the innkeeper and said, "Take care of him; and whatsoever thou shalt spend over and above, I, at my return, will repay thee" (Luke 10:35).

to save his own life, not Lucynell's or her mother's or anyone else's, and consequently he is in danger of losing it.

The story draws to an end, as it began, with a sunset, this time "directly in front of the automobile. It was a reddening ball that through his windshield was slightly flat on the bottom and top" and in its glare Shiftlet saw the hitch-hiker he was looking for, "a boy in overalls and a gray hat standing on the edge of the road," with his hat "set on his head in a way to indicate that he had left somewhere for good." With his "moral intelligence" fully in gear, Shiftlet picks up the runaway and tries to teach him a lesson: "I got the best old mother in the world, so I reckon you only got the second best." "It's nothing so sweet," he continues, "as a boy's mother. She taught him his first prayers at her knee, she give him love when no other would, she told him what was right and what wasn't, and she seen that he done the right thing." And "Son," he adds, "I never rued a day in my life like the one I rued when I left that old mother of mine." Finally, echoing the boy at the lunch counter: "My mother was a angel of Gawd" (182–83). The maudlin display is too much for the runaway hitch-hiker: "'You go to the devil!' he cried. 'My old woman is a flea bag and yours is a stinking polecat!' and with that he flung the door open and jumped out with his suitcase into the ditch."

Nothing less than an exorcism, not unlike "Go back to hell where you came from, you old wart hog" in a doctor's waiting room (646), and it too finds its mark. The bride he passed off as a "hitch-hiker" and left at the diner is now avenged by a real hitch-hiker, and the sky seems to agree: "A cloud, the exact color of the boy's hat and shaped like a turnip, had descended over the sun, and another, worse looking, crouched behind the car. Mr. Shiftlet felt that the rottenness of the world was about to engulf him. He raised his arm and let it fall again to his breast. 'Oh, Lord!' he prayed. 'Break forth and wash the slime from this earth!' " Be careful what you pray for: "The turnip continued slowly to descend. After a few minutes there was a guffawing peal of thunder from behind and fantastic raindrops, like tin-can tops, crashed over the rear of Mr. Shiftlet's car" (183). If the stories in *A Good Man is Hard to Find* are read "canonically" (that is, as parts of a collection), the "guffawing peal of thunder" may signal divine laughter answering Mr. Paradise's "loud guffaw" at the end of "The River," the story just preceding it in the collection. God has the last laugh, on Mr. Paradise and Mr. Shiftlet alike.

As the story ends, Shiftlet steps on the gas, and "with his stump sticking out the window he raced the galloping shower into Mobile," a name carefully chosen. His spirit is taking him to "Mobile," in an automobile ("always on the move, always . . ."), but his true destination, in O'Connor's words, is "everywhere and nowhere," or in the hitch-hiker's words, "to the devil." In the New Testament, "Every spirit which confesseth that Jesus Christ is come in the flesh is of God; And every spirit that dissolveth Jesus is not of God; and this is Antichrist" (1 John 4:2–3). No such confessional test is evident in this story, or in any of O'Connor's stories. Instead she leaves it to her readers to "try the spirits if they be of God." In Shiftlet's case the outlook is not promising. O'Connor in one of her letters lumps him right alongside Meeks, the copper flue salesman who gives Tarwater a lift in *The Violent Bear It Away*, as "one of those comic characters" who are "of the Devil because nothing in him resists the Devil" (*Collected Works*, 1119). Within the story, the hitch-hiker says it for her.

She Who Loses Her Life

The companion story, "Good Country People," has a gentleman caller and a victim as well. The victim, introduced first, is Hulga (*née* Joy) Hopewell, like Lucynell Crater "a large blonde girl," thirty-two instead of "nearly thirty," by no means mute or mentally challenged, but by contrast a PhD and an intellectual, yet just as "afflicted," with a wooden leg, a heart condition, and a bad disposition (263). There, however, the similarities stop. Where Lucynell was a mere object, the "prize" Shiftlet had to accept in order to gain what he really wanted, Hulga is emphatically the subject of this story, which unfolds almost entirely through her eyes and from her perspective. The "modern hero" or "outsider" in the story is "just a country boy," an earnest and polite young Bible salesman, "carrying a large black suitcase" that made him as lopsided as the one-armed Mr. Shiftlet (269). When Hulga's mother, Mrs. Hopewell, answers the door, he tells her that "you're a good woman. Friends have told me," and she assures him that "good country people are the salt of the earth!" He introduces himself as "Manley Pointer from out in the country around Willohobie, not even from a place, just from near a place" (270–71).[3] She does not buy a Bible, but invites him to stay for dinner. Like Hulga he has a heart condition, and instead of going to college he plans to devote his life to Christian service

3. That is, belonging "everywhere and nowhere," like the modern hero or outsider. As O'Connor once said of those she met in New York literary circles, "You know what's the matter with all that kind of folks? They ain't *frum* anywhere!" (as remembered by Drake, *Flannery O'Connor*, 11).

as a missionary because, as he puts it, "He who losest his life shall find it" (271–72). The same biblical text that confronted Shiftlet shines through Pointer's faulty grammar, this time focusing on the second half of the verse, the promise that "whosoever shall lose his life for my sake and the gospel shall save it" (Mark 8:35).

Hulga, an atheist, is not impressed, but when the young man finally leaves that evening Mrs. Hopewell sees the two of them talking together at the gate. As Hulga remembers the scene later, "He had stopped in front of her and had simply stood there," with a look "different from what it had been at the dinner table. He was gazing at her with open curiosity, with fascination, like a child watching a new fantastic animal at the zoo, and he was breathing as if he had run a great distance to reach her. His gaze seemed somehow familiar but she could not think where she had been regarded with it before" (275). Where had she felt that gaze before? The reader might remember, even though she does not. Like Manley Pointer, the Freemans, who had worked for Mrs. Hopewell for four years, were "good country people" whom she had hired even in the face of a warning that Mrs. Freeman was "the nosiest woman ever to walk the earth," and had to be "into everything" (264). Every morning Mrs. Freeman and Hulga's mother would linger in the kitchen exchanging clichés and idle chatter ("Everybody is different," for example, and "Yes, most people is," and "It takes all kinds to make the world"). Unlike her mother, who insisted on calling her Joy instead of Hulga, the name she had given herself, Mrs. Freeman abruptly began calling her Hulga, as if it were a secret between them. Instead of pleasing her it only irritated her: "It was as if Mrs. Freeman's beady steel-pointed eyes had penetrated far enough behind her face to reach some sacred fact. Something about her seemed to fascinate Mrs. Freeman and then one day Hulga realized that it was the artificial leg" (266–67). Manley Pointer's fascination with Hulga is similar, though with an added note of flattery: "'I see you got a wooden leg,' he said. 'I think you're real brave. I think you're real sweet'" (275). She tells him her name and lies about her age ("Seventeen," almost matching Lucynell Crater's lie about the age of her daughter), and they agree to meet again at the gate the next morning for a walk in the woods and a picnic.

In the night Hulga fantasizes about seducing Manley in "the storage barn beyond the two back fields," and then dealing with his remorse: "She imagined that she took his remorse in hand and changed it into a deeper understanding of life. She took all his shame away and turned it into something useful" (276). She meets him at the gate next morning, with Vapex on her collar "since she did not own any perfume," but without bringing food, "forgetting that food is usually taken on a picnic." He appears from behind a bush still carrying the black valise. "Why did you bring your Bibles?" she asks, and he reminds her, "You can never tell when you'll need the word of God, Hulga." He swings it as if it is lighter than before, and after they have crossed half the pasture asks her "Where does your leg join on?" When Hulga turns red and glares at him, he backs off. " 'I didn't mean you no harm,' he said, 'I only meant you're so brave and all. I guess God takes care of you,' " and for the first time she tells him, "I don't even believe in God" (277). Pointer "stopped and whistled. 'No!' he exclaimed as if he were too astonished to say anything else," adding "That's very unusual for a girl," and shortly afterward, seizing the moment, he "drew her against him without a word and kissed her heavily." The "surge of adrenalin" that the kiss produced goes right to her brain, so that "her mind, clear and detached and ironic anyway, was regarding him from a great distance, with amusement but with pity. She had never been kissed before and she was pleased to discover that it was an unexceptional experience and all a matter of the mind's control." Nothing more is said until they come out on a sunny hillside from which the storage barn she had fantasized about comes into view.

Pointer now resumes the conversation: "'Then you ain't saved?' he asked suddenly, stopping." Hulga smiled: "'In my economy,' she said, 'I'm saved and you are damned but I told you I didn't believe in God'" (278). She explains this only later, when they are together upstairs in the barn. After they have climbed the ladder into the loft, Pointer "began methodically kissing her face" and when her glasses got in the way he "took them off her and slipped them into his pocket' (279). He demands that she must say that she loves him: "In a sense," she begins, "if you use the word loosely, you might say that. But it's not a word I use. I don't have illusions. I'm one of those people who see *through* to nothing." When he repeats his demand, "You poor baby," she tells him, "It's just as well you don't understand," and pulls him close to her. " 'We are all damned,' she said, 'but some of us have taken off our blindfolds and see that there's nothing to see. It's a kind of salvation.'"[4] Ignoring her nihilism, he presses her yet again: "'Okay,' he almost whined, 'but do you love me or don'tcher?'" (280). "Yes, she replies,

---

4. Her musings revisit a passage from Heidegger that her mother had discovered in one of the books Hulga had been reading: "If science is right, then one thing stands firm: science wishes to know nothing of nothing. Such is after all the strictly scientific approach to Nothing. We know it by wishing to know nothing of Nothing." To Hulga's mother it sounded "like some evil incantation in gibberish" (269).

"in a sense," and then—after confessing her true age and that she has "a number of degrees," and after he "wildly planted her face with kisses"— finally "Yes, yes." "Okay then," Pointer continues, "Prove it," and at that moment Hulga felt that she had "seduced him without even making up her mind to try."

When he then whispers in her ear, "Show me where your wooden leg joins on," she feels nothing she is willing to call shame, only a kind of shock: "As a child she had sometimes been subject to shame but education had removed the last traces of that as a good surgeon scrapes for cancer." Thanks to her education she could no more feel shame over the "obscenity" of his suggestion than she could believe in his Bible" (280–81). Shame she attributes to Pointer himself and others like him who had not yet learned to "see through to nothing." She convinces herself that it is not so much a sexual matter as an invasion of privacy, something akin to the unease she had felt at Mrs. Freeman's casual use of her name and curiosity about her wooden leg. So she tells Pointer "No," but the "No" gives way almost at once to further negotiation: "It joins on at the knee. Only at the knee. Why do you want to see it?" "Because," he replies, "it's what makes you different. You ain't like anybody else."

A revelation of sorts, yet another "message in the bottle," not unlike "God made me thisaway," or "I am a Temple of the Holy Ghost," and its effect on Hulga is profound: "She decided that for the first time in her life she was face to face with real innocence. This boy, with an instinct that came from beyond wisdom, had touched the truth about her. When after a minute, she said in a hoarse high voice, 'All right,' it was like losing her own life and finding it again, miraculously, in his" (281). Without quite intending to, Hulga is echoing Pointer's own sentiment, "so sincere, so genuine and earnest," from Mark 8:35, expressed the night before at dinner, that "He who losest his life shall find it." And it is safe to say that the sentiment is more genuine and earnest on her part than on Manley Pointer's. Hulga is "face to face with real innocence" all right, but the innocence is hers and hers alone. Despite her PhD and her atheism, she is, in her way, every bit as innocent as young Lucynell Crater.

This becomes clearer and clearer in all that follows. She takes off the wooden leg and puts it back on, then allows Pointer to take it off. Instead of putting it back he begins kissing her again. "Without the leg she felt entirely dependent on him," but finally she demands, "Put it back on me now." He refuses, and instead opens the black valise, unveiling within it two Bibles, one of which is hollow, concealing condoms, a small flask of whiskey, and a pack of cards with obscene pictures. "Aren't you," she murmurs, sounding oddly like her mother, "aren't you just good country people?" Pointer sees only irony in the phrase "good country people," and takes it as an insult. "Yeah," he replies, "but it ain't held me back none." Ringing the changes on the word "good," he continues, "I'm as good as you any day in the week," and "Come on now, let's begin to have us a good time," and "We ain't got to know one another good yet" (282). He has his own definition of "good," a definition merely confirming O'Connor's principle that "a good man is hard to find." As for Hulga, he finds her not so "good" by his definition: "What's the matter with you all of a sudden?" he demanded. "You just a while ago said you didn't believe in nothing. I thought you was some girl!" (282–83). And in return she begins to insult him in earnest: "You're a fine Christian! You're just like them all—say one thing and do another. You're a perfect Christian, you're . . ."

Pointer interrupts her: "'I hope you don't think,' he said in a lofty indignant tone, 'that I believe in that crap!'" and in a torrent of clichés that would have done justice to Mrs. Hopewell and Mrs. Freeman combined, "I may sell Bibles but I know which end is up and I wasn't born yesterday and I know where I'm going!" (283). With these words he throws the cards and the condoms into the fake Bible, and the Bible and the wooden leg into the valise. The fake Bible stuffed with condoms, pornography, and liquor recalls Jesus' comparison of the "hypocrites" of his day to "whited sepulchres, which outwardly appear to men beautiful, but within are full of dead men's bones and of all filthiness" (Matt 23:27), driving home the point of Hulga's outburst at Pointer and at all who "say one thing and do another." For an instant Hulga can see her leg "slanted forlornly across the inside of the suitcase with a Bible at either side of its opposite ends," trapped as it were between the word of God and its Satanic counterfeit. As for Manley Pointer, he at last reveals himself, the "modern hero" or "outsider" that O'Connor described and dreaded: "And you needn't to think you'll catch me because Pointer ain't really my name. I use a different name at every house I call at and don't stay nowhere long."[5] The last thing she hears are his parting words, "'I'll tell you another thing, Hulga,' he said, using the name as if he didn't think much of it, 'you ain't so smart. I been

5. The modern hero again, like Mr. Shiftlet: "I can tell you my name is Tom T. Shiftlet and I come from Tarwater, Tennessee, but you never have seen me before: how you know I ain't lying? How you know my name ain't Aaron Sparks, lady, and I come from Singleberry, Georgia, or how you know it's not George Speeds and I come from Lucy, Alabama, or how you know I ain't Thompson Bright from Toolafalls, Mississippi?" (174).

believing in nothing ever since I was born'" (*Collected Works*, 283). The last thing she sees of him is "his blue figure struggling successfully over the green speckled lake"—that is, the sunlit "pink-speckled hillsides" over which they had come, which looked to her without her glasses like "two green swelling lakes" (279–80).

The story is not quite over.[6] Mrs. Hopewell and Mrs Freeman, digging up onions in the back pasture, see the same thing. Mrs. Hopewell identifies him as "that nice dull young man that tried to sell me a Bible yesterday." She guesses that "He must have been selling them to the Negroes back in there. He was so simple," and that "the world would be better off if we were all that simple." But Mrs. Freeman, the very embodiment of "good country people," has the last word. The story began with Mrs. Freeman, and her "forward expression" that was "steady and driving, like the advance of a heavy truck" (263). She deploys it here as she delivers her verdict on Manley Pointer: "'Some can't be that simple,' she said. 'I know I never could'" (283–84). Here, in contrast to some of O'Connor's other stories, manners and mystery, in the persons of the "outsider" and "good country people," are *not* on a collision course but kindred spirits. Mystery thrives even in the bosom of traditional Southern manners. "Good country people" are not what they seem, for Manley Pointer and Mrs. Freeman are cut from the same cloth. That was the case even in the companion story, "The Life You Save May Be Your Own," where Mr. Shiftlet's schemes were almost but not quite matched by those of the victim's mother, Lucynell the elder.

As for Hulga, she has "lost her life" along with her wooden leg, *without* "finding it again" in the person of Manley Pointer. Is she on her way to finding it at all? There are no clear redemptive signals, only the "dusty sunlight" in the old barn and Hulga's "churning face" (283), but the sunlight, often a signal that God is watching, may offer a faint clue. As always, self-knowledge is the first step toward redemption, and Hulga's own angry words to her mother earlier in the story "in the middle of a meal with her face purple and her mouth half full" are the prophetic words she now needs to hear: "'Woman! do you ever look inside? Do you ever look inside and see what you are *not*? God!' she had cried sinking down again and staring at her plate, 'Malebranche was right: we are not our own light. We are not our own light!'" (268). Strange words from a professed atheist. "God!" on Hulga's lips is an expletive, but it is just as easily read as her

6. In a note in *A Habit of Being*, Sally Fitzgerald remembers that Robert Giroux, O'Connor's publisher, wrote to her, suggesting "that an appearance by the mother and Mrs. Freeman at the end might improve it. Flannery recognized the value of the suggestion and added the sentences that are now part of the story" (75).

answer to the preceding question, "Do you ever look inside and see what you are *not*?" What Mrs. Hopewell was not, what Hulga was not, what none of us are, is "God." Malebranche merely puts it another way: "We are not our own light!"

The words of this French philosopher—an unlikely source for an atheist to be quoting[7]—can be traced to Augustine: "And for that the soul of man, though it gives testimony of the light, yet itself is not that light, but the Word, God himself, is that true light that lighteth every man that cometh into the world."[8] Nothing new under the sun: Hulga citing Malebranche, citing Augustine, citing the Gospel of John. Augustine was simply interpreting John 1:6–8: "There was a man sent from God, whose name was John. This man came for a witness, to give testimony of the light, that all men might believe through him. He was not the light, but was to give testimony of the light." Augustine's reading draws on the very next verse, "That was the true light, which enlighteneth every man that cometh into this world" (John 1:9), to make the point that what was just said about one man, John the Baptist, is true of everyone, every "soul of man." Mrs. Hopewell, Mrs. Freeman, Manley Pointer, Hulga herself—none of them are their own light, but as Augustine put it, "the Word, God himself, is that true light that lighteth every man." When Hulga told Pointer, "I'm one of those people who see *through* to nothing," and "some of us have taken off our blindfolds" (280), she thought she was her own light. What she now needs to hear again are her own words to her mother coming back at her like an echo, much as Ruby Turpin's defiant words to God, "Who do you think you are?" in another story "returned to her clearly like an answer from beyond the wood" (653). No such echo here, but Hulga has given "testimony of the light" at least once to her mother, and all "good country people" stand indicted, herself included. Now in the storage barn, the "dusty sunlight" is there to remind her at last of her own angry words. She has only to remember, and listen.

7. Nicolas Malebranche (1638–1715) was a philosopher and Roman Catholic priest who attempted to combine the rationalism of Descartes with Augustinian theology.

8. *St. Augustine's Confessions* 7.9. Loeb Classical Library, 1.367.

9

More Visitations

L IKE CERTAIN OTHER STORIES we have discussed, "A Circle in the Fire" and "The Displaced Person," published just a few months apart in 1954, can be read as a matched pair. Both deal with a farm run by a widow, and with a visitation of some kind that throws "everything off balance"—to borrow The Misfit's words about Jesus. In one it is a visitation of evil or the demonic in the persons of three teenage boys from a housing development in Atlanta, in the other a visitation of the good in the person of a Polish immigrant, but the results are much the same. Nothing much is left of either farm, and the widow who owns and runs it is changed forever. O'Connor's words about the "modern hero" or "outsider" are apt: "don't attempt to rebuild until he is gone. He soon will be; then you can take stock of what is left."

SONGS OF THE THREE CHILDREN

"A Circle in the Fire" is seen and told through the eyes of a young girl with an ugly disposition not unlike the child in "A Temple of the Holy Ghost," only with a name, Sally Virginia Cope. "A pale fat girl of twelve with a frowning squint and a large mouth full of silver bands" (238), Sally Virginia could easily have been Hulga Hopewell at an early age. It is both her coming-of-age story and her mother's story, as she watches it begin to unfold from an upstairs bedroom window in her mother's farmhouse. Below, her mother and Mrs. Pritchard are carrying on a rambling conversation much like that between Hulga's mother and Mrs. Freeman, different only in that instead of random clichés it centers on one bizarre tale of a woman who had a baby in an iron lung, and the death and funeral of both. While they talked, Mrs. Cope "worked at the weeds and nut grass as if they were an evil sent directly by the devil to destroy the place" (232). But what she really fears will "destroy the place" are fires in her woods. On summer evenings when she tells the child to "Get up and look at the sunset, it's gorgeous," Sally Virginia is fond of taunting her mother with words like "It looks like a fire. You better get up and smell around and see if the woods ain't on fire" (233).

From the window, it is Sally Virginia who first sees three boys get out of a pick-up truck and start walking toward the house single file. The three of them could be younger versions of The Misfit, Bobby Lee, and Hiram in "A Good Man is Hard to Find." The middle-sized one is "bent to the side carrying a black pig-shaped valise," not unlike Manley Pointer, and when they arrive at the house he is seen to wear the obligatory "silver-rimmed spectacles" of The Misfit. Another "outsider" or "modern hero," perhaps, of the kind O'Connor more than once described, yet he and his companions seem far too young. "He looked to be about thirteen," only a year older than Sally Virginia herself (235). They are three displaced country boys living in "one of those nice new developments" in Atlanta, where "The only way you can tell your own is by smell," as one of them puts it, "They're four stories high and there's ten of them, one behind the other" (239). Their story is that Powell Boyd, the ringleader with the silver-rimmed spectacles, had once lived as a tenant on this farm. His father has since died and his mother is remarried. He remembers riding the horses here, and has told his two friends that "he had the best time of his entire life right here on this place," and "when he died he wanted to come here!" (237). Mrs. Cope extends hospitality to the three young visitors, just as Abraham did to his three mysterious guests at Mambre (Gen 18:1-8), but the outcome is very different. The boys, it seems, have come to stay, bringing with them a series of increasingly outrageous encroachments on Mrs. Cope's rather naïve hospitality, from smoking in the barn and drinking out of the milk cans, to riding the horses bareback all afternoon, to the most feared transgression of all, smoking in the woods. "I can't have people smoking in my woods," she tells them, and the oldest boy (Garfield Smith) mutters to himself, "Her woods" (240). Later he tells Hollis, Mrs. Pritchard's husband who helps in the farm: "She don't own them woods." They speak in tandem, as if finishing each other's senteneces, as the littlest one (W. T. Harper) adds, "Man, Gawd owns them woods and her too," and Powell chimes in sarcastically," "I reckon she owns the sky over this place too" (242–43).

The reader knows they are speaking the truth, even if Mrs. Cope does not. At the beginning of the story, the woods were "a solid gray blue wall" turned almost black, and "the sky was a livid glaring white" (232), not a reassuring sign of her ownership. Sally Virginia "thought the blank sky looked as if it were pushing against the fortress wall, trying to break through" (232). Sarah Gordon (*Obedient Imagination*, 165), finds here "a mythic suggestion of sexual intercourse whereby the sky (male) penetrates the female earth." While there are sexual hints in the story,[1] inevitable perhaps, in that the victims are female and the young perpetrators male, it is more plausibly read as human self-assertion and property rights under the judgement of a sovereign God displayed in the sky, and above all in the sun. Sally Virginia's mother was oblivious to all this when she admired the "gorgeous" sunsets on summer evenings, but when she first served the boys a plate of sandwiches, she stood "looking at the sun which was going down in front of them, almost at the top of the tree line. It was swollen and flame-colored and hung in a net of ragged cloud as if it might burn through any second and fall into the woods." From the window, Sally Virginia "saw her shiver and catch both arms to her sides," but she expressed no fear, only thanksgiving. "We have so much to be thankful for," she exclaims. "Do you boys thank God every night for all He's done for you? Do you thank Him for everything?" They ignored her, and so did the threatening sun: "The sun burned so fast that it seemed to be trying to set everything in sight on fire. The white water tower was glazed pink and the grass was an unnatural green as if it were turning into glass" (241).

So who really threatens the woods, the three displaced boys from the development, or the sun in an angry sky, representing "Gawd," who "owns them woods and her too"? In the end it amounts to the same thing, for the three young vagrants will carry out exactly what the sun was attempting to do. Still Mrs. Cope convinces herself that "this is my place" (242), and when she is certain the boys are finally gone for good, she continues her litany of thanksgiving. She reminds Sally Virginia "how much they had to be thankful for, for she said they might have had to live in a development themselves or they might have been Negroes or they might have been in iron lungs or they might have been Europeans ridden in boxcars like cattle." Sally Virginia, unconvinced, sets off the next morning looking for

---

1. These center largely on the oldest boy, Garfield. When he is asked, "do you have men teachers or lady teachers at your school? he replies, "Some of both and some you can't tell which" (241). When Sally Virginia sticks her head out the window, "'Jesus,' he growled, 'another woman'" (242), and he tells Mr. Pritchard, "I never seen a place with so many damm women on it, how do you stand it here?" (243).

the three boys, armed with two toy pistols, overalls over her dress, and a man's felt hat pulled tightly over her head (247). She is "off to the woods as if she were stalking out an enemy, her head thrust forward and each hand gripped on a gun," a comic scene, but one that quickly turns serious: "Suddenly she heard a laugh. She sat up, prickle-skinned. It came again." Then she saw the boys swimming naked in the cow trough, and heard what each of them said in turn, all echoing the same refrain. "If this place was not here any more," Powell said, "you would never have to think of it again." Then Garfield: "it don't belong to nobody." Then the littlest boy: "It's ours." And Garfield again: "I'd build a big parking lot on it, or something" (248–49). Finally, as she watches, they pull out matches and start a fire: "They began to whoop and holler and beat their hands over their mouths and in a few seconds there was a narrow line of fire widening between her and them." At first, "she stood there, weighted down with some new unplaced misery that she had never felt before. But finally she begins to run."

By this time Mrs. Cope and Mrs. Pritchard can see "smoke rising from the woods across the pasture, and Sally Virginia "loping heavily, screaming, 'Mama, Mama, they're going to build a parking lot here!" (250). Her mother quickly summons Mr. Pritchard and the black hired help, as Sally Virginia "came to a stop beside her mother and stared up at her face as if she had never seen it before. It was the face of the new misery she felt, but on her mother it looked old and it looked as if it might have belonged to anybody, a Negro or a European or to Powell himself" (250–51). She and her mother, alienated through much of the story, now have something in common, as she comes of age in what O'Connor once called "the world of guilt and sorrow" (*Collected Works*, 500). Both mother and daughter are now displaced or dispossessed, just as surely as the three young refugees from "one of those nice new developments" in Atlanta.

The final scene unfolds through the child's eyes and hers alone, as she "turned her head quickly, and past the Negroes' ambling figures she could see the column of smoke rising and widening unchecked inside the granite line of trees. She stood taut, listening, and could just catch in the distance a few wild high shrieks of joy as if the prophets were dancing in the fiery furnace, in the circle the angel had cleared for them" (251). This closing sentence that gives the story its name is also its only biblical clue, linking the three perpetrators with Shadrach, Meshach, and Abednego, the three "holy children" who survived Nebuchadnezzar's fiery furnace in the third chapter of Daniel. O'Connor draws the imagery not from the canonical book of Daniel in Protestant Bibles, but from the longer Roman

Catholic version of Daniel found in her Douay Bible. In the Protestant version, the three men were "cast into the midst of the burning fiery furnace," and "fell down bound" into it (Dan 3:21, 23, KJV). So far the Catholic Bible agrees, but follows this with a long addition taken from a section of the Greek Old Testament that has no known Hebrew or Aramaic equivalent (Dan 3:24–90 in the Douay Bible). It is in this lengthy addition, and only there, that we find the imagery of "prophets" dancing with "shrieks of joy" as if "in the circle the angel had cleared for them." In the Protestant version the three men are hardly prophets, for they say nothing, but in O'Connor's Bible, "they walked in the midst of the flame, praising God and blessing the Lord" (Dan 3:24, Douay). Then Abednego (suddenly renamed Azarias, the Hebrew equivalent), prays a very long prayer (3:25–45), until the flames mounted above the furnace and "burnt such of the Chaldeans as it found near the furnace" (3:48).

At once the source of O'Connor's unexpected image of a "circle the angel had cleared for them" becomes clear, as "the angel of the Lord went down with Azarias and his companions into the furnace: and he drove the flame of the fire out of the furnace, And made the midst of the furnace like the blowing of a wind bringing dew, and the fire touched them not at all, nor troubled them, nor did them any harm" (Dan 3:49–50). Then all three "as with one mouth praised and glorified, and blessed God in the furnace," and another long hymn of praise ensues (3:51–90).[2] Finally, the Douay text rejoins the Hebrew Bible and the Protestant versions, so that Daniel 3:91–92 in the Catholic Bible agrees almost word for word with 3:24–25 in the King James version, where there is no explicit "angel of the Lord," but "four men loose, walking in the midst of the fire, and they have no hurt, and the form of the fourth is like the Son of God" (Dan 3:25, KJV). In Protestant interpretation, the "fourth man" is sometimes an angel, sometimes the pre-incarnate Christ, but in the Douay version he is unmistakably "the angel of the Lord" of Daniel 3:50, with his gentle "wind bringing dew," so that "the fire touched them not at all."

None of this would have been known to Sally Virginia or her mother. Nothing in the story identifies them as Roman Catholics, much less Bible-reading Catholics. Whatever knowledge Sally Virginia had would have come from the King James version, where there are no "shrieks of joy,"

---

2. In early editions of the King James version that contained the Apocrypha, these additions to Daniel were called "The Song of the Three Holy Children," while in contemporary Protestant edtions of the Apocrypha (for example *The New Oxford Annotated Bible*) they are designated "The Prayer of Azariah and the Song of the Three Jews."

no prayers, no prophecies. This is O'Connor, therefore, not Sally Virginia, telling us just as clearly as if she had written it in a letter, how to regard the three boys setting fire to the woods. They are "prophets," sending Mrs. Cope the message that "Gawd owns them woods and her too," and carrying out the judgement of the "glaring" sky and the "swollen and flame-colored" sun against her, and against her claim that "this is my place." They have literally "displaced" her. They are no less demonic than their older compatriots, The Misfit and his two companions, no less so than Rufus Johnson, or Mary Grace in "Revelation." And yet, like Rufus, Mary Grace and the demoniacs in the New Testament, they speak the truth, which is all that a prophet is called to do. Consequently they stand, at least for the moment, under divine protection, like the three young men in Daniel "in the circle the angel had cleared for them."

MRS. SHORTLEY'S VISIONS

The longest O'Connor story aside from her novels, "The Displaced Person" is divided into three chapters. Its first chapter is all about the enormous Mrs. Shortley, the dairyman's wife who "might have been the giant wife of the countryside" (285), a larger version of Ruby Turpin, the "country female Jacob." The events of the chapter are seen through her eyes, and the chapter ends with her death. But unlike Ruby, she is not blessed with a good disposition. As the story begins, she watches from a hill as a car arrives driven by an aged parish priest, carrying the Guizacs (or Gobble-hooks as she calls them), Polish refugees from the holocaust and the farm's new hired help. The priest gets out of the car first, then "two children, a boy and a girl," then "a woman in brown, shaped like a peanut," finally "the man, the Displaced Person. He was short and a little sway-backed and wore gold-rimmed spectacles" (286). Not "silver-rimmed" like Powell's, or The Misfit's when he got out of another car in another story (146), but gold-rimmed ones. Yet the scene, while not unexpected, is almost as ominous to her as The Misfit's appearance was to the grandmother and her family: "These people who were coming were only hired help, like the Shortleys themselves or the Negroes. Yet here was the owner of the place out to welcome them. Here she was, wearing her best clothes and a string of beads, and now bounding forward with her mouth stretched" (285).

The owner is Mrs. McIntyre, "a small woman of sixty with a round wrinkled face and red bangs that came almost down to two high orange-colored eyebrows." She introduces the Guizacs to Mrs. Shortley, who quickly sizes them up. She remembers a newsreel she had once seen, of "a small room piled high with bodies of dead naked people all in a heap, their arms and legs tangled together, a head thrust in here, a head there, a foot, a knee, a part that should have been covered up sticking out, a hand raised clutching nothing," and she muses that "If they had come from where that kind of thing was done to them, who was to say they were not the kind that would also do it to others?" Looking at the priest, she remembers as well "that these people did not have an advanced religion. There was no telling what all they believed since none of the foolishness had been reformed out of it. Again she saw the room piled high with bodies" (287–88).

Mrs. Shortley fears the worst. She explains to the black hired help, Astor and Sulk, that these were "Displaced Persons," because they "ain't where they were born at and there's nowhere for them to go—like if you was run out of here and wouldn't nobody have you," and she issues a warning of "ten million billion more just like them" (290). And after she and her husband assess the capabilities and especially the limitations of the Guizacs, "I rather have a nigger if it was me," Mr. Shortley concludes, "I give them three weeks here." But three weeks later, the verdict is in. Ironically, the displaced European with his foreign ways and no "advanced religion," turns out to embody all the stereotypical American virtues of hard work, efficiency, and initiative: "Mr. Guizac could drive a tractor, use the rotary hay-baler, the silage cutter, the combine, the letz mill, or any other machine she had on the place. He was an expert mechanic, a carpenter and a mason. He was thrifty and energetic. Mrs. McIntyre said she figured he would save her twenty dollars a month on repair bills alone. She said getting him was the best day's work she had ever done in her life. He could work milking machines and he was scrupulously clean. He did not smoke" (292).

Mrs. McIntyre is delighted. "At last," she says, "I've got somebody I can depend on. For years I've been fooling with sorry people. Sorry people." Pointing to Mr. Guizac, she tells Mrs. Shortley, "That man is my salvation" (293–94). Mrs. Shortley calls it "salvation got from the devil," even though she "had never given much thought to the devil for she felt that religion was essentially for those people who didn't have the brains to avoid evil without it," but she felt that "if she had ever given it much thought, she would have considered the devil the head of it and God the hanger-on." Still, in light of the arrival of these strangers from abroad, she is "obliged to give new thought to a good many things" (294), and in time she undergoes a conversion of sorts. Fearing that the priest was trying to bring yet another Polish family to the farm, she imagines a day when "there would be almost nothing spoken but Polish!"—a "war of words," with "the Polish words, dirty and all-knowing and unreformed, flinging mud on the clean English words until everything was equally dirty. She saw them all piled in a room, all the dead dirty words, theirs and hers too, piled up like the naked bodies in the newsreel. God save me! she cried silently, from the stinking power of Satan!" This drove her "to read her Bible with a new attention":

> She pored over the Apocalypse and began to quote from the Prophets and before long she had come to a deeper understanding of her existence. She saw plainly that the meaning of the world was a mystery that had been planned and she was not surprised to suspect that she had a special part in the plan because she was strong. She saw that the Lord God Almighty had created the strong people to do what had to be done and she felt that she would be ready when she was called.

For the moment, her job was simply "to watch the priest," because he was "leading foreigners over in hoards to places that were not theirs, to cause disputes, to uproot niggers, to plant the Whore of Babylon in the midst of the righteous!" (300–301),[3] but a greater, more prophetic call is in store for her as well, and she is ready.

Her readiness is rewarded with a vision on a Sunday afternoon as she stands atop a small hill she has just climbed in the pasture, aware of "her heart, like a child's fist, clenching and unclenching inside her chest," and gazing at "low-lying clouds that looked like rows and rows of white fish washed up on a great blue beach." There suddenly "the sky folded back in two pieces like the curtain to a stage and a gigantic figure stood facing her. It was the color of the sun in the early afternoon, white-gold. It was of no definite shape, but there were fiery wheels with fierce dark eyes in them, spinning rapidly all around it." Then it "turned blood-red and the wheels turned white," and "A voice, very resonant, said the one word, 'Prophesy!'" Standing there, "tottering slightly but still upright, her eyes shut tight and her fists clenched," Mrs. Shortley is indeed ready: "'The children of wicked nations will be butchered,' she said in a loud voice. 'Legs where arms should be, foot to face, ear in the palm of hand. Who will remain whole? Who will

3. That is, the "great Whore" of the King James version, the translation Mrs. Shortley would have known (Rev 17:1; also vv. 15 and 16), further identified as "MYSTERY, BABYLON THE GREAT," and in some Protestant fundamentalist interpretations linked with the Roman Catholic Church.

remain whole? Who?'" When she opens her eyes again, the sky is still "full of white fish carried lazily on their sides by some invisible current and pieces of the sun, submerged some distance beyond them, appeared from time to time as if they were being washed in the opposite direction" (301).

Mrs. Shortley's vision is vaguely biblical, with its "fiery wheels with fierce dark eyes" (see Ezek 1:15–21 and 10:9–19), but something is wrong. The "gigantic figure" that she sees is an "it," with "no definite shape," not a Person, much less "the Lord," as in Ezekiel. And while the command to "Prophesy" is quite common in the book of Ezekiel, it is almost invariably followed by a verbatim message to deliver, introduced by "And say," or "Thus saith the Lord God," or something similar (see Ezek 6:2; 11:4; 13:2, 17; 20:46; 21:2, 9, 28; 25:2; 28:21; 29:2; 30:2; 34:2; 35:2; 36:1, 3, 6; 37:4, 9, 12; 38:2; 39:1). In the New Testament, when Jesus was told simply, "Prophesy" (Mark 14:65), it was not a call from God but a mockery on the lips of his tormentors just after his hearing before the Sanhedrin. And as for Mrs. Shortley, she is given no prophecy to prophesy, no message from above, so that her words too are a kind of mockery. She is left with her own musings, the same images of the holocaust that have haunted her all along. Her final words, "Who will remain whole? Who will remain whole? Who?" sounds vaguely like a warning of judgement to come, not unlike the words of the "the kings of the earth, and the princes, and the tribunes, and the rich, and the strong" in the book of Revelation at the breaking of the sixth seal, as they "hid themselves in the dens and in the rocks of mountains," saying to the mountains and the rocks, "Fall upon us and hide us from the face of him that sitteth upon the throne and from the wrath of the Lamb. For the great day of their wrath is come. *And who shall be able to stand?*" (Rev 6:15–17, italics added). Not a prophecy at all, but a cry of despair from those under divine judgment. Another way of saying, "Who will remain whole? Who will remain whole? Who?"

Who indeed? Not Mrs. Shortley. As in the case of old Mason Tarwater, who discovered one day that "the destruction he had been waiting for had fallen on his own brain and his own body" (332), the judgment falls first on the prophet of judgment. Even her name tells us that her judgment is coming soon. To her it seemed that "the Lord God Almighty had created the strong people to do what had to be done" and that she was among the strong (300), but in the Bible even (or especially) "the rich, and the strong" tremble before "the wrath of the Lamb." As soon as her vision is over, Mrs. Shortley returns to the house and sees the priest's car in the driveway. "'Here again,' she muttered. 'Come to destroy'" (302). Hiding herself in the feed house, she listens to Mrs. McIntyre's conversation with the priest about the need to raise Mr. Guizac's wages and the consequent need to get rid of some of the other help. Finally she overhears Mrs. Mc-Intyre say, "I've decided to give Mr. Shortley his month's notice tomorrow." Without hesitation, her face an "almost volcanic red," Mrs. Shortley goes off and tells her husband. "Bring the car around to the back door," because "You ain't waiting to be fired!" (303). By four o'clock in the morning, while Mrs. McIntyre is still asleep, the Shortleys with their two daughters have packed all their earthly possessions into the car and left the farm. "Where we goin?" Mr. Shortley asks, once and then again, as Mrs. Shortley's face keeps changing "from red to white and back again." She sits erect in the car "in spite of the fact that one leg was twisted under her and one knee was almost into her neck," and "there was a peculiar lack of light in her icy blue eyes," as if they were "turned around, looking inside her" (304). Suddenly she grabs her husband's elbow and her daughter's foot simultaneously, "as if she were trying to fit the two extra limbs onto herself." She lurches "forward and backward, clutching at everything she could get her hands on and hugging it to herself." Finally "her fierce expression faded into a look of astonishment," as she lets go of all she had been holding on to. "One of her eyes drew near to the other and she seemed to collapse quietly and she was still" (304–5). Her two daughters, we are told, "didn't know that she had had a great experience or even been displaced in the world from all that belonged to her." All they can do is take up the chorus, "Where we goin, Ma? Where we goin?" over and over, as "their mother, her huge body rolled back still against the seat and her eyes like blue painted glass, seemed to contemplate for the first time the tremendous frontiers of her true country" (305).

In this closing scene of chapter one, Mrs. Shortley's self-generated "prophecy" finds its fulfillment: "Legs where arms should be, foot to face, ear in the palm of hand. Who will remain whole? Who will remain whole? Who?" And yet it is fair to ask, Is redemption a matter of "remaining whole"? Jesus thought not, for he told his disciples, "And, if thy hand scandalize thee, cut if off; it is better for thee to enter into life, maimed, than having two hands to go into hell, into unquenchable fire," and "if thy foot scandalize thee, cut it off; it is better for thee to enter lame into life everlasting than having two feet to be cast into the hell of unquenchable fire," and "if thy eye scandalize thee, pluck it out; it is better for thee with one eye to enter into the kingdom of God than having two eyes to be cast into the hell of fire" (Mark 9:42, 44, 46). Mrs. Shortley does not "remain whole" as her story ends, and yet she is given a glimpse of her "true country," leaving us with the question, What is her true country?

O'Connor herself, not once but twice, wrote about her own calling as a writer in terms strangely reminiscent of Mrs. Shortley and her fate. In her essay, "The Fiction Writer and His Country," she defines a writer's "country" as "everything from the actual countryside that the novelist describes, on, to, and through the peculiar characteristics of his region and his nation, and on, through, and under all of these to his true country, which the writer with Christian convictions will consider to be what is eternal and absolute" (*Collected Works*, 801). In much the same way Mrs. Shortley, introduced as a "giant wife of the countryside" (285), in the end glimpses her "true country." Not her region, not America in contrast to Europe and its millions, not even the whole world, but a country with even more "tremendous frontiers."

There is an even more explicit connection. In a January 1956 letter to Betty Hester, O'Connor testifies to how the Lord helped her overcome her fierce aversion to angels:

> In fact I forgot that angels existed until a couple of years ago the Catholic Worker sent me a card on which was printed a prayer to St. Raphael. It was sometime before it dawned on me Raphael was an arch angel, the guide of Tobias. The prayer had some imagery that I took over and put in The Displaced Person—the business about Mrs. Shortley looking on the frontiers of her true country. The prayer asks St. Raphael to guide us to the province of joy so that we may not be ignorant of the concerns of our true country. (*Collected Works*, 983–84)

In July 1964, less than a month before she died, O'Connor sent a copy of the prayer to her friend Janet McKane, in which we see that its actual wording is "the concerns of our country" (*Collected Works*, 1281). "True country" was O'Connor's embellishment from memory, whether from "The Displaced Person" or her essay about the fiction writer's "true country." What "dawned on" her was that Raphael was not just a saint on a prayer card but a character in a story she knew well from the book of Tobit, or Tobias, in her Catholic Bible. There the angel Raphael guides Tobias on a long journey "to the province of joy," in the sense that it is on behalf of his blind father, who asks "What manner of joy shall be to me who sit in darkness, and see not the light of heaven?" (Tob 5:12), and on his return cures the father's blindness, so that "the rest of his life was in joy" (Tob 14:4).

The other operative text, one that O'Connor does not explicitly acknowledge but must have known, speaks of the family of Abraham as "pilgrims and strangers on the earth," who look for "a better, that is to say, a heavenly country" (Heb 11:13, 16). As the chapter ends, Mrs. Shortley, like Hazel Motes and Enoch Emery, is "saved" in the sense that she is moving toward what O'Connor might have called her "true end," that is, what she was always meant to be. As Flannery once wrote to John Hawkes, "everything works toward its true end, or away from it, everything is ultimately either saved or lost" (*Collected Works*, 1107). Whether or not Mrs. Shortley's destiny is in any way equivalent to Christian salvation is another question altogether. It is perhaps O'Connor's firm belief in Purgatory that allows her to leave the matter ambiguous, for even in death Mrs. Shortley is still a pilgrim and a stranger, "not having received the promises, but beholding them afar off" (Heb 11:13).

Mrs. McIntyre's Purgatory

This first chapter of "The Displaced Person" could almost stand alone as a short story in its own right. It is virtually self-contained except for a hint of something more to come in Mrs. Shortley's recollection that "she had found out what the Displaced Person was up to through the old man, Astor, and she had not told anybody but Mr. Shortley" (299). What was this momentous piece of news? What *was* Mr. Guizac "up to"? We find out only in the next chapter, when Mrs. McIntyre sees him hand a photograph to Sulk, the younger Negro. She finds out that it is a photograph of his young cousin in Poland, whose only hope of escape from a life in concentration camps is marriage to an American, and Sulk is Mr. Guizac's only hope (310–11).

By this time Mrs. McIntyre has already begun to take on something of the persona of Mrs. Shortley, with the help of a number of factors. For one thing, the comments of Astor, the older black man: "He from Pole," and "In Pole it ain't like it is here," because "They got different ways of doing." When Mrs. McIntyre said, "If you have anything to say about him, say it and say it aloud," Astor is silent until he finally adds, "We ain't never had one like him before is all" (307). For another, "the Judge," Mrs. McIntyre's deceased first husband, buried "in the family graveyard, a little space fenced in the middle of the back cornfield," who liked to say, as Astor is quick to remind her, that "the devil he know is better than the devil he don't" (299, 308). Consequently, Mrs. McIntyre is already uneasy with the

Displaced Person, despite his energy and efficiency, and the news of his plan to marry his cousin to a black American in her employ is the last straw.

She finds Mr. Guizac in the cornfield and gives him an ultimatum: "I don't want to have to speak to you about this again. If I do, you'll have to find another place yourself. Do you understand?" And after he drives off on the tractor, she seems to channel the dead Mrs. Shortley, as she "climbed to the top of the slope and stood with her arms folded and looked out grimly over the field." Finally she "narrowed her gaze until it closed around the diminishing figure on the tractor as if she were watching him through a gunsite. All her life she had been fighting the world's overflow and now she had it in the form of a Pole." She spoke to him as if he were still within earshot: "You're just like all the rest of them," she said out loud, "—only smart and thrifty and energetic but so am I," adding, in words she might have borrowed from Mrs. Cope, "And this is my place" (315).

The third and last chapter shifts the scene to Mrs. McIntyre's front porch, where she is sipping ginger ale with the the aged priest, Father Flynn (a not-so-distant cousin to Father Finn in "The Enduring Chill"), who has been instructing her about Purgatory. "I'm not theological. I'm practical!" she tells him "I want to talk to you about something practical!" Her "practical" concern is that the Displaced Person was unsatisfactory. "He's extra," she tells the priest. "He doesn't fit in. I have to have somebody who fits in." But the priest is more interested in her peacock, which he has admired from the start. "Give him time," he replies, "He'll learn to fit in," but the peacock quickly claims his attention: "Where is that beautiful birrrrd of yours?" and then, "Arrrr, I see him!" as he stands up to get a closer look at the peacock and two hens. Ignoring this, Mrs. McIntyre admits the Displaced Person's efficiency, but insists that "he doesn't understand how to get on with my niggers" (316). "Arrrr, I must be off," the old priest replies, but pauses long enough to tell her "He has nowhere to go," and "Dear lady, I know you well enough to know you wouldn't turn him out for a trifle!" At that moment the peacock spreads his tail, and the priest exclaims, "Christ will come like that!" Mrs. McIntyre tries to ignore his words, for "Christ in the conversation embarrassed her the way sex had her mother." Instead, she pursues "practical" matters: "'It is not my responsibility that Mr. Guizac has nowhere to go,' she said. 'I don't find myself responsible for all the extra people in the world.'" But the two are talking past each other, as the old priest, still looking at the spread tail, murmurs "The Transfiguration," thinking of that moment on a mountain with three of his disciples, when Jesus's "face did shine as the sun: and his garments became white as snow" (Matt 17:1–2; also Mark 9:1–2, Luke 9:28–29), an event closely linked to a promise that "Christ will come like that!" (see Matt 16:28, "the Son of man coming in his kingdom"; also 2 Pet 1:16–17). Mrs. McIntyre, with "no idea what he was talking about," keeps on complaining about Mr. Guizac, the Displaced Person who "didn't have to come here in the first place," and smiling, the priest replies, "He came to redeem us," shakes her hand and leaves (317).

A few weeks later Mr. Shortley returns with the news that his wife has died, adding yet another voice to the chorus calling for Mr. Guizac's departure: "'I figure that Pole killed her,' he said. 'She seen through him from the first. She known he come from the devil. She told me so'" (318). Mrs. McIntyre rehires Mr. Shortley, and once again, manners and mystery are on a collision course—mystery in the person of the Displaced Person and manners in the persons of Mrs. McIntyre, Mr. Shortley, and the Negro help. This time the collision will be lethal for all concerned, albeit in different ways. The priest had reminded her of a "moral obligation," but Mrs. McIntyre insisted that "*her* moral obligation was to her own people, to Mr. Shortley, who had fought in the world war for his country and not to Mr. Guizac, who had merely arrived here to take advantage of whatever he could" (319). The priest, on his next visit, seems more interested in converting Mrs. McIntyre than in dealing with the issue of the Guizacs. Paraphrasing John 3:16 as if it were "something that had happened yesterday in town," he confides to her that "when God sent his Only Begotten Son, Jesus Christ Our Lord"—here bowing his head—"as a Redeemer to mankind, He . . ." But she angrily interrupts him: "Father Flynn!"—calling him by name for the first time—"I want to talk to you about something serious!" and "As far as I'm concerned," she adds, "Christ was just another D.P." (320).

In one sense, of course, Mrs. McIntyre is right, for Jesus himself said "The foxes have holes and the birds of the air nests; but the Son of man hath not where to lay his head" (Matt 8:20). Yet this remark of hers, perhaps more than anything else, has prompted readers of the story to conclude that Mr. Guizac is in some way a "Christ figure"—this of course in the wake of certain other broad hints, such as the priest's remark (in the crossfire of their conversation) that "He came to redeem us," or Mrs. McIntyre's own acknowledgement that "That man is my salvation." Yet even if Christ was in some way a Displaced Person, is every displaced person is a stand-in for Christ? Well, yes and no. There are no other obvious "Christ figures" in O'Connor's fiction, at least no human ones, and while Mr. Guizac seems like a plausible candidate, he also resembles O'Connor's "modern hero" or "outsider," of whom she wrote, "He can go anywhere. He belongs nowhere" (*Collected Works*, 856). Mrs. McIntyre complains that she has always been "just making it against people who came from nowhere and were going nowhere, who didn't want anything but an automobile. She said she had found out that they were the same whether they came from Poland or Tennessee" (321).

In short, even if the Displaced Person is a Christ figure of sorts, he is at the same time another version of a Tom T. Shiftlet or a Manley Pointer, or a Rufus Johnson—or The Misfit. Like Christ and like them all, Mr. Guizac in The Misfit's words "thown everything off balance" (151). Or in Mrs. McIntyre's words: "He's extra and he's upset the balance around here" (322). Like Christ too, he dies a violent death, the victim of a run-away tractor and a conspiracy of inaction on the part of Mrs. McIntyre, Mr. Shortley, and Sulk, the younger Negro: "She had felt her eyes and Mr. Shortley's eyes and the Negro's eyes come together in one look that froze them in collusion forever, and she had heard the little noise the Pole made as the tractor wheel broke his backbone. The two men ran forward to help and she fainted" (325–26). While O'Connor rightly ridiculed all the early attempts to see Christ in The Misfit or Shiftlet or Pointer, in Mr. Guizac's case she acknowledged to Betty Hester that "The displaced person did accomplish a kind of redemption in that he destroyed the place, which was evil, and set Mrs. McIntyre on the road to a new kind of suffering" (*Collected Works*, 970). Does destroying what was evil amount to Christ-like goodness? Not necessarily. Nothing in the story characterizes Mr. Guizac as an intrinsically "good" person, that elusive "good man" who is hard to find. No attempt is made to get inside his head. He is simply there, "extra," as Mrs. McIntyre is fond of reminding us, "Just one too many" (322), or "the world's overflow" (315), one of those who, in the Apostle Paul's words, "are made as the refuse of this world, the offscouring of all even until now" (1 Cor 4:13). He is, in short, not Christ or necessarily Christ-like, but simply one of those "least" with whom Christ identifies himself in the Gospel of Matthew (25:40, 45), and only in that sense a "Christ figure." He is not so much a person as a kind of icon, a vehicle of mystery, like the hermaphrodite in "A Temple of the Holy Ghost," or a piece of Negro statuary in another story. If we must have a "Christ figure" in this story, let it be the peacock, in whose spread tail the priest sees Christ's Transfiguration and Second Coming.

In the end, Mrs. McIntyre herself becomes a "displaced person," as if she were "in some foreign country where the people bent over the body were natives, and she watched like a stranger while the dead man was carried away in the ambulance" (326). Mr. Shortley and Sulk both leave. The old man Astor cannot run the farm alone. The cattle are sold at auction. Mrs. McIntyre is hospitalized and returns home, blind and bedridden, with only an unnamed colored woman to wait on her, and without visitors "except the old priest. He came regularly once a week with a bag of bread crumbs and, after he had fed these to the peacock, he would come in and sit by the side of her bed and explain the doctrines of the church" (326–27). Mrs. McIntyre's displacement, her "Purgatory" if you will, is very different from Mrs. Shortley's. Like Asbury Fox, she is condemned not to die but to live. In her letter to Betty Hester, O'Connor went on to ask if Mrs. McIntyre's "new kind of suffering" was not something "very like that of souls in Purgatory? I missed making this clear but how are you going to make such things clear to people who don't believe in God, much less in Purgatory?" (*Collected Works*, 971).

From a biblical perspective, O'Connor's "Purgatory" is not unlike the present world in which we all live. If the world is, as O'Connor herself believed, "territory held largely by the devil" (*Mystery and Manners*, 118), those who belong to God are to that extent strangers in the world. Biblical examples include Abraham and his descendants, likened in the Old Testament to strangers "in a land not their own" (Gen 15:13) and remembered in the New as "pilgrims and strangers on the earth" (Heb 11:13), Israel's twelve tribes, exiled in Babylon and "scattered abroad" in the world ever since (Jas 1:1), and New Testament Christians similarly addressed as "strangers and pilgrims" in Roman society (1 Pet 2:11). Displaced persons all, and O'Connor's fiction too has displacement or homelessness as a major theme. Both Hazel Motes and Enoch Emery were "strangers" in the strange world in which they lived, as was Tarwater on his way to "the dark city, where the children of God lay sleeping." Some of O'Connor's displaced persons are the outsiders who appear as if out of nowhere and going nowhere, agents of mystery such as The Misfit, or Rufus Johnson, or Sarah Ham, or Shiftlet, or Manley Pointer, or Powell and his companions, or Mr. Guizac. Others, at home in their communities and comfortable with their manners, are displaced in the course of the story and set adrift, like the grandmother, or Sheppard, or Lucynell Crater, or Hulga, or Mrs. Cope, or Mrs. Shortley or Mrs. McIntyre. "Where is there a place for you to be?" Haze asks, and for the moment his answer stands: "No place" (93).

Passing by the Dragon

Some are headed toward heaven, some toward hell, but for now they are all in a kind of Purgatory, still on the way to their "true country," wherever and whatever it might be.

10

Men and Monsters

Mrs. Shortley's dying vision of her "true country" raises the possibility of revelation, even redemption, at the moment of death. O'Connor, at the end of her lecture on "The Catholic Novelist in the Protestant South," compared herself to the blind man whom Jesus touched twice (Mark 8:22–25), who at the first touch saw only "men as if they were trees—but walking. Christ touched him again, and he saw clearly. We will not see clearly until Christ touches us in death, but this first touch is the beginning of vision . . ." (*Collected Works*, 864). In context, she was referring to "deeper and deeper visions that we shall have to accept if we want to realize a Catholic literature," but her words are just as applicable to several characters in her stories. Mrs. Shortley's "first touch" was hardly a touch at all, a self-generated "prophecy" so ambiguous that it sounded more like the voice of the devil than of God. But in death it was as if her eyes were "turned around, looking inside her,"[1] viewing "for the first time the tremendous frontiers of her true country" (304–5). And two other tales from O'Connor's second collection, "Greenleaf" and "A View of the Woods," make the same point, that "We will not see clearly until Christ touches us in death." In each there is at least one previous touch as well, a "beginning of vision" heralding a final journey to either heaven or hell.

---

1. "Woman! do you ever look inside?" (Hulga to her mother in "Good Country People," 268).

Greenleaf's Gentleman

In "Greenleaf," a widow much like Mrs. Cope or Mrs. McIntyre is asleep in her bedroom, dreaming of something outside her window eating its way into her house, "eating her and the boys, and then on, eating everything but the Greenleafs, on and on, eating everything until nothing was left but the Greenleafs on a little island all their own in the middle of what had been her place" (501–2). The widow is Mrs. May, this is "her place," and the Greenleafs are her tenant family, husband and wife. The chewing sound outside her window turns out to be a scrub bull on the loose, belonging to the Greenleafs' grownup twin boys. The "little island all their own" is Mrs. May's version of a "circle in the fire" protecting the Greenleafs, who, as she saw it, "had no worries, no responsibilities. They lived like the lilies of the field, off the fat that she struggled to put into the land." (509). "Consider the lilies of the field, how they grow," Jesus said: "they labour not, neither do they spin: But I say to you, that not even Solomon in all his glory was arrayed as one of these" (Matt 6:28–29). To Mrs. May, the Greenleafs are something close to white trash, yet also, mysteriously and maddeningly, somehow the Chosen of God. The twin sons, O. T. and E. T., have served their country overseas, married French wives, and now send their children to convent school, run a clean and efficient dairy farm. "They never quarls," one of their hired hands testifies. "They like one man in two skins" (516). Her own two boys, Scofield and Wesley, are by contrast shiftless and self-absorbed, quarreling constantly with each other and with her. "O. T. and E. T. are fine boys," she tells one them in a rage. "They ought to have been my sons," and "you two should have belonged to that woman" (511). Worst of all, Mr. Greenleaf will not let her forget it.

The scrub bull, therefore, is no abrupt visitation throwing "everything off balance." So far as Mrs. May is concerned, everything is already off balance, and has been for fifteen years, ever since the Greenleafs arrived. The bull is merely the latest in a series of small aggravations. The one-word title, "Greenleaf," calls attention not to the bull but to Mr. Greenleaf, implying that he is the real thorn in her side. The story traces a power struggle between Mrs. May and Greenleaf, who, as she puts it,

> walked with a high-shouldered creep and he never appeared to come directly forward. He walked on the perimeter of some invisible circle and if you wanted to look him in the eye you had to move and get in front of him. She had not fired him because she had always doubted she could do better. He was too shiftless to go out and look for another job; he didn't have the initiative

to steal, and after she had told him three or four times to do a thing, he did it; but he never told her about a sick cow until it was too late to call the veterinarian and if her barn had caught on fire, he would have called his wife to see the flames before he began to put them out. (503)

Still, compared to his wife, Mrs. May thought, Greenleaf was "an aristocrat." Mrs. Greenleaf was "large and loose. The yard around her house looked like a dump and her five girls were always filthy; even the youngest one dipped snuff." But the oddest thing of all about Mrs. Greenleaf was "her preoccupation was what she called 'prayer healing'":

> Every day she cut all the morbid stories out of the newspaper—the accounts of women who had been raped and criminals who had escaped and children who had been burned and of train wrecks and plane crashes and the divorces of movie stars. She took these to the woods and dug a hole and buried them and then she fell to the ground over them and mumbled and groaned for an hour or so, moving her huge arms back and forth under her and out again and finally just lying down flat and, Mrs. May suspected, going to sleep in the dirt. (505)

Her behavior recalls the "horrifying love" that threatened to engulf Rayber "in an act of idiot praise" (401), or the "daredevil charity" of Thomas's mother in "The Comforts of Home" (573). Mrs. Greenleaf, it seems, is a victim of just such reckless love, as if the whole world, with all its pain and suffering, has become her own "idiot child" (442), for which she must groan and agonize in prayer.[2]

Once, just a few months after the Greenleafs first arrived, Mrs. May had discovered Mrs. Greenleaf in the woods, sprawled on the ground screaming "Jesus! Jesus!" a sound so piercing that it seemed to Mrs. May "as if some violent unleashed force had broken out of the ground and was charging toward her." So far as she was concerned, "the word, Jesus, should be kept inside the church building like other words inside the bedroom. She was a good Christian woman with a large respect for religion, though she did not, of course, believe any of it was true." She asked the woman, "What's the matter with you?" and was told "You broken my healing," and "I can't talk to you until I finish" (506). Then, in desperation over her broken healing: " 'Oh, Jesus, stab me in the heart!' Mrs. Greenleaf shrieked.

2. Not surprisingly, O'Connor saw Mrs. Greenleaf as "a sympathetic character. She and the sun and the bull were connected and sympathetic. At one point Mrs. May sees the bull as the sun's shadow cast at an oblique angle moving among the cows, and of course he's a Greenleaf bull!" (*Collected Works*, 989–90).

'Jesus, stab me in the heart!' and she fell back flat in the dirt, a huge human mound, her legs and arms spread out as if she were trying to wrap them around the earth" (506–7). The imagery of "Jesus, stab me in the heart!" recalls John's vision in the book of Revelation, of Jesus with "a sharp two edged sword" sticking out of his mouth (Rev 1:16, 19:15). O'Connor's familiarity with such passages is evident in one of her last stories, "Why Do the Heathen Rage?" in which a woman stumbles across a similar passage from St. Jerome which her son had underlined, words that to her "made no sense for now"—until "it came to her, with an unpleasant little jolt, that the General with the sword in his mouth, marching to do violence, was Jesus" (800). The "sword" is in Jesus's mouth instead of his hand because it is not a literal sword but the spoken word by which he conquers his enemies. In another text the word of God is said to be "living and effectual, and more piercing than any two edged sword; and reaching into the division of the soul and the spirit, of the joints also and the marrow" (Heb 4:12). On Mrs. Greenleaf's lips, "Oh, Jesus, stab me in the heart!" sounds like a prayer for just such a "word" from above, a revelation piercing to the very heart of her being. But Mrs. May, unimpressed, tells her that Jesus "would be *ashamed* of you. He would tell you to get up from there this instant and go wash your children's clothes!" (507).

Mrs. Greenleaf, although her "prayer healings" are a regular occurrence, has no part in the story beyond the one incident remembered in a flashback. She is by no means a sidekick to Mrs. May (like Mrs. Pritchard was to Mrs. Cope, or Mrs. Freeman to Mrs. Hopewell), only a chronic irritant. One of Mrs. May's sons, a sickly Asbury Fox type named Wesley, torments his mother with such lines as "You ought to start praying, Sweetheart," and "Why don't you pray for me like Mrs. Greenleaf would?" (509–10), and Greenleaf defends his wife with the information that "She cured a man oncet that half his gut was eat out with worms" (522). For the most part, Mrs. May's dealings are with Greenleaf alone, who seems to her to embody the whole Greenleaf clan, including the twin sons and their wives (none of whom ever appear in the story at all), and not least, the scrub bull.

It is the bull, of course, who captures the reader's imagination, from the moment Mrs. May first glimpses him from her window, "his head raised, as if he listened—like some patient god come down to woo her—for a stir inside the room." Wearing "a hedge-wreath that he had ripped loose caught in the tip of his horns," he is "standing about four feet from her, chewing calmly like an uncouth country suitor" (501–2). The imagery of courtship evokes O'Connor's "gentleman callers," as Greenleaf, and even Mrs. May herself, repeatedly personify him as "the gentleman." The bull's encroachments continue. A visit to the twin sons' farm finds them not around, and yields no results, only a glimpse of their spotlessly white milking room "filled with sunlight that came from a row of windows head-high along both walls," brighter even than the light outside. And yet when she stepped back and closed the door, "she was conscious that the sun was directly on top of her head, like a silver bullet ready to drop into her brain" (515).

Finally another dream about the bull triggers her resolve to get rid of it once and for all. She dreams of hearing a grinding noise as she walked "over a succession of beautiful rolling hills," a noise that turned out to be "the sun trying to burn through the tree line," then turning "narrow and pale until it looked like a bullet. Then suddenly it burst through the tree line and raced down the hill toward her." When she woke up, it was, once again, "the bull munching under her window. Mr. Greenleaf had let him out" (519). "That gentleman torn out of here last night," Greenleaf acknowledges the next morning, and Mrs. May orders him, not once but four times, "Go get your gun" (519–20). Greenleaf is not happy. The gun is in the harness room, and before he comes out with it she hears "a crash as if he had kicked something out of the way." The silent clash of wills between Greenleaf and Mrs May continues in the car, as they drive to the far pasture. Greenleaf "held the gun between his knees and looked straight ahead. He'd like to shoot me instead of the bull, she thought, and turned her face away so that he could not see her smile." Exhilarated, she exclaims, "Spring is here!" and " 'The gentleman is waiting on you,' she said and gave Mr. Greenleaf's furious profile a sly look. 'Run him into that next pasture and when you get him in, I'll drive behind you and shut the gate myself' " (520–21).

Greenleaf flings himself angrily from the car, and sets out across the pasture to open the gate: "He seemed to throw himself forward at each step and then pull back as if he were calling on some power to witness that he was being forced." In characteristic Greenleaf fashion he "circled around to open the gate first," and when he had opened it he "began circling back" so as to approach the bull from the rear (521). Mrs. May suspects that he will simply pretend to lose the bull in the woods. If he does, she will tell him, "You are going to shoot him if I have to pull the trigger for you," and she remains confident that "When he saw she meant business he would return and shoot the bull quickly himself." She decides to wait ten minutes at the car and then honk. She lies back against the hood of the car, "tired because she had been working continuously for fifteen years. She decided she had every right to be tired, and to rest for a few minutes before she began working again. Before any kind of judgement seat, she would be able to say: I've worked, I have not wallowed" (522).

After ten minutes Mrs. May honks the horn three times and sits down again on the bumper. Not a good place to be, in light of Greenleaf's account earlier of how this bull had once "run his head into their pickup truck. He don't like cars and trucks" (512). Greenleaf still does not appear, but "something emerged from the tree line, a black heavy shadow that tossed its head several times and then bounded forward. After a second she saw that it was the bull. He was crossing the pasture toward her at a slow gallop, a gay almost rocking gait as if he were overjoyed to find her again." All she can do is shout, "Here he is, Mr. Greenleaf!" to someone who is still not in view. She stares in "freezing unbelief"

> at the violent black streak bounding toward her as if she could not decide at once what his intention was, and the bull had buried his head in her lap, like a wild tormented lover, before her expression changed. One of its horns sank until it pierced her heart and the other curved around her side and held her in an unbreakable grip. She continued to stare straight ahead but the entire scene in front of her had changed—the tree line was a dark wound in a world that was nothing but sky—and she had the look of a person whose sight has been suddenly restored but who finds the light unbearable. (523)

Once again, the "second touch" comes in the moment of death. Mrs. May has been touched before, by Mrs. Greenleaf's shrieks of "Jesus, stab me in the heart!" and by the sun overhead, outside O. T. and E. T.'s milking room and again in her most recent dream. Always something "charging toward her," or aimed at her like a bullet. Now at last the sun has conspired with the bull to "stab her in the heart," just as it conspired with the three young "prophets" to deprive Mrs. Cope of her woods in "A Circle in the Fire." But is it indeed a revelation, the "sharp two edged sword" of the word of God? Or is it merely the horns of a rogue bull, just another horrific news item for Mrs. Greenleaf to cut out, bury in the ground, and pray over in the woods? Is it "the terrible speed of mercy," or of something else? The redemptive signals are not as clear as Mrs. Shortley's glimpse of her "true country." Mrs. May's eyes are at last open, but the light, presumably the light of the sun, is unbearable.

The story could have ended here, but does not. There is one more paragraph, in which Greenleaf, characteristically, makes his belated appearance, and he and Mrs. May are each seen through the other's eyes. First, even in her dying moment, she sees him as she has always seen him, "approaching on the outside of some invisible circle, the tree line gaping behind him and nothing under his feet." He is "running toward her from the side with his gun raised," and at last, when it is too late, he shoots the bull "four times through the eye." The animal's weight pulls her body forward onto its head, and the point of view abruptly changes. Mrs. May is now seen through Greenleaf's eyes: "she seemed, when Mr. Greenleaf reached her, to be bent over whispering some last discovery into the animal's ear" (524). But is Greenleaf a reliable witness to his antagonist's "last discovery"? And is a "last discovery" a revelation? Has she seen her "true country" after all? Once again, we are left to wonder. In any event, there is a certain mutuality in this final paragraph, hinting at a reconciliation between two sworn enemies, a subtle convergence, if you will, right alongside the more obvious, and lethal, "convergence" of Mrs. May and the bull.

It is surely no coincidence that this story comes second, just after the title story, in a collection entitled *Everything That Rises Must Converge*. Of this lethal convergence, O'Connor told Betty Hester, "My preoccupation is how I am going to get this bulls horns into this womans ribs," yet in the end she leaves us to make of the story what we will, for she was quick to add, "Of course why his horns belong in her ribs is something more fundamental but I can't say I give it much thought. Perhaps you are able to see things in these stories that I can't see because if I did see I would be too frightened to write them. I have always insisted that there is a fine grain of stupidity required in the fiction writer" (*Collected Works*, 990).

FORTUNE'S PROGRESS

The third story in the collection, "A View of the Woods," is arguably, if not the most violent at least the most disturbing of O'Connor's stories, a tragedy of almost Shakespearean proportions. It begins where the preceding story left off, on the bumper of a car. Mr. Fortune is sitting on the bumper of his "battered mulberry-colored Cadillac," parked on an embankment overlooking what had once been his cow pasture. He and his nine-year-old granddaughter Mary Fortune Pitts, seated on the hood with her feet planted firmly on his shoulders, are watching a huge machine digging up dirt in order to to build a fishing club. Mary Fortune is fascinated as she sees the giant bulldozer "gorge itself on the clay, then, with the sound of a deep sustained nausea and a slow mechanical revulsion, turn and spit it up." Mr. Fortune has sold the lot to a developer, and is taking great satisfaction in the march of progress. "Any fool that would let a cow pasture interfere with progress is not on my books," he tells her, with her father (his son-in-law) Mr. Pitts in mind. When he had sold it, "Pitts had nearly had a stroke; and as far as Mr. Fortune was concerned, he could have gone on and had it" (525).

Like Mrs. May, Mr. Fortune sees his family as highly dysfunctional. His daughter "had married an idiot named Pitts and had had seven children, all likewise idiots except the youngest, Mary Fortune, who was a throwback to him." She was "short and broad like himself, with his very light blue eyes, his wide prominent forehead, his steady penetrating scowl and his rich florid complexion; but she was like him on the inside too. She had, to a singular degree, his intelligence, his strong will, and his push and drive. Though there was seventy years' difference in their ages, the spiritual distance between them was slight. She was the only member of the family he had any respect for" (526). He allowed them to live on his farm, but was careful to maintain control: "every now and then he gave the Pittses a practical lesson by selling off a lot." It was all in the name of progress, for Mr. Fortune had long dreamed of "a paved highway in front of his house," and "a supermarket store across the road from him," and "a gas station, a motel, a drive-in picture show within easy distance." Now at last,

> Progress had suddenly set all this in motion. The electric company had built a dam on the river and flooded great areas of the surrounding country and the lake that resulted touched his land along a half-mile stretch. Every Tom, Dick and Harry, every dog and his brother, wanted a lot on the lake. There was talk of their getting a telephone line. There was talk of paving the road that ran in front of the Fortune place. There was talk of an eventual town. He thought this should be called Fortune, Georgia. He was a man of advanced vision, even if he was seventy-nine years old. (527–28)

Mary Fortune, by contrast, is thinking something quite different as they watch the bulldozer from the embankment. "If you don't watch him," she shouts above the noise as she runs along the embankment, "he'll cut off some of your dirt!" She is jealously guarding the border of what is still his property from the bulldozer's encroachment. "Don't run so near the edge," he cautions her, watching her with pride and noticing that "Her glasses were silver-rimmed like his and she even walked the way he did, stomach forward, with a careful abrupt gait, something between a rock and a shuffle" (528).

Something is wrong. The reader can sense, even if Mr. Fortune does not, that he and his granddaughter do not see things the same way. There are troubling clues, troubling even to him. Pitts was "a man of nasty temper and of ugly unreasonable resentments," and on occasion he would "abruptly, for no reason, with no explanation, jerk his head at Mary Fortune and say, "'Come with me,' and leave the room, unfastening his belt as he went" (529–30). What bothered Mr. Fortune even more than the knowledge that her father was about to beat her was the look on her face, "a look that was part terror and part respect and part something else, something very like cooperation." Once when this happened he had followed them and had seen her father beat her around the ankles and leave her crying in the woods, and she denied it to his face. "Nobody is here and nobody beat me," she insisted, "Nobody's ever beat me in my life and if anybody did, I'd kill him. You can see for yourself that nobody is here" (530).

Mr. Fortune was furious, for he knew that "This was Pitts' revenge on him. It was as if it were *he* that Pitts was driving down the read to beat and it was as if *he* were the one submitting to it." It would be no use putting them off his land, for Pitts would say, "Put me off and you put her off too. Go right ahead." Instead, Mr. Fortune had "a little scheme up his sleeve that was going to be a considerable blow to Pitts." Now, sitting on the bumper of his car with her feet on his back, he tells Mary Fortune that "he might be selling another lot soon and that if he did, he might give her a bonus but not if she gave him any sass." She says, "I don't want no bonus," but he ignores the signal: "He had frequent little verbal tilts with her but this was a sport like putting a mirror up in front of a rooster and watching him fight his reflection." So he plunges on, now much more explicitly: "I'm going to start you an account just as soon as I complete this deal. Won't anybody be able to check on it but me and you," and finally, "'I'm going to sell the lot right in front of the house for a gas station,' he said. 'Then we won't have to go down the road to get the car filled up, just step out the front door'" (531).

It is the first turning point in the story. "You mean," Mary Fortune asks, "the lawn?" "Yes, mam!" her grandfather replies enthusiastically, "I mean the lawn." "That's where we play," she objects, and then finally the real issue, "We won't be able to see the woods across the road," and with this the battle is joined—a litany of mutual disbelief:

> The old man stared at her. "The woods across the road?" he repeated.
> "We won't be able to see the view," she said.
> "The view?" he repeated.

"The woods," she said; "we won't be able to see the woods from the porch."

"The woods from the porch?" he repeated.

Then, "My daddy grazes his calves on that lot," and for the second time he calls her father a fool: "Do you think I give a damn hoot where that fool grazes his calves?" This triggers a comic duel of biblical references, quoted freely (and in the old man's case, ungrammatically) from memory: "'He who calls his brother a fool is subject to hell fire,' she said. 'Jedge not,' he shouted, 'lest ye be not jedged!'" (532). Her text was from Matthew 5:22, his from Matthew 7:1. O'Connor worried that she might be thought to have plagiarized Mary Fortune's text from Caroline Gordon, who in one of her stories has the line, "She who calleth her brother a fool is in danger of hell fire,"[3] but in the end O'Connor kept the reference in because, as she wrote to Betty Hester, "Some prediction of hell for the old man is essential to my story" (*Collected Works*, 1011).

The duel continues, as the old man tells her, "You let him beat you any time he wants to and don't do a thing but blubber and jump up and down!" Mary Fortune flatly insists that "He nor nobody else has ever touched me," and "if anybody did, I'd kill him." Furious, her grandfather tells her, "Walk home by yourself. I refuse to ride a Jezebel!" and she counters, "And I refuse to ride with the Whore of Babylon," getting out of the car and starting off across the pasture. "A whore is a woman!" the old man shouts, "That's how much you know!" (532–33). The comic exchange does not shake Mr. Fortune's pride in his granddaughter, a pride marred only by her refusal to stand up to her father. That, he thought, "was the one point on which she did not resemble him" (533). That noon at dinner, when he announces his plan to sell "the lawn," Pitts blames Mary Fortune, and takes her off in the truck for yet another beating. Her apparent cowardice continues to affect Mr. Fortune "as if it were his own," and ironically we learn almost immediately that in fact it is his own. "Not one of you lifts a hand to stop him," he protests to his daughter, and one of the boys mutters, "You ain't lifted yours neither." "I'm an old man with a heart condition," he replies, "I can't stop an ox" (534). The heart condition at least is real: "His heart, whenever he knew the child had been beaten, felt as if it were slightly too large for the space that was supposed to hold it" (534).

3. The contexts were very different, for in the 1929 Caroline Gordon story, "Summer Dust," the pronouncement was an actual brother's self-serving attempt to intimidate and control his sister. One would think that in any case the Bible is in the public domain!

The next morning, it all seems forgotten as Mr. Fortune wakes up and finds his granddaughter "sitting astride his chest ordering him to make haste so that they would not miss the concrete mixer," a large machine "about the size and color of a circus elephant." They spend half an hour watching it, but he does not tell her that he has an appointment to meet with Tilman, the prospective developer, "an up-and-coming man—the kind, Mr. Fortune thought, who was never just in line with progress but always a little ahead of it so that he could be there to meet it when it arrived" (535). The narrator describes Tilman differently in a later scene, as "a man of quick action and few words," who "sat habitually with his arms folded on the counter and his insignificant head weaving snake-fashion above them." Those who look for St. Cyril's "Dragon by the side of the road" in every O'Connor story are sure to find him here, in the serpent-like Mr. Tilman, whose "eyes were green and very narrow and his tongue was always exposed in his partly opened mouth" (542). Mary Fortune accompanies her grandfather, knowing "only that he had to see a man," not that this was the man to whom he was about to sell the lot. He tells her to wait in the car, but when he comes back from his dealings with Tilman he finds her gone, and when he returns home he finds her sitting on the porch, "looking glum-faced in front of her across the field he was going to sell." Beyond the field lay woods and more woods beyond those and beyond both the sky, and "She looked into this scene as if it were a person that she preferred to him" (537).

The personification of the woods began already at the beginning of the story, where the two of them had seen from the embankment "a black line of woods which appeared at both ends of the view to walk across the water and continue along the edge of the fields" (525). Not "men as if they were trees, walking," but "trees as if they were men," walking across the water. O'Connor once wrote to Betty Hester that "the woods, if anything, are the Christ symbol. They walk across the water, they are bathed in a red light, and they in the end escape the old man's vision and march off over the hills. The name of the story is a view of the woods and the woods alone are pure enough to be a Christ symbol if anything is" (*Collected Works*, 1014). Even Mr. Fortune is given a glimpse of this personification. Disgusted at Mary Fortune's behavior, he goes to his room and looks out the window at the lawn in front of the house and the line of woods beyond. "The sunlight was woven through them at that particular time of the afternoon so that every thin pine trunk stood out in all its nakedness."

The sight merely confirms to him that "A pine trunk is a pine trunk." and that selling the lot is indeed the right thing to do. Yet the third time he looks out as the sun is going down, "the gaunt trunks appeared to be raised in a pool of red light that gushed from the almost hidden sun setting behind them." It was "as if for a prolonged instant he were caught up out of the rattle of everything that led to the future and were held there in the midst of an uncomfortable mystery that he had not apprehended before. He saw it, in his hallucination, as if someone were wounded behind the woods and the trees were bathed in blood." The two "as ifs" signal the "uncomfortable mystery," an unmistakable offer of grace, but just as unmistakably an offer refused, as Mr. Fortune "returned to his bed and shut his eyes and against the closed lids hellish red trunks rose up in a black wood" (538). He has mistaken a redemptive vision of a suffering Christ for something "hellish." His mind is made up, and no "hallucination" is going to change it. Before going to bed he looks out the window again "at the moon shining over the woods across the road and listened for a while to the hum of crickets and treefrogs, and beneath their racket, he could hear the throb of the future town of Fortune" (539).

Next morning the old man tells Mary Fortune, "I thought you and me'd go into town and have us a look at the boats in the new boat store." She asks him "What else are you going for?" and he lies: "Nothing else." She agrees to go but seems to know he is lying, for she shows no interest in the boats. His real destination is the courthouse, where he will locate the deed and draw up papers for the sale of the land. Mary Fortune sulks, and he sees in her face "the Pitts look, pure and simple, and he felt personally stained by it, as if it had been found on his own face." When he returns to the car from the courthouse, the expression on her face is both "foreboding and withdrawn," and the face of the darkened sky matches it, for "there was a hot sluggish tide in the air, the kind felt when a tornado is possible" (540–41). One more stop: Tilman's, where he closes the deal, and where the "tornado" strikes. Just as the two men finish shaking hands on the deal, Tilman "disappeared completely under the counter as if he had been snatched by the feet from below. A bottle crashed against the line of tinned goods behind where he had been. The old man whirled around. Mary Fortune was in the door, red-faced and wild-looking, with another bottle lifted to hurl." In a moment she was screaming and throwing everything within reach, until her grandfather finally caught her, pulled her out of the store and drove away: "His heart felt as if it were the size of the car and was racing forward, carrying him to some inevitable destination faster than he had ever been carried before" (542–43).

The "inevitable destination" is not far off. Mr. Fortune makes up his mind that the time for discipline is long overdue: "She respected Pitts because, even with no just cause, he beat her; and if he—with his just cause—did not beat her now, he would have nobody to blame but himself if she turned out a hellion" (543). So he drives her to the exact spot in the woods where he had once seen Pitts beat her, "a place where the road widened" to form "an ugly red bald spot surrounded by long thin pines that appeared to be gathered there to witness anything that would take place in such a clearing." "Get out," he tells Mary Fortune, "Now I'm going to whip you!"—this as he begins to take off his belt. "Nobody has ever beat me," she says, just as she has said before, "and if anybody tries it, I'll kill him." She takes off her glasses and invites her grandfather to do the same. "Don't give me orders!" he replies and begins to slap at her ankles with the belt (544). She is all over him in an instant, "coming at him from all directions at once. It was as if he were being attacked not by one child but by a pack of small demons all with stout brown shoes and small rocklike fists. His glasses flew to the side. 'I toljer to take them off,' she growled without pausing." Finally, "with horror he saw her face rise up in front of his, teeth exposed, and he roared like a bull as she bit the side of his jaw. He seemed to see his own face coming to bite him from several sides at once but he could not attend to it for he was being kicked indiscriminately in the stomach and then in the crotch." At last she asked him, "Have you had enough?" and "The old man looked up into his own image. It was triumphant and hostile. 'You been whipped,' it said, 'by me,' and then it added, bearing down on each word, 'and I'm PURE Pitts.' "

Yet all in a moment the tables are turned. As his granddaughter pauses to declare victory and loosens her grip, the old man suddenly grabs her by the throat, reversing their positions so that now he is "looking down into the face that was his own but had dared to call itself Pitts. With his hands still tight around her neck, he lifted her head and brought it down once hard against the rock that happened to be under it. Then he brought it down twice more. Then looking into the face in which the eyes, slowly rolling back, appeared to pay him not the slightest attention, he said, "There's not an ounce of Pitts in me" (545). His last words are, "This ought to teach you a good lesson," words spoken "in a voice that was edged with doubt." These are indeed his last words, for the story ends with two deaths, not one. We are not told what Mary Fortune saw, only that her grandfather saw "no look of remorse" on her face, and that her eyes "were set in a fixed glare that did not take him in." But we are told what the old man saw. As he tried to get up, "the enlargement of his heart which had begun in the car was still going on. He turned his head and looked behind him for a long time at the little motionless figure with its head on the rock." Then, as he looked up at the bare pine trunks overhead, "his heart expanded once more with a convulsive motion":

> It expanded so fast that the old man felt as if he were being pulled after it through the woods, felt as if he were running as fast as he could with the ugly pines toward the lake. He perceived that there would be a little opening there, a place where he could escape and leave the woods behind him. He could see it in the distance already, a little opening where the white sky was reflected in the water. It grew as he ran toward it until suddenly the whole lake opened up before him, riding majestically in little corrugated folds toward his feet. He realized suddenly that he could not swim and that he had not bought the boat. On both sides of him he saw that the gaunt trees had thickened into mysterious dark files that were marching across the water and away into the distance. He looked around desperately for someone to help him but the place was deserted except for one huge yellow monster which sat to the side, as stationary as he was, gorging itself on clay. (546)

An extraordinary ending. So detailed and vivid is the old man's last vision that it is by no means clear to the reader that it is in fact a death vision like Mrs. Shortley's or Mrs. May's. Is the old man dying, or not?

If there was ever a passage in O'Connor's fiction that needed what Plato called its "father" or "parent" to come to its rescue, it is this one, and O'Connor does exactly that in the same letter in which she told Betty Hester that the woods were her Christ symbol. With the publication of her letters, her private explanation has passed into the public domain: "Part of the tension of the story," she wrote, "is created by Mary Fortune and the old man being images of each other but opposite in the end. One is saved and the other is dammed [sic] and there is no way out of it, it must be pointed out and underlined. Their fates are different." Within the story, even Mr. Fortune recognized that "With grown people, a road led either to heaven or hell," but he thought that "with children there were always stops along the way where their attention could be turned with a trifle" (538). He could not have been more wrong. O'Connor in her letter goes on to clarify yet another point: "One has to die first because one kills the other, but you have read it wrong if you think that they die in different places.

The old man dies by her side; he only thinks he runs to the edge of the lake, that is his vision. I changed the verb to the conditional which makes that clearer now. He runs in imagination" (*Collected Works*, 1014–15).

It is important to notice that this letter was written December 28, 1956, almost a year before the story appeared in print in the Fall 1957 issue of *Partisan Review*. The verb O'Connor claimed to have "changed to the conditional" has to be the verb "running" in the last paragraph of the story. Just as it is *as if* Mr. Fortune were being pulled through the woods by his expanding heart, so it is *as if* he were "running as fast as he could" toward the lake. "As if" is surely one of O'Connor's very favorite expressions, not least in visionary or climactic scenes like this one. Here more specifically it echoes the old man's earlier vision of pine trunks in the glare of the evening sun, *as if* someone were "wounded behind the woods" (538), evoking once more the woods as Christ symbol, and an offer of grace refused.

O'Connor's insistence that Mr. Fortune runs only in his imagination is also supported by the last line of the story, in which the "huge yellow monster" is said to be "as stationary as he was." What is less clear is whether or not he dies at all, for at the end he still "looked around desperately for someone to help him." O'Connor's reply to Hester obviously assumes his death. She goes on to speak of an "old last-paragraph," which she had once considered adding, either in place of, or after, what she calls "the new ending"—presumably of the story as published. In the letter as it appears in *The Habit of Being*, Sally Fitzgerald inserts a note (not found in the *Collected Works*), in which this longer ending is quoted in full:

> Pitts, by accident, found them that evening. He was walking home through the woods about sunset. The rain had stopped but the polished trees were hung with clear drops of water that turned red where the sun touched them; the air was saturated with dampness. He came on them suddenly and shied backward, his foot not a yard from where they lay. For almost a minute he stood still and then, his knees buckling, he squatted down by their sides and stared into their eyes, into the pale blue pools of rainwater that the sky had filled. (190)

The addition would obviously have removed all doubt that "The old man dies by her side," but O'Connor wrote to Hester that since it "was only an appendage anyhow, that it might have been added to the new ending, but I don't really think it does anything for it. You can see what you think" (*Collected Works*, 1015). Sally Fitzgerald, in a rare disagreement with O'Connor, thought otherwise. She considered O'Connor's insistence that the old man was damned a "rather extreme verdict, given his unawareness of the nature of what he was doing all along, and the killing of the child was clearly accidental. The paragraph she omitted seems to suggest that although both were doomed, having destroyed each other, in the end both had their eyes opened and filled with rain, even possibly with tears" (*Habit of Being*, 190).[4]

So we have here an O'Connor story with a shorter and a longer ending, not unlike the Gospel of Mark in the New Testament.[5] O'Connor, like Mark, seems to have decided that "less is more." Her shorter version leaves to our imaginations the old man's actual death, and a number of other things as well, not least his eternal destiny. If O'Connor's own interpretation is to be accepted, he is headed for hell just as surely as Mary Fortune is headed for heaven, and nowhere that I know of is O'Connor quite so explicit about any of her characters. But is this "rather extreme verdict" (as Sally Fitzgerald called it) justified? And if it is justified, what exactly does hell look like for the old man? If there is a biblical text at work in the story, it is the second great commandment according to Jesus, "Thou shalt love thy neighbour as thyself" (Matt 22:39, Mark 12:31, Luke 10:27), said to be "like," or equal to, the first, to "love the Lord thy God with thy whole heart, with thy whole soul, and with thy whole mind." (Matt 22:37). The latter comes from Deuteronomy 6:5, the former from Leviticus 19:18, and only in the New Testament Gospels are they explicitly brought together. Elsewhere in the New Testament, "Thou shalt love thy neighbour as thyself" stands alone, twice in Paul's letters (Rom 13:9 and Gal 5:14), and once in James (2:8). Consistently present in all these occurrences is the phrase, "as thyself" (or yourself), directly traceable to the divine command given through Moses in Leviticus 19:18, and undergirded with the reminder,

4. This longer ending also shows Pitts in a somewhat more sympathetic light, for the reader is allowed to see things through his eyes, just as one sees Mrs. May through Greenleaf's eyes at the end of that story. Concerning Pitts, O'Connor even entertained seriously Betty Hester's suggestion that he, of all people, might have been a Christ figure. She characterizes him first as "a Christian and a sinner, pathetic by virtue of his sin" (*Collected Works*, 1014), yet later concedes that Hester might be right after all (*Habit of Being*, 196). Another instance in which O'Connor was unsure about the meaning of one of her own stories.

5. The most reliable manuscripts of Mark end at 16:8, where after the women have come to the tomb of Jesus and met a young man who told them to notify the male disciples that Jesus had risen and would meet them in Galilee, "they said nothing to any man; for they were afraid." Other, later manuscripts continue to 16:20 with accounts of several appearances of the risen Jesus to his disciples. But whether O'Connor knew of these variations is uncertain. While the King James and her Douay Bible simply print the longer text without note or comment, her Ronald Knox translation has a note calling attention to the variants.

"I am the Lord." Later in the same chapter we read, "If a stranger dwell in your land, and abide among you, do not upbraid him: But let him be among you as one of the same country: and you shall love him *as yourselves*: for you were strangers in the land of Egypt. I am the Lord your God" (Lev 19:33–34; emphasis added). At issue here is the relationship between love of self and love of the "neighbor," however defined. Self love is tacitly acknowledged as part and parcel of the human condition, but these texts command something more: love of the "other." When Jesus is asked, "Who is my neighbor," he tells the story of the Good Samaritan (Luke 10:29–37), defining the neighbor unmistakably as the "other," even as the enemy. Paul applies the principle to a man's love for his closest "neighbor," his wife: "So ought men to love their wives *as their own bodies*. He that loveth his wife, *loveth himself*. For no man ever hated his own flesh; but nourisheth and cherisheth it, as also Christ doth the church" (Eph 5:28–29), and consequently, "let every one of you in particular love his wife *as himself*" (5:33; emphasis added).

What has any of this to do with Mr. Fortune? In a strange way, "A View of the Woods" is a love story, the only love story except for "Parker's Back" in the whole O'Connor canon, and yet different from most in that the love is not between lovers, or a husband and wife, but between a grandfather and a granddaughter. More importantly, and tragically, it is about a love that parodies and mocks the biblical principle of "love your neighbor as yourself." Mr. Fortune loves his granddaughter "as himself" only in the sense that loving her is his way of loving himself. Like Narcissus of old, he loves her as his mirror image, a projection of himself, never as the "other," always as a Fortune, never as a Pitts. If love is the greatest virtue (as Paul claimed in 1 Cor 13:13), the greatest and most hellish vice is arguably not so much hatred as rather the perversion and mockery of love itself. Mary Fortune, by contrast, loves the old man authentically and unconditionally as "the other," knowing deep inside that she—in her own words that bring about her death—is "PURE Pitts" (545). This is why O'Connor could say with such confidence that the two are "images of each other but opposite in the end" (*Collected Works*, 1014–15). She even quoted with approval Robert Lowell's comment implying that Mary Pitts was Flannery herself: "He has wonderful insights, and is probably right that this one was written by Mary Pitts herself, playing Jehovah," she wrote to Betty Hester. "Mary Pitts can't be anybody but Mary Pitts and can't write anything but what Mary Pitts would write" (*Habit of Being*, 250).

As for Mr. Fortune, the one thing he loves more than his granddaughter is Progress, eventuating in a town called Fortune, Georgia (528)—self-love in yet another form. The enemy of Progress, and its victim, is the empty weed-infested lot that served as the Pitts' lawn, and in particular the black line of woods beyond. Mr. Fortune resolutely closed his eyelids against a vision of those woods "bathed in blood" by the dying afternoon sun (538), but in the end he is made to face them again, drawn through them, "running as fast as he could with the ugly pines toward the lake." His death vision is itself a "progress" in the now almost archaic sense of a journey, his own visionary journey like that of Christian in Bunyan's *Pilgrim's Progress*, but collapsed into a moment of time. Is it then yet another instance of "the terrible speed of mercy"? If the woods are, as O'Connor claimed, a "Christ symbol," the journey is at least potentially redemptive, like the earlier vision of the bloody trees, "as if someone were wounded behind the woods." But again redemption is refused, for the old man's only thought is to "escape and leave the woods behind him," and he succeeds, for on either side of him "the gaunt trees had thickened into mysterious dark files that were marching across the water and away into the distance." Like the blind man who at Jesus' first touch saw "men as it were trees, walking" (Mark 8:24), Mr. Fortune at this second and last touch sees trees "marching across the water and away into the distance." But in stark contrast to the blind man his sight is not restored and never will be. As O'Connor explained to Betty Hester, the woods "in the end escape the old man's vision and march over the hills" (*Collected Works*, 1014). Whether they escape him or he escapes them, he is free of them, and thus free of any hope of redemption. Hell makes its appearance at the end of the story as the embodiment of Progress, the same "huge yellow monster" to which we were introduced at the story's beginning, still "gorging itself on clay" (525, 546). Ironically, the two stories under discussion in this chapter are framed together by Mrs. May's opening dream of a monstrous bull eating her shrubbery and everything else in her world except for the Greenleafs, and the final stark reality of the monster Progress devouring the woods and worlds of Pitts and Fortune alike.

What then of the woods, the "Christ symbol"? Are they in some sense the real protagonist? This story is O'Connor's most explicit foray into ecology, or environmentalism, and it is indeed tempting to make that its overarching theme. Yet at the end of the day, "A View of the Woods" is about just that—not the woods but people, and how people "view" the woods. The "lawn" in front of the house is important only because, as Mary

Fortune put it, "That's where we play," and "My daddy grazes his calves on that lot," and the woods matter only because she and her family value them and want to look at them. O'Connor cares for the environment, and even invites the reader to weep over it, but she is not an environmentalist in any strict ideological sense of the word.[6] To misapply slightly a well-known saying of Jesus, "The environment was made for people, not people for the environment." Moreover, like the sky and the sun in O'Connor's fiction, the woods matter not for their own sake but as a stand-in for their Creator. The question "Who owns the woods?" was raised already in "A Circle in the Fire," where Mrs. Cope's three young tormentors gave the right answer, "Gawd owns them woods," and from it drew all the wrong conclusions: "it's ours," and "I'd build a big parking lot on it or something." Mr. Fortune comes to much the same conclusion, but by a different route. He does not own the woods, nor does he claim them for himself. At first they are a matter of indifference: "woods—not a mountain, not a waterfall, not any kind of planted bush or flower, just woods" (538). But in his first "unpleasant vision" through his bedroom window they take on the shape of an enemy with "hellish red trunks," something to be feared and resisted. In his last vision, his only wish is for the "ugly pines" to leave him alone. They do finally leave him alone, and that is his very own brand of hell.

6. In answer to the question, "Would she have held common cause with the various 'green' activists and organizations that have sprouted up in the last forty years," even Mark Graybill, who makes a strong case for her "deep ecological vision," acknowledges that "Given O'Connor's iconoclastic and skeptical disposition about movements and most forms of social do-goodery, it seems unlikely" (Graybill, "O'Connor's Deep Ecological Vision," 1).

11

Getting Home

"IGUESS YOU'RE GOING home," Mrs. Wally Bee Hitchcock said to Hazel Motes at the beginning of *Wise Blood* (3), and he was, even though he said he was not. All of O'Connor's characters will get home one way or another, wherever and whatever home might be. Some do so in death, like Haze, or Mrs. May, or Mr. Guizac, or Mr. Fortune and Mary Pitts, or Bevel, or Norton, or the Grandmother. Others, like Rayber or Sheppard or Thomas, or Mrs. McIntyre or Mrs. Cope, through a kind of death in the midst of life. Still others, like Tarwater, Hulga, or Asbury, through a life renewed yet still on its way toward death. The same options are at work in one story, "The Artificial Nigger," from O'Connor's first collection, and three from her second, "Everything That Rises Must Converge," "Revelation," and "Judgement Day," all with an additional common theme, that elephant in the living room in O'Connor's world, the issue of race.

THERE AND BACK AGAIN

The line "there and back again," traceable to the nursery rhyme, "How many miles to Babylon?" served as the title of a children's book by the New Testament scholar C. H. Dodd in 1932, and in 1937 as the subtitle of J. R. R. Tolkien's *The Hobbit*. It would have made an admirable, and far less provocative, title for "The Artificial Nigger," a story O'Connor called "my favorite" (*Collected Works*, 953), and "probably the best thing I'll ever write" (1027).[1] Published in 1955, it anticipates "A View of the Woods" in

---

1. Some were uneasy with the title, but O'Connor stood firm. She once said of the poet John Crowe Ransom, "I have always listened to what he has had to say about

166

having to do with a grandfather and a grandchild at odds with each other, and yet in certain ways mirror images. Mr. Head, aged sixty, and Nelson, aged ten, were "grandfather and grandson but they looked enough alike to be brothers and brothers not too far apart in age, for Mr. Head had a youthful expression by daylight, while the boy's look was ancient, as if he knew everything already and would be pleased to forget it" (212).

The story unfolds in a single day, beginning at two a.m. in a bedroom "full of moonlight," and ending in the evening, "just as the moon, restored to its full splendor, sprang from a cloud and flooded the clearing with light" (210, 230). In between, the long planned journey "there and back again": from a place so rural and remote that they "would have to leave the house at four to get to the railroad junction by five-thirty," to Atlanta, the big city where Nelson had been born. Mr. Head wakes up briefly, as Nelson sleeps on in a fetal position, "hunched over on his side, his knees under his chin and his heels under his bottom" (210–11). The journey will have a moral purpose, Mr. Head decides. He will teach his grandson "a lesson that the boy would never forget." Nelson would "find out that the city is not a great place." He would "see everything there is to see in a city so that he would be content to stay at home for the rest of his life" (211–12). Mr. Head, aptly named, sees himself as "a suitable guide for the young," and the narrator, looking at him with a touch of irony and an eloquence quite exceeding the old man's capabilities, confirms that his qualifications could even "be seen plainly in his features. He had a long, tube-like face with a long rounded open jaw and a long depressed nose. His eyes were alert but quiet, and in the miraculous moonlight they had a look of composure and of ancient wisdom as if they belonged to one of the great guides of men. He might have been Vergil summoned in the middle of the night to go to Dante, or better,[2] Raphael, awakened by a blast of God's light to fly to the side of Tobias" (210).[3]

---

my stories—except when he wanted me to change the title of "The Artificial Nigger" (*Habit of Being*, 297).

2. Why "better"? Not because the Bible is necessarily more important in the story than Dante, but (as we have seen) because O'Connor herself learned to depend on Raphael, the angel of healing, "to guide us to the province of joy so that we may not be ignorant of the concerns of our true country" (*Collected Works*, 983–84).

3. The Douay Bible is less flamboyant: "And the holy angel of the Lord, Raphael, was sent to heal them both" (Tob 3:25). The phrases, "summoned in the middle of the night" and "awakened by a blast of God's light" owe more to Mr. Head's own nocturnal awakening than to either Dante or the Bible.

It matters not that Mr. Head is unlikely to have ever heard of Vergil or Dante, or that his King James Bible did not contain the book of Tobias, or Tobit. This is O'Connor looking at Mr. Head in his moonlit room, not Mr. Head remembering his Bible, much less his *Divine Comedy*. She is not telling us what is literally going on in his mind, but simply evoking for us his self-image as what the Apostle Paul called "a guide of the blind, a light of them that are in darkness, an instructor of the foolish, a teacher of infants, having the form of knowledge and of truth in the law" (Rom 2:19–20), an image that quickly deconstructs itself in Paul's argument: "Thou therefore that teachest another, teachest not thyself: thou that preachest that men should not steal, stealest: Thou thay sayest, men should not commit adultery, commitest adultery: thou that abhorrest idols, commitest sacrilege: Thou that makest thy boast of the law, by transgression of the law dishonourest God" (Rom 2:21–23). In our story as well, any claims Mr. Head might have to the "ancient wisdom" of "the great guides of men," are dubious, and Nelson knows it.

Mr. Head wakes up again at three thirty to find Nelson already up and fixing breakfast. Nelson insists this will not be his first trip to Atlanta because, as his grandfather had told him, he was born there. But now he is duly warned. "You may not like it a bit," Mr. Head tells him, "It'll be full of niggers"—to him the major reason it was "not a great place." "You ain't never seen a nigger," he reminds the boy, "There hasn't been a nigger in this county since we run that one out twelve years ago and that was before you were born" (212). Nelson insists he must have seen them in Atlanta as a baby, and Mr. Head, exasperated, fires back, "If you seen one you didn't know what he was," and in a rare moment of truth-telling, adds "A six-month old child don't know a nigger from anybody else" (213). At ten Nelson is still colorblind, until instructed by his faithful mentor and guide.

The train turns out be a kind of microcosm of the city itself, and the train ride something of a farce. "A conductor with the face of an ancient bloated bulldog" ushers them on board as the train comes to a stop right where they are standing at a pre-arranged signal crossing. As they enter the car filled with sleeping passengers, Mr. Head tells Nelson where to sit "in his normal voice which was very loud at this hour in the morning," and then "sat down and settled himself and took out his ticket and started reading aloud everything that was printed on it. People began to stir. Several woke up and stared at him" (214). Introducing Nelson to a man half asleep across the aisle, "First time this boy has ever been on a train," he explains, "Ignorant as the day he was born, but I mean for him to get his fill once and for all." The only response is "Yeah," as the man tries to wake himself up and Nelson interrupts. "I was born in the city," he chimes in, "This is my second trip." But then something catches Mr. Head's attention: "A huge coffee-colored man was coming slowly forward. He had on a light suit and a yellow satin tie with a ruby pin in it. One of his hands rested on his stomach which rode majestically under his buttoned coat, and in the other he held the head of a black walking stick." He had a white mustache and white hair, and was proceeding slowly down the aisle, accompanied by "two young women, both coffee-colored, one in a yellow dress and one in a green" (215).

"What was that?" Mr. Head asks the boy. "A man," Nelson replies. "What kind of a man?" "A fat man." "You don't know what kind?" "An old man"—this from Nelson, with "a sudden foreboding that he was not going to enjoy the day." Finally the revelation: "'That was a nigger,' Mr Head said and sat back." His moment of triumph, as he says to Nelson, "I'd of thought you'd know a nigger since you seen so many when you were in the city on your first visit," and (to the man across the aisle), "That's his first nigger." He might have added, "and his second and third," but oddly enough the two "coffee-colored" young women are not on Mr. Head's radar screen. Who were they? The man's daughters? His employees? Nelson may or may not have noticed them. "You said they were black," he told his grandfather. "You never said they were tan." His attention too centers on the man, who he felt must have "deliberately walked down the aisle in order to make a fool of him" (216).

The humor trumps Mr. Head's obvious racism and his not-so-obvious sexism. He blunders on, taking Nelson on a tour of the train, to "see the parts of it" (217)—just as he will later show him the sewer system in Atlanta in order to see the city's "lower parts" (220). He "wanted the boy to see the toilet so they went first to the men's room and examined the plumbing." Then "the ice-water cooler as if he had invented it," and "the single spigot where the travelers brushed their teeth." Only then the elegant dining car, where they encounter three more blacks waiting on tables, and in the near corner, "set off from the rest by a saffron-colored curtain" the huge white-haired old man they had seen before, with his two female companions. The "tremendous Negro" is now seen to have "a heavy sad face," yet he is obviously prosperous and comfortable in his own tan skin as he speaks 'in a soft voice to the two women while he buttered a muffin." All Mr. Head can say is "They rope them off," as he and Nelson move on toward the kitchen. When the black head waiter insists, "Passengers are NOT allowed in the kitchen!" Mr. Head shouts back that this is "because the cockroaches would run the passengers out!" drawing general laughter from the passengers, and from Nelson "a sudden keen pride" in his grandfather's wit and wisdom (217–18). And even though Mr. Head continues to make a fool of himself as the train pulls into Atlanta, reading out loud the name of every building they pass, Nelson suddenly wants to "take hold of Mr. Head's coat and hold on like a child," realizing for the first time "that his grandfather was indispensable to him."

Unknown to Nelson, the "indispensable" Mr. Head carries with him the scars of a previous visit to Atlanta, when he had gotten off by mistake at Emory, the suburban stop ("Firstoppppppmry," shouts the conductor), and "had had to pay a man fifteen cents to take him into the heart of town," then had got lost in a store and "found his way out only after many people had insulted him" (218–19). This time Mr. Head knows better, but in the excitement of getting off the train, neither of them notice that their sack lunch ("some biscuits and a can of sardines," [213]), still sits on the seat where they had left it. The city itself turns out to be not so much dark and surreal, like Taulkinham in *Wise Blood*, as merely indifferent to two strangers from the deep woods. It is by no means "Babylon the great" in the book of Revelation, nor is it the great city "called spiritually Sodom and Egypt," nor are Mr. Head and Nelson by any means the "two witnesses" whose bodies will lie in its streets (Rev 11:3, 8). It is merely the Atlanta that O'Connor herself knew, going about its daily business with crowds hurrying to work, oblivious to Mr. Head and his great moral lesson for young Nelson.

Still, in Mr. Head's eyes the city is the Other, and as the Other it takes on for him an almost apocalyptic quality. Because of his bad experience earlier, he resolves to stay out of the stores. Instead, he and Nelson pay to learn their weight and their fortune on a machine outside a store. Mr. Head learns that he is "upright and brave and all your friends admire you," while Nelson has "a great destiny ahead of you but beware of dark women." Mr. Head calls Nelson's attention to the sewer system, and squatting on the curb explains to him "how the entire city was underlined with it, how it contained all the drainage and was full of rats and how a man could slide into it and be sucked along down endless pitchblack tunnels. At any minute any man in the city might be sucked into the sewer and never heard from again." Nelson, shaken by this, "connected the sewer passages with the entrance to hell and understood for the first time how the world was put together in its lower parts." Mr. Head's apocalyptic city is beginning to sound more like Dante's *Inferno* than the book of Revelation.

Nelson, despite his dependence on his grandfather, is undeterred, Drawing back from the curb, he assures himself that "you can stay away from the holes," and stubbornly reminds his grandfather, "This is where I come from!" "You'll get your fill," Mr. Head replies, and with the crowds, the two walk and walk some more, circling ever to the left but keeping the "putty-colored terminal with a concrete dome on top" always in sight (219–20). But after a half-hour they pass the railroad station again, and stores they have seen before. "We done been here!" Nelson exclaims, "I don't believe you know where you're at!" Mr. Head then changes directions several times until they begin to see more and more black people. "Niggers live in these houses," Nelson concludes, and they turn down another street only to find "colored men in their undershirts standing in the doors and colored women rocking on the sagging porches. Colored children played in the gutters and stopped what they were doing to look at them" (221). Soon they discover they have left their lunch on the train, and the station is no longer in sight. They are tired, with not even a place to sit down, and they begin trading accusations. "Whyn't you ast one of these niggers the way?" Nelson says to his grandfather, "You got us lost," and "This is where you were born," Mr. Head fires back, "You can ast one yourself if you want to."

If the first iconic or revelatory moment in the story was Mr. Head's sighting of the "huge coffee-colored man" on the train with his two young female companions, the second is Nelson's and his alone: "Up ahead he saw a large colored woman leaning in a doorway that opened onto the sidewalk. Her hair stood straight out from her head for about four inches all around and she was resting on bare brown feet that turned pink at the sides. She had on a pink dress that showed her exact shape." Nelson asks her how to get back to town "in a voice that did not sound like his own," and she tells him "You in town now"—this "in a rich low tone that made Nelson feel as if a cool spray had been turned on him." (222–23). Transfixed, he "stood drinking in every detail of her":

> His eyes traveled up from her great knees to her forehead and then made a triangular path from the glistening sweat on her neck down and across her tremendous bosom and over her bare arm back to where her fingers lay hidden in her hair. He suddenly wanted her to reach down and pick him up and draw him against her and then he wanted to feel her breath on his face. He wanted to look down and down into her eyes while she held him tighter and tighter. He had never had such a feeling before. He felt as if he were reeling down through a pitchblack tunnel.

The "pitchblack tunnel" evokes for him the sewers under Atlanta that had seemed the very entrance to hell, but the woman's words are commonplace and reassuring: "You can go a block down yonder and catch you a car take you to the railroad station, Sugarpie."

This woman, with her "great knees" and "tremendous bosom," stands as a kind of sequel to Mr. Head's "tremendous Negro" on the train who had fascinated him and frustrated Nelson. This revelatory moment far exceeds Mr. Head's, for Nelson's vision of the woman is not just one more sighting of a colored person, but an example of what O'Connor in her later stories might have called convergence, a traumatic union with the Other–black to be sure, but female as well, erotic and at the same time maternal. The irony is that if Nelson had been a more privileged white boy he might have had just such a memory of a black Nanny. But as it is, the vision he has and the feeling it evokes come as a frightening mystery, something akin to the "horrifying love" that Rayber felt for Bishop, or the grandmother's sudden realization that The Misfit was "one of my babies" (152). This time the vision is that of the "baby" unexpectedly meeting his alien "mother" in an alien city. Nelson's repeated claim that "I was born here!" and "This is where I come from!" abruptly takes on ample, maternal and very black flesh, and Nelson, terrified, "would have collapsed at her feet if Mr. Head had not pulled him roughly away." The woman is nothing to Mr. Head, who mocks the boy for acting "like you don't have any sense!" and "standing there grinning like a chim-pan-zee while a nigger woman gives you direction. Great Gawd!" (223–24).

Remembering the warning about "dark women" that came with his weight, and convinced that his grandfather was indeed "upright and brave," Nelson slips into a more dependent mode as the two continue their journey. Instead of following the black woman's advice and boarding a streetcar ("Mr. Head had never boarded a streetcar"), they decide to follow the trolley tracks on foot to the railroad station. Before long, they are back in a white neighborhood, but still well out of sight of the station and possibly lost. Half apologetically (but only half), Nelson tells Mr. Head, "I never said I would or wouldn't like it. I never said I wanted to come. I only said I was born here and I never had nothing to do with that. I want to go home. I never wanted to come in the first place. It was all your big idea. How you know you ain't following the tracks in the wrong direction?" (224). How indeed? They are lost and tired and hungry. Nelson, exhausted, sits on the pavement, then falls over on his side in a fit of sleep. His knees are tucked "up under his chin" in a fetal position, just as when the story began, but now as if he is again about to be born in the dark city into a very different life, for he is "half conscious of vague noises and black forms moving up from some dark part of him into the light." Mr. Head meanwhile, ever the faithful mentor and guide, resolves to teach him "a lesson he won't forget, particularly when the child is always reasserting his position with some new impudence." Hiding around the corner seated on a covered garbage can, he waits for Nelson to wake up alone and panic.

It does not turn out well. When he feels he has waited long enough, Mr. Head kicked his foot back against the can so that "a hollow boom reverberated in the alley. Nelson shot up onto his feet with a shout. He looked where his grandfather should have been and stared. He seemed to whirl several times and then, picking up his feet and throwing his head back, he dashed down the street like a wild maddened pony" (225). Mr. Head follows but cannot keep up. By the time the boy is in sight, it is too late: "Nelson was sitting with both legs spread out and by his side lay an elderly woman, screaming, and groceries scattered on the sidewalk." Mr. Head, hidden behind a trash box, sees a crowd of women gathered, and the old woman on the pavement calling for the police. Finally he approaches, very slowly, and when he is within ten feet, "Nelson saw him and sprang. The child caught him around the hips and clung panting against him." The injured woman said "You sir! You'll pay every penny of my doctor's bill that your boy has caused. He's a juve-nile delinquent! Where is an officer?" Mr. Head stares at the women: "'This is not my boy,' he said, 'I never seen him before.' "

This incident is supposed to evoke the Gospel accounts of Peter's denial of Jesus, a notion traceable to O'Connor's reference to a letter in which "I was asked if Mr. Head didn't represent Peter and Nelson the Christ-Child." Her answer was guarded: "I had to say that Mr. Head's behaviour certainly resembled Peter's a little but that I found it harder to gin up Nelson's character so he could suitably represent the Christ-Child" (*Collected Works*, 931). Yet later, in the same letter in which she called the story her favorite, she added, "And then there's Peter's denial. They all got together in that one" (*Collected Works*, 954). Still, the differences outweigh the similarities. Most obviously, Peter denied the adult Jesus, his Lord and Teacher, not "the Christ-Child." And Mr. Head denies Nelson once, not three times. Like Peter, he does it out of fear, but the point of the story, as even the women who watched are quick to notice, is that here was "a man who would deny his own image and likeness" (226). Jesus was by no means Peter's "image and likeness," but in this story we are expected to remember that Mr. Head and Nelson "looked enough alike to be brothers" (212). If

Mr. Fortune's mortal sin in "A View of the Woods" was *destroying* "his own image and likeness" in the person of his granddaughter, Mr. Head's sin is *denying* his own image in the person of his grandson. Serious indeed but not mortal, and this story unlike the other will have a happy ending.

The denial marks a turning point, in that from here on the reader is allowed more and more into the inner world of its two main characters, inside Mr. Head's head (as it were), and to a lesser extent inside Nelson's. Mr. Head's guilt is seen first in his body language as he walks on with Nelson following twenty paces behind: his "shoulders were sagging and his neck hung forward at such an angle that it was not visible from behind." Finally he turns his back and calls out to Nelson, "Let's go get us a Co' Cola somewheres!" When that is ignored, Mr. Head "began to feel the depth of his denial. His face as they walked on became all hollows and bare ridges. He saw nothing they were passing but he perceived that they had lost the car tracks. There was no dome to be seen anywhere and the afternoon was advancing. He knew that if dark overtook them in the city, they would be beaten and robbed. The speed of God's justice was only what he expected for himself, but he could not stand to think that his sins would be visited upon Nelson and that even now, he was leading the boy to his doom." He almost stumbles over an open water spigot on the edge of the grass, and although he feels he does not deserve it he calls out to Nelson, "Come on and getcher some water!" in the hope "that they would both drink and be brought together" (227). The momentary hint is that the ancient biblical symbol of water, the water of life, will bring about reconcilation and redemption (see Isa 55:1, Zech 14:8; John 4:13–14, 7:37–38), but it does not happen: "Nelson, though he had not had water since some he had drunk out of a paper cup on the train, passed by the spigot, disdaining to drink where his grandfather had." Something else will have to bring them together.

When Mr. Head, he saw that not even "living water" (much less a "Co' Cola"!) could achieve reconciliation, "lost all hope. His face in the waning afternoon light looked ravaged and abandoned. He could feel the boy's steady hate, traveling at an even pace behind him and he knew that (if by some miracle they escaped being murdered in the city) it would continue just that way for the rest of his life. He knew that now he was wandering into a black strange place where nothing was like it had ever been before, a long old age without respect and an end that would be welcome because it would be the end." Nelson, for his part, had "his mind frozen around his grandfather's treachery as if he were trying to preserve it intact to present at the final judgment," and yet he is conflicted, for at the same time he can feel, "from some remote place inside himself, a black mysterious form reach up as if it would melt his frozen vision in one hot grasp" (228). The "blackness" that holds only despair for Mr. Head offers Nelson just the glimmer of a hope of reconciliation.

The irony in all this is that the "black strange place" that Mr. Head so hates and fears has been by no means hostile or unforgiving. The "huge coffee-colored" man on the train had not so much as noticed them; the "large colored woman" in the doorway had given Nelson the right directions willingly, if with a touch of amusement; and although the elderly white woman whom Nelson had knocked down had been furious, it had surely been with good reason. Now Mr. Head, who had come to the point that "if he saw a sewer entrance he would drop into it and let himself be carried away," encounters yet another stranger whose behavior can hardly be faulted, "a fat man"—evidently white in this white neighborhood, bald and wearing golf knickers and followed by two bulldogs. This potential Good Samaritan looks prosperous and comfortable in his own skin, reminding us just a little of the fat colored man on the train, followed instead by two young women (are the two bulldogs a deliberately comic touch?). But Mr. Head sees him quite differently from the way he saw the colored man, crying out in desperation. "'I'm lost!' he called. 'I'm lost and can't find my way and me and this boy have got to catch this train and I can't find the station. Oh Gawd I'm lost! Oh hep me Gawd I'm lost!'" The fat man looks at Mr Head's tickets and patiently explains, "you won't have time to get back to town to make this but you can catch it at the suburb stop. That's three blocks from here" (228–29). Without so much as a "Thank you," Mr. Head stares "as if he were slowly returning from the dead and when the man had finished and gone off with the dogs jumping at his heels, he turned to Nelson and said breathlessly, 'We're going to get home!'" Nelson, by contrast, is unmoved: "His eyes were triumphantly cold. There was no light in them, no feeling, no interest. He was merely there, a small figure, waiting. Home was nothing to him."

Mr. Head finally grasps something of the theological meaning of being "lost," for he "felt he knew now what time would be like without seasons and what heat would be like without light and what man would be like without salvation," and suddenly home means nothing to him either: "He didn't care if he never made the train and if it had not been for what suddenly caught his attention, like a cry out of the gathering dusk, he might have forgotten there was a station to go to." What caught his attention was something that would accomplish what even "living water" could not, "the plaster figure of a Negro sitting bent over on a low yellow brick fence that curved around a wide lawn"—an ornamental lawn jockey gracing some white person's suburban yard: "The Negro was about Nelson's size and he was pitched forward at an unsteady angle because the putty that held him to the wall had cracked. One of his eyes was entirely white and he held a piece of brown watermelon." He looked neither young nor old, but "too miserable to be either. He was meant to look happy because his mouth was stretched up at the corners but the chipped eye and the angle he was cocked at gave him a wild look of misery." Mr. Head can only say, "An artificial nigger!" and Nelson repeats after him in the same tone of voice, "An artificial nigger!" (229).

The two are transfixed, as Mr. Head had been by the huge black man on the train, and as Nelson had been by the huge black woman who gave him directions. This time they are in it together, and they too look neither young nor old: "Mr. Head looked like an ancient child and Nelson like a miniature old man. They stood gazing at the Negro as if they were faced with some great mystery, some monument to another's victory that brought them together in their common defeat. The could both feel it dissolving their differences like an action of mercy." The iconic moment is seen mainly through the eyes of the old man: "Mr. Head had never known before what mercy felt like because he had been too good to deserve any, but he felt he knew now." He had feared and felt already "the speed of God's justice" but now he begins to understand that in the end justice and mercy amount to the same thing, for mercy teaches us that we are by no means "too good to deserve any."

Ever the faithful mentor and guide, Mr. Head struggles to "say something to the child to show that he was still wise and in the look the boy returned he saw a hungry need for that assurance. Nelson's eyes seemed to implore him to explain once and for all the mystery of existence." But all he can manage is "They ain't got enough real ones here. They got to have an artificial one." The contrast between the profundity of his thoughts and the banality of his words is stunning. Here if anywhere he does resemble the Apostle Peter, who when he saw the transfigured Jesus on the mountain conversing with Moses and Elijah, said, "Rabbi, it is good for us to be here: and let us make three tabernacles, one for thee, and one for Moses, and one for Elias." Even the Gospel writer could not resist adding, "For he knew not what he said: for they were struck with fear" (Mark 9:4–5). As for Nelson, he has had no profound thoughts, at least none that we are told, yet his words are more to the point than his grandfather's, for they demonstrate that what he has just seen has changed him. A moment before, "Home was nothing to him," but now he says, "Let's go home before we get ourselves lost again" (230).

The reader is impelled to ask, "What just happened here?" O'Connor in her correspondence comes to the rescue, but just barely. "What I had in mind to suggest with the artificial nigger," she wrote, "was the redemptive quality of the Negro's suffering for us all" (*Collected Works*, 931). If that is indeed what she had in mind, she is content to leave it implicit in the story, while making much else very explicit. Certainly Mr. Head and Nelson, mirror images of each other, see the "artificial nigger" as a mirror image of themselves. In the statue's "wild look of misery" they see their own misery. This lawn ornament which signals, or had once signaled, the affluence of its owner ("some monument to another's victory") now brings them "together in their common defeat," common both to the two of them and to the race they ridiculed and despised as the Other. This jarring revelation of solidarity with the Other is the "mystery" for which Mr. Head cannot find the right words, the "action of grace" that reconciles him with Nelson and will change them both forever.

The train picks them up at the Emory suburban station, and the trip home is uneventful. As it lets them off, "the moon, restored to its full splendor, sprang from a cloud and flooded the clearing with light." The story ends as it began, in moonlight, for it is the moon that prompts Mr. Head's "second touch" of grace, this time a touch (in contrast to Mrs. May's and Mr. Fortune's) that is *not* lethal:

> Mr. Head stood very still and felt the action of mercy touch him again, but this time he knew there were no words in the world that could name it. He understood that it grew out of agony, which is not denied to any man and which is given in strange ways to children. He understood that it was all a man could carry into death to give his Maker and he suddenly burned with shame that he had so little of it to take with him. He stood appalled, judging himself with the thoroughness of God, while the action of mercy covered his pride like a flame and consumed it. He had never thought himself a great sinner before but he saw now that his true depravity had been hidden from him lest it cause him despair. He realized that he was forgiven for sins from the beginning of time, when he had conceived in his own heart the sin of Adam, until the present, when he had denied poor Nelson. He saw that no sin was too monstrous for him to claim

as his own, and since God loved in proportion as He forgave, he
felt ready at that instant to enter Paradise. (230–31)

Much has been written about whether this is true repentance or mere self-deception, but there is little doubt that O'Connor intends it seriously. In the same letter in which she spoke of "the redemptive quality of the Negro's suffering" she went on to comment that her friend Caroline Gordon "is always telling me that I must gain some altitude and get a larger view. Well the end of The Artificial Nigger was a very definite attempt to do that and in those last two paragraphs I have practically gone from the Garden of Eden to the Gates of Paradise" (*Collected Works*, 931). It must be said that O'Connor has indeed "gained some altitude" in these musings of Mr. Head at the story's end. It is all far beyond what he is able to put into words, and by now he knows enough not to try, so O'Connor has done it for him. The "action of mercy" consuming his pride "like a flame" exemplifies once again her apparent conviction that purgatory begins already in the present life.

Still, we see little in Mr. Head's remarkable soliloquy of "the redemptive quality of the Negro's suffering for us all." If racism is the sin that takes him to the brink of despair and for which he is now forgiven, it is a sin that dare not speak its name. Presumably it is included in his sweeping reference to no sin "too monstrous to claim as his own," but it lies buried under the more general heading of Original Sin "from the beginning of time, when he had conceived in his own heart the sin of Adam." His only named transgression, it seems, is that "he had denied poor Nelson." Doubtless he was already thinking of Nelson when he spoke of agony as something "given in strange ways to children." Possibly O'Connor viewed racism as corporate sin, the sin of a particular culture and a particular time, not the sin of an individual, at least not this individual. Mr. Head's "confession," if we may call it that, is highly individualistic. It is not that he shares in the corporate guilt of the human race because of Adam's transgression long ago, but rather that he himself at the "beginning of time" had "conceived in his own heart the sin of Adam." He sounds less like the Apostle Paul[4] than like the anonymous second century Jewish writer who said, "Adam is, therefore, not the cause, except only for himself, but each of us has become our own Adam" (2 *Baruch* 54.19; *Old Testament Pseudepigrapha*, 1.640).[5]

4. In Romans 5:12 for example: "Wherefore as by one man sin entered the world, and by sin death; and so death passed upon all men, in whom all have sinned."

5. O'Connor is unlikely to have read *Second Baruch*, but she might well have read Thomas Aquinas, who insisted that "the flesh cannot be the subject of original sin, but

The irony of the story is that Mr. Head and Nelson's vision of their solidarity with the Other bears relatively modest fruit, bringing the two of them together without any explicit effect on their perception of the world in which they live. The command in John's Gospel to "Love one another" (John 13:34–35; 15:12, 17) trumps the command in Luke and Matthew to love the "Other," in the persons of one's perceived enemies (Matt 5:44–46; Luke 6:27, 35; 10:29–37). More specifically, the generational reconciliation of grandfather and grandson trumps any sustained vision of reconciliation between the races. We are not privy to Nelson's thoughts as we are to those of the old man, and O'Connor does not help us out here. All we have to go on is the expression on his face, "a mixture of fatigue and suspicion," as the train that had brought them home "glided past them and disappeared like a frightened serpent into the woods," and his parting words, a far cry from his grandfather's lofty meditations: "I'm glad I've went once, but I'll never go back again!" (231). O'Connor hinted at least twice in her letters that she herself was a lot like Nelson, just as she was like Hulga Hopewell, Hazel Motes and Enoch Emery (and she could have added Mary Pitts). "My disposition is a combination of Nelson's and Hulga's," she wrote to Betty Hester in 1955 (*Collected Works*, 954), and again about a year later, "And of course I have thrown you off by informing you that Hulga is like me. So is Nelson, so is Haze, so is Enoch" (*Collected Works*, 1000).

Nelson's last words are as worthy of close exegesis as Mr. Head's lengthy reflections on sin and forgiveness. Most immediately, they echo what he said as he stared at the Artificial Nigger, "Let's go home before we get ourselves lost again." Whatever his infatuation with the city and whatever his pride at having been born there, he now wants to go home to stay. He acknowledges that he has now been to the city "once," not "twict" as he insisted before (211). His grandfather wanted him to "get his fill once and for all," and he has done just that. He has met the Other, first in the huge black woman whom he envisioned as his mother, and then in the piece of statuary in whose face he saw reflected the "misery" that is humanity's common lot. Even though at some level he is changed forever by that other world, he has no desire to be a part of it. All he wants is to "get home" and get on with his young life. "I'm glad I've went once, but I'll never go back again!" are his words about Atlanta in the story, but they could as easily be O'Connor's own words about New York City and the northeast.

---

only the soul," and that "'The soul of any individual man was in Adam in respect of his seminal principle" (*Summa Theologica* II, 1, 3, Q. 82,"On the Subject of Original Sin"), in *Great Books of the Western World*, 20.171–72.

Consequently the story's message about race is muted at best, in keeping with her confession in an unpublished letter to Maryat Lee three months before she died: "You know, I'm an integrationist by principle and a segregationist by taste anyway."[6] One suspects that this pretty much describes Nelson and his grandfather as well, even *after* their memorable encounter with "the artificial nigger."

The Last and the First

The issue of race is addressed more fully in O'Connor's second collection, *Everything That Rises Must Converge*, a title drawn from Teilhard de Chardin and hinting at racial reconciliation. Still, whatever "rising and convergence" of race, class, or generations is visible either in the title story or the collection as a whole is imperfect at best, as O'Connor's close friend, Robert Fitzgerald, was quick to point out. Fitzgerald, in his introduction to the collection in 1965, a year after O'Connor's death, compared but also contrasted O'Connor's vision with Teilhard's: "Quite as austere in its way as his, her vision will hold us down to earth where the clashes of blind wills and the low dodges of the heart permit any rising or convergence only at the cost of agony. At that cost, yes, a little" (Fitzgerald, "Introduction, xxx). As to the title story in particular, Fitzgerald added that it shows "young and old and black and white to be practically sealed off against one another, struggling but hardly upward or together in a welter of petty feelings and cross purposes, resolved only slightly even by the tragic blow. 'Slightly,' however, may mean a great deal in the economy of this writer" (xxxi). In short, we should not expect too much "rising and convergence" in these stories, but just be grateful for what we do find.

The title story is told by Julian, a college graduate who wants to be a writer but is reduced to living with his mother and selling typewriters. He has agreed to accompany his mother to her weight reducing class because she "would not ride the buses by herself at night since they had been integrated" (485). O'Connor makes only three references to this story in her published letters, all of them accenting race. She comments in the first that it "touches on a certain topical issue in these parts and takes place on a bus" (*Habit of Being*, 436), in the second that it applies Teilhard's principle to "a

6. The letter, dated May 3, 1964, is available in the Flannery O'Connor Collection at Georgia College and State University in Milledgeville. Possibly the reason it has never been published is the way it continues: "I don't *like* negroes. They all give me a pain and the more of them I see, the less I like them. Particularly the new kind."

certain situation in the Southern states & indeed in all the world" (*Habit of Being*, 438), and in the third (two years later) that it casts "a plague on everybody's house as far as the race business is concerned" (*Habit of Being*, 537). And indeed it does. Julian and his mother are on opposite sides on the race issue, as on almost everything else. Their relationship recalls that of Asbury Fox with his mother, or Mrs. May and her two sons, especially John Wesley, in "Greenleaf," or Thomas and his mother in "The Comforts of Home." In simplest terms, she gets on his nerves. He waits "like Saint Sebastian for the arrows to begin piercing him" as she fusses over whether to wear the new hat she has bought for seven dollars and fifty cents: "It was a hideous hat. A purple velvet flap came down on one side of it and stood up on the other; the rest of it was green and looked like a cushion with the stuffing out." Rolling his eyes, Julian reassures her: "'Yes, you should have bought it,' he said, 'Put it on and let's go'" (485). She rationalizes that "you only live once and paying a little more for it, I at least won't meet myself coming and going" (486), and when she has second thoughts and threatens to take it back, Julian grabs her arm and tells her to "Shut up and enjoy it." She finally agrees, and turns to more serious issues: "'With the world in the mess it's in,' she said, 'it's a wonder we can enjoy anything. I tell you, the bottom rail is on top.'" Julian heaves a sigh, for with one simple remark his mother has opened up the dreaded topics of class and especially race, topics he wants at all costs to avoid.

The metaphor of the bottom rail on top recalls the scene in "Revelation" where Ruby Turpin shouts at the Almighty from her pig parlor, "Put that bottom rail on top. There'll still be a top and bottom!" (653). In her world, the rise of blacks can only take place at her expense. Like Ruby, Julian's mother visualizes a world carefully structured both by class ("'Your great-grandfather was a former governor of this state,' she said. 'Your grandfather was a prosperous landowner. Your grandmother was a Godhigh'") and by race ("Your great-grandfather had a plantation and two hundred slaves"). When Julian reminds her that "There are no more slaves," she replies, "They were better off when they were." "It's ridiculous," she continues, "It's simply not realistic. They should rise, yes, but on their own side of the fence" (487–88). Rising but no convergence. Separate but equal. A perspective not unlike Nelson's, perhaps even a bit like O'Connor's own.

For Julian's mother herself it has not been a matter of rising (much less convergence) but quite the opposite. She remembers better days, at her grandfather's house with its double stairways and kitchen walls fragrant with the smell of home cooking. "Actually the place belonged to the God-highs," she tells Julian, "but your grandfather Chestny paid the mortgage and saved it for them." They were, she recalls, in "reduced circumstances," yet "they never forgot who they were." She goes on to reminisce about "the old darky who was my nurse, Caroline. There was no better person in the world. I've always had a great respect for my colored friends." Julian cuts her short: "Will you for God's sake get off that subject?" He remembers the house too, for even though he has seen it only in a state of decay, "it remained in his mind as his mother had known it. It appeared in his dreams regularly. He would stand on the wide porch, listening to the rustle of oak leaves, then wander through the high-ceilinged hall into the parlor that opened onto it and gaze at the worn rugs and faded draperies. It occurred to him that it was he, not she, who could have appreciated it" (488).

It is Julian, not his mother, who mourns the family's "reduced circumstances." On the bus, hiding behind his newspaper, he muses, "All of her life had been a struggle to act like a Chestny without the Chestny goods, and to give him everything she thought a Chestny ought to have; but since, said she, it was fun to struggle, why complain?" She had sacrificed to put him through college, and felt she had won because he had turned out well. "She excused his gloominess on the grounds that he was still growing up and his radical ideas on his lack of practical experience. She said he didn't know a thing about 'life,' that he hadn't even entered the real world—when already he was as disenchanted with it as a man of fifty" (491–92). So far as he was concerned, "in spite of all her foolish views, he was free of prejudice and unafraid to face facts. Most miraculous of all, instead of being blinded by love for her as she was for him, he had cut himself emotionally free of her and could see her with complete objectivity" (492).

The idle conversation on the half-filled bus is both comic and racially tinged. "I see we have the bus to ourselves," Julian's mother says out loud, and a woman across the aisle replies, "I come on one the other day and they were thick as fleas—up front and all through." A well-dressed black man carrying a briefcase gets on, and Julian's mother pokes Julian in the ribs whispering, "Now you see why I won't ride on these buses by myself." Julian, not only ignoring a NO SMOKING sign, but forgetting that he had no cigarettes, crosses the aisle, sits down next to the man and asks him, "Do you have a light?" (492–93). Embarrassed and retreating into a world of his own, he fantasizes about different ways he might teach his mother a lesson about race, either by making friends with "some of the better types," like the man with the briefcase, or participating in a sit-in, or best of all, bringing home "a beautiful suspiciously Negroid woman" and telling his mother "This is the woman I've chosen. She's intelligent, dignified, even good, and she's suffered and she hasn't thought it *fun*" (494).

His reverie is interrupted by the sight of an unmistakably "Negroid woman" getting on the bus with a little boy. She is "large, gaily-dressed, sullen-looking," a "giant of a woman," with "a mammoth red pocketbook" and a face "set not only to meet opposition but to seek it out." The little boy climbs onto the vacant seat beside Julian's mother, while the woman sits next to Julian, and he is relieved that this seems to annoy his mother even more than it annoys him. On the woman's head sits "a hideous hat. A purple velvet flap came down on one side of it and stood up on the other; the rest of it was green and looked like a cushion with the stuffing out" (495), a description matching verbatim that of his mother's hat ten pages earlier. Julian sees "something familiar-looking about her," and it takes him awhile to realize that it is the hat. "The vision of the two hats, identical, broke upon him with the radiance of a brilliant sunrise. His face was suddenly lit with joy. He could not believe that Fate had thrust upon his mother such a lesson." But Julian is wrong, for almost as soon as his mother notices the hat, "an amused smile came over her face as if the woman were a monkey who had stolen her hat." No lesson at all. She has "met herself coming and going," but to Julian's chagrin it doesn't seem to matter.

Meanwhile Carver, the little boy, looks up at Julian's mother, hungry for her attention, and a minor courtship ensues. "I think he likes me," she tells the woman with "the smile she used when she was being particularly gracious to an inferior." The black mother angrily retrieves Carver, slaps him across the leg and tells him to "Be-have." But he plays peekaboo with Julian's mother until the black woman slaps his hand down: "'Quit yo' foolishness,' she said, 'before I knock the living Jesus out of you!'" (496). The danger signals are in place, and Julian fears disaster. To his relief the next stop is theirs, but it is the black woman's as well, and he knows that his mother is going to "open her purse and give the little boy a nickel. The gesture would be as natural to her as breathing." He tries to grab her purse but too late. Once off the bus she has the purse open. She can only find a penny, but she runs and catches up them. "Oh little boy!" she calls out, "Here's a bright new penny for you," as she holds out the coin. A black fist and a red pocketbook punctuate a shout, "He don't take nobody's pennies!" Julian cringes and shuts his eyes, and when he opens them, "the woman was disappearing down the street with the little boy staring wide-eyed over her shoulder. Julian's mother was sitting on the sidewalk" (498).

"I hope this teaches you a lesson," he tells her, but on her part there is a strange disconnect, as she "leaned forward and her eyes raked his face. She seemed to be trying to determine his identity. Then, as if she found nothing familiar about him, she started off with a headlong movement in the wrong direction," not to her weight reducing class but, as she insists, "Home." She sets off walking, as if to walk all the way home, and Julian follows, still intent on teaching her a lesson. "Don't think that was just an uppity Negro woman," he tells her. "That was the whole colored race which will no longer take your condescending pennies. That was your black double." He tries to make her stop and at least wait for a bus, but "Home" she says again, plunging on as if she has not heard him. Finally Julian catches her arm and stops her. "Tell Grandpa to come get me," she commands him, "Tell Caroline to come get me," and when Julian, stunned, lets go, she "lurched forward again, walking as if one leg were shorter than the other," and fell to the pavement (499–500).

Julian is changed: "A tide of darkness seemed to be sweeping her from him." Like his mother, he reverts to childhood: "Mother!" he cries even as she falls. "Darling, sweetheart, wait!" and falling at her side, "Mamma, Mamma!" He finds her face "fiercely distorted. One eye, large and staring, moved slightly to the left as if it had become unmoored. The other remained fixed on him, raked his face again, found nothing and closed." Julian runs for help toward lights in the distance drifting "further away the faster he ran." Like the dying Mr. Fortune, he races on a journey that takes him nowhere. Instead, the same "tide of darkness seemed to sweep him back to her, postponing from moment to moment his entry into the world of guilt and sorrow" (500). Unlike Mr. Fortune, Julian is condemned to live and not die, consigned by "the terrible speed of mercy" not to hell but to O'Connor's purgatory, "the world of guilt and sorrow" in which we all live. His mother was right: "he hadn't even entered the real world." The story is Julian's story, not his mother's. She has no dying vision that we know of, nor, despite her limitations on the subject of race, does she need one. She is "Home," with her grandfather and her colored nurse Caroline, the only rising or convergence she will know. In her end is her beginning.

Such a reading of "Everything That Rises Must Converge" requires that we revisit its companion story, "Revelation," in which Ruby Turpin agrees that "the bottom rail is on top." And although she never meets her black double, Ruby imagines that if she had had the choice of being created either Negro or white trash, she would have said to God, "All right, make me a nigger then—but that don't mean a trashy one." And God would have

made her "a neat clean respectable Negro woman, herself but black" (636).
Like Julian's mother too, Ruby is struck with an unconventional weapon
hurled at her in rage, not a red pocketbook wielded by a black woman but
a very large book in the hands of a white Wellesley girl who calls her "a
wart hog from hell" (644–46). Yet in contrast to Julian's mother, and more
like Julian himself, Ruby has ample time to learn a lesson, take it to heart,
and go on living in this "world of guilt and sorrow." The lesson comes
to full realization in her "purgatorial" vision of souls "rumbling toward
heaven"—white trash, blacks, freaks and lunatics, and some like herself
and Claud—all of them together "climbing upward into the starry field
and shouting hallelujah" (654).

The point is not the reversal of social classes as some critics have
thought. Ruby herself saw it that way when she tried to tell God that when
the bottom rail is on top "There'll still be a top and a bottom!" But Ruby
was wrong. Reversal is not the point, for behind both stories stands the
Gospel saying of Jesus, "So shall the last be first and the first last" (Matthew
20:16), a pronouncement that, if one really thinks about it, deconstructs
itself. That is, if the first are last and the last first, the very terms "first"
and "last" have lost their meaning altogether.[7] In the parable to which the
pronouncement is attached in Matthew, the workers hired first and those
hired last all received *the same* wages (see 20:12, "thou hast made them
equal to us"). The saying promises not reversal but equality, or convergence if you will, and Ruby, in much the same way, envisions one human
family "rumbling toward heaven," warts and all. The point is not that she
and Claud and those like them are bringing up the rear, but that Ruby, the
"wart hog from hell," is there at all. Mary Grace, the enraged girl who called
her that and is "going to be a lunatic" (647) is likely there as well, among
all the other "freaks and lunatics" who inhabit O'Connor's pages, and we
can imagine Enoch Emery or the hermaphodite in "A Temple of the Holy
Ghost" somewhere in the procession. O'Connor's stories stop well short
of affirming that everyone will make it, even by way of purgatory, but this

---

7. This is not necessarily true of all the New Testament occurrences of the saying.
Mark 10:31, Matthew 19:30 and Luke 13:30, for example, do promise a reversal of
sorts, but in each instance there is a qualifying word or phrase, such as "many," or
"there are [some]," implying not total reversal (as if *all* the last will be first and *all* the
first last), but simply that there will be plenty of surprises when the Kingdom of God
comes. The Apostle Paul applies the principle even to equality between the living and
the dead (see 1 Thess 4:15, where the dead [that is, "the last"] will not only be present
at the last day, but will rise "first." See for further discussion my article, "Everything
That Rises Must Converge: Paul's Word from the Lord."

is about as close to Teilhard de Chardin's universalism as she ever comes. Not everything rises, but everything that rises must converge.

THE MONKEY AND THE BEAR

T. C. Tanner, like Mr. Head and Nelson, and like Julian's mother, wants to get home. In "Judgment Day," the last story in O'Connor's last collection, Tanner is "conserving all his strength for the trip home. He meant to walk as far as he could get and trust to the Almighty to get him the rest of the way." The old man, from Corinth, Georgia lives with his only daughter and her husband in a New York apartment overlooking an alley "full of New York air, the kind fit for cats and garbage" (676). Tanner remembers raising "three boys and her. The three boys were gone, two in the war and one to the devil and there was nobody who felt a duty toward him but her, married and childless, and living in New York City like Mrs. Big" (679). Now he sits by the window ready to leave, with his "blue shirt buttoned at the collar, his coat on the back of the chair, and his hat on his head," waiting only for his daughter to go off shopping, for he "couldn't leave until she got out of the way." It is only a few minutes from this opening scene to the end of the story, when he finally does leave, but most of the story unfolds in a series of flashbacks in Tanner's mind to "two days ago," then to the past summer when his daughter had come south to offer him a home with her in New York, then thirty years back, and finally to the several weeks that had passed since he first arrived in the big city.

In the first flashback, Tanner remembers overhearing a conversation between his daughter and her husband, a long distance truck driver off for three days with a moving van. She advised her husband to get a hat because "People that are somebody wear hats. Other kinds wear those leather caps like you got on." But her husband only made fun of "him in there," who does nothing but "sit all day with that hat on. Sits all day with that damn black hat on his head. Inside!" To Tanner's delight, his daughter had defended him. "He was somebody when he was somebody," she had said, remembering that "He never worked for nobody in his life but himself, and he had people—other people—working for him." It comes out that the "other people" were blacks: "'Niggers is what he had working for him,' the son-in-law said, 'That's all. I've worked a nigger or two myself,' and the daughter replied, "Those were just nawthun niggers you worked" and she added, "It takes brains to work a real nigger. You got to know how to handle them" (677). An argument almost started that would have warmed

Tanner's heart, but it did not end well when the son-in-law finally changed the subject: "Where you going to bury him?" "Right here in New York," the daughter replied. "Where do you think? We got a lot. I'm not taking that trip down there again with anybody." Satisfied, her husband said as he left, "I just wanted to make sure." Old Tanner was furious. "You promised you'd bury me there," he said when his daughter came back into the room. "Your promise ain't any good. Your promise ain't any good. Your promise ain't any good," and shaking all over said, "Bury me here and burn in hell" as he fell back in his chair. "You ain't dead yet!" she answered. "And don't throw hell at me. I don't believe in it. That's a lot of hardshell Baptist hooey," she added as she finally retreated to the kitchen, talking to herself (678).

To old Tanner, hell is not "hooey," Baptist or otherwise. This becomes clear in the second flashback, recalling his daughter's visit down south the previous summer, when he was living in a shack with a drunken black man named Coleman Parrum, a shack the two of them had built together, located precariously on land that was up for sale. Tanner now remembers that "When Coleman was young, he had looked like a bear; now that he was old he looked like a monkey. With Tanner it was the opposite: when he was young he had looked like a monkey but when he got old, he looked like a bear" (679). His daughter had come South to invite him to live with her, and was shocked by the sight of old Coleman "a stinking skin full of bones," sleeping on the floor. "If you don't have any pride I have," she had said, "and I know my duty and I was raised to do it. My mother raised me to do it. She was from plain people but not the kind that likes to settle in with niggers." Tanner had told her, "Who do you think cooks? Who do you think cuts my firewood and empties my slops? He's paroled to me. That scoundrel has been on my hands for thirty years. He ain't a bad nigger." He had refused her offer, but learned later that summer that the land had been bought by another black man, Doctor Foley, part Indian and part white as well, a prosperous wheeler dealer who was "everything to the niggers—druggist and undertaker and general counsel and real estate man and sometimes he got the evil eye off them and sometimes he put it on" (680). When Foley came, looking over his newly acquired property, Tanner saw the inevitable coming. "This shack ain't in your property," he had said. "Only on it, by mistake," and the Doctor had replied, "It ain't my mistake," and started looking for the still where Tanner and Coleman made hard liquor. "This would have been the time to kill him," Tanner reasoned, but "he had been weakened for that kind of violence by the fear of hell." He had never killed a Negro, but had "always handled them with his wits and with luck" (681).

All of which triggers yet a third flashback, to thirty years earlier when Tanner first met Coleman Parrum. He had been working a group of six blacks at a sawmill deep in the woods when he kept noticing a surly Coleman off to the side, either sleeping "like a gigantic bear on his back" or watching the others work, and by his very presence tempting them not to. When they began taking their lunch break a half hour early, Tanner had without hesitation "gone to the source of the trouble" (682). His first thought was to threaten the intruder with his knife and send him on his way, but something changed his mind, back then not the fear of hell but the thought that this stranger might have a knife of his own. Instead, Tanner used his knife for something he had gotten into the habit of doing, whittling a piece of bark to conceal a shaking in his hands. He never knew what his idle whittling would produce, and this time, before he knew it, he had made "two holes the size of half dollars in the piece of bark." To his surprise, he had the makings of a pair of spectacles. "You can't see so good, can you boy?" Tanner said, fashioning the spectacles from two pieces of wire he found underfoot. "'Put these on,' he said, 'I hate to see anybody can't see good.'" Coleman could have crushed the glasses in his hand, or grabbed the knife and stabbed him, but he did not. Tanner could see "the exact instant in the muddy liquor-swollen eyes when the pleasure of having a knife in this white man's gut was balanced against something else, he could not tell what." Instead, the black man took the glasses: "He attached the bows carefully behind his ears and looked forth. He peered this way and that with exaggerated solemnity. And then he looked directly at Tanner and grinned, or grimaced, Tanner could not tell which, but he had an instant's sensation of seeing before him a negative image of himself, as if clownishness and captivity had been their common lot. The vision failed him before he could decipher it" (683).

A comic moment, like Julian's mother "meeting herself coming and going" on a bus, but a revelatory moment as well, like Mr. Head and Nelson gazing at a piece of statuary. Unlike other such moments in O'Connor's fiction, it is the beginning of a negotiation, a kind of rhetorical dance, a rare instance in which Southern manners cross racial lines. "Preacher," Tanner began, "what are you hanging around here for?" And, carving another piece of bark, "This ain't Sunday." Coleman, willing to play the game, replies, "This here ain't Sunday?" "This is Friday," Tanner told him, "That's the way with you preachers—drunk all week so you don't know when

Sunday is. What you see through those glasses?" "See a man." "What kind of a man?" "See the man make theseyer glasses." "Is he white or black?" "He white!" Coleman decided, "as if only at that moment was his vision sufficiently improved to detect it." "Yessuh, he white!" he repeated, and Tanner said, "Well, you treat him like he was white" (683–84).

The racism behind Tanner's strategy is undeniable, but the outcome had not been what he planned. What prevailed over the years was not his supposed racial superiority, but the vision he could not decipher, the vision of Coleman as his own mirror image and the "common lot" the two men shared, of "clownishness and captivity." Doctor Foley was a different matter altogether. Thirty years later, as Tanner watched the Doctor searching for his still, he remembered that he had never gotten rid of Coleman: "You make a monkey out of one of them and he jumps on your back and stays there for life, but let one make a monkey out of you and all you can do is kill him or disappear. And he was not going to hell for killing a nigger." And so another negotiation began, with a very different black man and a very different outcome. "Where's your still?" Foley asked. Tanner played dumb, and the Doctor offered to let him stay on the land on one condition. "If you want to run the still for me, that's one thing," he said. "If you don't, you might as well be packing up." Tanner replied, "The government ain't got around yet to forcing the white folks to work for the colored" (684). For him, as for Ruby Turpin and Julian's mother, the issue was whether or not "the bottom rail is on top." So far as he was concerned it was not, but the Doctor told him that the day was coming "when the white folks IS going to be working for the colored and you might's well to git ahead of the crowd." "That day ain't coming for me," Tanner said. "Done come for you," Foley replied, "Ain't come for the rest of them." Tanner played his last card: "I got a daughter in the north," he finally said, "I don't have to work for you." The Doctor "appeared to have measured and to know secretly the time it would take the world to turn upside down." His parting shot was, "I be back here next week," and "if you still here, I know you going to work that still for me."

So it was that Tanner had come north, but now he regrets it: "If he had known it was a question of this—sitting here looking out the window all day in this no-place, or just running a still for a nigger, he would have run the still for the nigger. He would have been a nigger's white nigger any day" (685). His daughter, still irritated by his "hardshell Baptist hooey," urges him to turn his chair away from the window and look at the TV instead, so as to "quit thinking about morbid stuff, death and hell and judgment. My Lord." But old Tanner will not be moved: "The Judgment is coming," he replies, "The sheep'll be separated from the goats. Them that kept their promises from them that didn't. Them that did the best they could with what they had from them that didn't. Them that honored their father and mother from them that cursed them. Them that . . ." His voice is drowned out by his daughter's loud sigh, asking herself "What's the use in me wasting my good breath?" (686). At some level the old man is remembering Matthew 25:32, "All the nations shall be gathered together before him, and he shall separate them one from another, as the shepherd separateth the sheep from the goats," but his criteria for judgment, above all promise keeping and honoring one's parents, are drawn more from the Bible in general than from any one passage, and above all from his own frustration with his daughter.

From here on, the old man revisits in his mind the weeks that have passed since his arrival in New York. He imagines his old friend Coleman by his side on a tour his daughter had taken him on through the streets of New York, with its "underground railroad," and the "steps that moved under you while you stood still," and the "elevator to the thirty-fourth floor." In his mind he heard Coleman say, "What we doing here? Where you get this fool idea coming here?" He knew what he would have said: "I come to show you it was no kind of place. Now you know you were well off where you were," and he could almost hear Coleman's answer: "I knowed it before, Coleman said. Was you didn't know it." That was the fantasy. The reality was a brief note from Coleman, written for him by W. T. Hooten, the white man at the railroad station: "This is Coleman–X–howyou boss," to which he had written back, "This place is alrite if you like it. Yours truly, T. C. Tanner" (686–87). But secretly he made plans, as soon as his pension check came, to go home and take Foley up on his offer.

Instead he encountered yet a third black man, one of "the new kind," as O'Connor might have put it. Driven by a conviction that he was gifted with the ability to "handle" blacks, he repeatedly tried to initiate a conversation or negotiation of some kind with this man, just as he had done successfully with Coleman and unsuccessfully with Doctor Foley. A series of encounters began just three weeks after he had come to live with his daughter. The people living next door had moved out and Tanner stood in the hall watching a new couple move in, "a large negro in a light blue suit" followed by "a young tan-skinned woman with bright copper-colored hair" (687). The woman noticed that "there's an old guy watching," and as they turned to look at him Tanner said "Had-do," and quickly slipped back into his daughter's apartment. "A South Alabama nigger if I ever saw one," he told his daughter with unconcealed glee. "And got him this high-yeller, high-stepping woman with a red wig and they two are going to live next door to you!" The second encounter came twenty minutes later. Confident that the stranger "would like to talk to someone who understood him," Tanner kept lurking in the hall until he saw him come out, having "put on a tie and a pair of horn-rimmed spectacles." "A real swell," Tanner thought, noticing the man's small but elegant goatee, and he said "Haddy John," but the black man seemed not to hear and hurried down the stairs (688). The third encounter was the next morning, when Tanner abruptly greeted the man coming out of his apartment and began the kind of negotiation that had worked so well with Coleman. "Good morning, Preacher," he began. "I seen you move in," he continued. "I ain't been up here long myself. It ain't much of a place if you ask me. I reckon you wish you were back in South Alabama." "I'm not from South Alabama," the man replied angrily. "I'm from New York city. And I'm not a preacher! I'm an actor." "It's a little actor in most preachers, ain't it," Tanner persisted. "I don't preach!" the stranger cried, and disappeared down the stairs (689–90).

The fourth encounter was the worst. Late that afternoon, Tanner was waiting for his black neighbor as he came up the stairs. "Good evening, Preacher," he greeted him, and the man grabbed Tanner by both shoulders. "I don't take no crap," he said, "off no wool-hat red-neck son-of-a-bitch peckerwood old bastard like you," and then added, as if channeling Hazel Motes, "And I'm not a preacher! I'm not a Christian. I don't believe in that crap. There ain't no Jesus and there ain't no God." All hope of negotiation or any kind of ritual of Southern manners was gone. "And you ain't black," the old man said, "And I ain't white!" It was the only Christian testimony of which he was capable, in the words of Ralph Wood, "his own unashamed testimony that the God of Jesus Christ is as real as skin color" (*O'Connor and the Christ-Haunted South*, 140). With that, the black man hurled him first against the wall and then against the edge of his own inside door. "Hard as his head was," he now remembered, "the fall cracked it and when he got over the concussion he had a little stroke" (690).

These then were the events leading up to the moment at which the story begins, with Tanner dressed up, waiting for his daughter to leave so that he could start out for home. Pinned to his pocket was a note that said, "If found dead ship express collect to Coleman Parrum, Corinth, Georgia," with instructions to "sell my belongings and pay the freight on me & the undertaker. Anything left over you can keep. Yours truly, T. C. Tanner.

P.S. Stay where you are. Don't let them talk you into coming up here. It's no kind of place" (676). He kept dreaming of arriving at the Corinth station in a pine box, hearing Coleman and Hooten getting ready to open it up, then pushing upward with both hands, sitting straight up in the box and yelling. "'Judgment Day! Judgment Day!' he would cry, 'Don't you two fools know it's Judgment Day?'" It was his own self-made death vision, fashioned well in advance and transformed into a prank (691–92).

As soon as his daughter was out the door, overcoming his fear that he would "never get there dead or alive," Tanner stood up, pushed a foot forward without falling and moved toward the sofa. "'The Lord is my shepherd,' he muttered, 'I shall not want.'" Psalm 23 in the King James version, just as we would expect from an old "hardshell Baptist." Tanner is certain at last that no one is going to bury him here, "as confident as if the woods of home lay at the bottom of the stairs" (693). But his legs give out under him as he heads toward the stairs, and he catches himself only by hanging on to the banister post with both hands. Then he falls, landing upside down halfway down the flight of stairs. As he loses consciousness, his prank turns back into a death vision: he is in the pine box again, listening for Coleman's footsteps. Finally he hears them "ratttling closer and closer," and then Coleman's voice: "'He in there,' Coleman said, 'one of his tricks,'" and "It's him. Git the crowbar." Then a shaft of light and Tanner crying out, "Judgment Day! Judgment Day. You idiots didn't know it was Judgment Day, did you?" At last, hesitantly: "Coleman?"

The black face looking down at him with "a large surly mouth and sullen eyes" is not Coleman's. "Oh," Tanner says, "it's you," and the actor grabs him by his shirt. " 'Judgment day,' he said in a mocking voice, 'There's not any judgment day, old man. Except this. Maybe this here is judgment day for you.'" Then, quite unexpectedly, Tanner resumes a playful negotiation that had never actually begun, as he "lifted his hand, as light as a breath, and said in his jauntiest voice, 'Hep me up, Preacher. I'm on my way home!'" This may be the closest we come anywhere in O'Connor's fiction to the grandmother's exclamation to The Misfit, "Why you're one of my babies. You're one of my own children!" Even Tanner's body language faintly recalls the grandmother's toward The Misfit, as "She reached out and touched him on the shoulder." In the same way that she rcognized The Misfit as one of her own, old Tanner has recognized the black actor. He knows who the actor is ("Oh, it's you"), and yet he can see in the black man's face the common humanity, the "clownishness and captivity" that we all share, as the face becomes that of his old friend Coleman, whom he knows he can call "Preacher" and who will gladly bring him home.

The actor's response to "Hep me up, Preacher. I'm on my way home!" is just as quick and just as deadly as The Misfit's response to the grandmother. Old Tanner ends up with his hat "pulled down over his face and his head and arms thrust between the spokes of the banister." In the end, "They cut him out with a saw and said he had been dead about an hour." And he is on his way home. His daughter "buried him in New York city, but after she had done it she could not sleep at night." His "hardshell Baptist" words, "Bury me here and burn in hell!" seem to have kept ringing in her ears, for "Night after night she turned and tossed and very definite lines began to appear in her face, so she had him dug up and shipped the body to Corinth. Now she rests well at night and her good looks have mostly returned" (695). The "crow-filled tree" which O'Connor once speculated might some day take root in The Misfit's heart (*Mystery and Manners*, 113), seems to have found its place not in the black actor's heart but in hers. Yet one way or another, white and black in the persons of T. C. Tanner and Coleman Parrum are reunited, in this world and the next. The rising and convergence that does not quite happen in "The Artificial Nigger," or even in "Everything That Rises Must Converge," is finally under way in this last O'Connor story.

12

The New Testament
Wedded to the Old

IF "JUDGMENT DAY" is O'Connor's last story, "Parker's Back" is a close second. Even though she had been working on both for quite some time—in the case of "Judgment Day" her whole writing career[1]—she was putting finishing touches on both almost to the day of her death. And because she was dying when she finished them, her letters offer fewer guidelines than usual for reading them. For example, her description of "Parker's Back" over three years before her death, seems to have little to do with the story as it actually turned out: "The latest I have got to add to my collection is one of a man who has just had Christ tattooed on his back. This is obviously for artistic and not religious purposes as he also has tiger and panther heads and an eagle perched on a cannon" (*Collected Works*, 1145). In fact, of course, the tattoo on Parker's back had everything to do with his, not to mention O'Connor's, "religious purposes."

HERETIC OR BIBLE BELIEVER?

O'Connor's last and better known comment on the story came just nine days before her death, as a clarification of something Caroline Gordon had said. "No Caroline didn't mean the tattoos were the heresy," she wrote to Betty Hester. "Sarah Ruth was the heretic—the notion that you can worship in pure spirit" (*Collected Works*, 1218; 25 July, 1964). The heresy

---

1. This is because "The Geranium," her very first story in the collection that comprised her 1947 Master's thesis at the University of Iowa, was in some sense already the first draft of "Judgment Day."

remark seems to have been something the dying O'Connor did not originate but simply accepted and passed along. Gordon had commended her on successfully "dramatizing a heresy," and O'Connor had replied that she did not set out to do so, even while admitting that "the spirit moveth where it listest" (*Collected Works*, 1217; 17 July, 1964). Yet that one brief comment has cast a very long shadow in O'Connor criticism. The heretic label stuck, and the reputation of O. E. Parker's wife, Sarah Ruth, has suffered accordingly. The nature of her heresy has even been spelled out by O'Connor scholars as "Gnostic" or "Manichaean," based on Caroline Gordon's comment. Typical of many are Ralph Wood, who calls Sarah Ruth a "gnostic believer" (*O'Connor and the Christ Haunted South*, 45, 49) and Helen Andretta, who defines her in terms of both Gnosticism and Manicheism. Andretta describes Gnosticism, more or less accurately, as "distinguishing the spiritual and good world from the evil and material world," and Manicheism as "a radical dualism," in which "spirit represents Light and matter represents Darkness" ("Hylomorphic Sacramentalism," 48–49).

All this is based solely on Sarah Ruth's comment to Parker near the end of the story that God is "a spirit. No man shall see his face" (674), giving voice to her shock, not simply at the tattoos with which her husband had covered his body, but at the one tattoo of the face of a "Byzantine Christ with all-demanding eyes" (667) that now decorated his back. Is it enough to brand Sarah Ruth Parker as a heretic? She is, after all, merely quoting Scripture. "Thou canst not see my face," God told Moses, "for man shall not see me and live" (Exod 33:20); and God *is* spirit according to the Old Testament, as even Jesus the Jew reminded a Samaritan woman (John 4:24).

While heretics are known for their ability to quote Scripture, Sarah Ruth's biblical allusions betray no obvious Gnostic or Manichaean tendencies. The Old Testament *does* forbid making "to thyself any graven thing, nor the likeness of any thing that is in heaven above, or in the earth beneath, nor of those things that are in the waters under the earth" (Exod 20:4), and the Israelites *were* reminded that "You saw not any similitude in the day that the Lord spoke to you in Horeb from the midst of the fire: Lest perhaps being deceived you might make you a graven similitude, or image of male or female, the similitude of any beasts, that are upon the earth, or of birds, that fly under heaven, or of creeping things, that move upon the earth, or of fishes, that abide in the waters under the earth" (Deut 4:15–18). When Sarah Ruth exclaims, "Vanity of vanities" (660), and charges Parker with "Enflaming yourself with idols under every green tree!" (674), she speaks with an Old Testament voice,[2] while the ancient heresy of Gnosticism hated and rejected the Old Testament as the revelation of an inferior and ignorant god. Moreover, contrary to conventional wisdom, one of our earliest witnesses to ancient Gnosticism (admittedly not a friendly witness) associates that heresy precisely with the use of images. Irenaeus in the second century speaks of those who

> style themselves Gnostics. They also possess images, some of them painted, and others formed from different kinds of material; while they maintain that a likeness of Christ was made by Pilate at the time when Jesus lived among them. They crown these images and set them up along with the images of the philosophers of the world; that is to say, with the images of Pythagoras, and Plato, and Aristotle, and the rest. They have also other modes of honouring these images, after the manner of the Gentiles. (Irenaeus, *Against Heresies* 1.25.6; ANF, 1.351)

Even Brian Abel Ragen, who follows the conventional wisdom in linking Sarah Ruth to the Gnostics and Manichaeans, nevertheless admits that she evidently "reads the Old Testament of her Bible more than the New," and that "Her faith is concerned more with the law than with the person of Jesus," so that she is, in short, "a Pharisee; she means to keep the law, but does not know Jesus" (*Wreck on the Road*, 47–48, 52).

Sarah Ruth Parker is not a "gnostic believer," therefore, but an Old Testament believer. This could mean an Israelite, a Jew, a Muslim, a Puritan, or a certain kind of Protestant fundamentalist, the last of which is what she actually is. Her father, we learn, is a "Straight Gospel preacher" who for the time being is "away, spreading it in Florida" (662). Fundamentalists, like Jews, Muslims, and Puritans, do tend to be iconoclasts, but none of them have any inherent distaste for material things, nor does Sarah Ruth. She hungers for the apples and peaches Parker brings her, and tells him, "You ought to go back to selling the fruits of the earth" (664). Nor is she, as has been charged, an ascetic like some ancient gnostics, scandalized by "erotic nakedness" (Wood, *O'Connor and the Christ Haunted South*, 45). She is, after all, pregnant with Parker's child, evidently because while she preferred him "dressed and with his sleeves rolled up," there was one exception: "in total darkness" (663). And at the end of the story when Parker

---

2. For the former, see Ecclesiastes 1:2 and the book of Ecclesiastes generally; for the latter, several passages, but most conspicuously Isaiah 57:5, "Who seek your comfort in idols under every green tree."

comes home and she tells him, "you ain't going to have none of me," she significantly adds a qualifying phrase: "this near morning" (674).

As an Old Testament believer, Sarah Ruth's closest kin in O'Connor's fiction is Francis Marion Tarwater, whose vision of what it meant to be a prophet was, as we have seen, a distinctly Old Testament vision. To be sure, his Old Testament was far more splendid, more imaginative than hers, with "wheels of light and strange beasts with giant wings of fire," and Moses's burning bush, and Joshua's long day, and Daniel in the lions' den. But his expectation was at least something she would have recognized: "a voice from out of a clear and empty sky," something "untouched by any fleshly hand or breath." He wanted nothing so physical or so humiliating as "the sweat and stink of the cross," or "spending eternity eating the bread of life." The point is not that an Old Testament vision disdains the flesh as evil. The flesh and the material world are God's creation. The point is rather that *because* the flesh is God's creation, it is not God. God is not flesh, as Sarah Ruth knew, but "a spirit," and consequently "No man shall see his face." With this even the New Testament agrees (John 1:18 and 1 John 4:10, "No man hath seen God at any time"). The Old Testament affirms both flesh and spirit, but keeps them distinct, and with this even Jesus agrees: "That which is born of the flesh is flesh, and that which is born of the Spirit is spirit" (John 3:7).

What then differentiates the New Testament from the Old? The Old Testament points toward a coming Messiah, or Anointed One, who will one day judge the world. Sarah Ruth knew all about that, for she told Parker, "At the judgement seat of God, Jesus is going to say to you, 'What you been doing all your life besides have pictures drawn all over you?'" (663–64). Yet nothing in the Old Testament quite prepares its readers for the resounding news, "And the Word was made flesh, and dwelt among us; and we saw his glory, the glory as it were of the only-begotten of the Father, full of grace and truth" (John 1:14). Nor does it fully prepare anyone for the New Testament corollaries added to the acknowledgement that "No man hath seen God at any time"—in one instance, "the only-begotten Son, who is in the bosom of the Father, he hath declared him" (John 1:18), and in another, "If we love one another, God abideth in us; and his charity is perfected in us" (1 John 4:10). When St. Augustine wrote in his *Confessions* that when he looked into "certain books of the Platonists" he did not find it written "that the Word was made flesh and dwelt among us" (7.9), he could as well have been referring to the Old Testament. It was by no means a foregone conclusion that Old Testament believers would be ready to accept the notion of the God of Israel coming into the world in human flesh, and in fact most of them were not ready. Just three verses before the notice that "the Word was made flesh," we are told that "He came unto his own, and his own received him not" (John 1:11). Sarah Ruth, accordingly, when she finally looks at the face of God enfleshed on her husband's back, can only reply, "It ain't anybody I know" (674).

The Love Story

How did Parker and Sarah Ruth get to this point? If she is in some sense an Old Testament believer, how does that affect our reading of the story? Sarah Ruth is first seen through Parker's eyes as she snaps beans on their front porch of the house they rented, "alone save for a single tall pecan tree," on an embankment overlooking a highway: "Parker was sitting on the step, some distance away, watching her sullenly. She was plain, plain. The skin on her face was thin and drawn as tight as the skin on an onion and her eyes were grey and sharp like the points of two icepicks" (655). From here on the story is told from Parker's viewpoint, up until the very end where the tables are turned and the point of view abruptly changes. Now we look at Parker through Sarah Ruth's "icepick" eyes, as "she looked toward the pecan tree and her eyes hardened still more. There he was— who called himself Obadiah Elihue—leaning against the tree, crying like a baby" (675). Two visions of each other, neither one flattering, yet framing a love story—except for "A View of the Woods," the only love story O'Connor ever wrote.

Parker's story, like old Tanner's, is told in flashbacks. In the first flashback, he remembers how his truck had broken down on the highway and when he noticed Sarah Ruth watching him he had—without quite knowing why—tried to get her attention by feigning an injury to his hand and yelling loud blasphemies: "Without warning a terrible bristly claw slammed the side of his face and and he fell backwards on the hood of the truck. 'You don't talk no filth here!' a voice close to him shrilled. Parker's vision was so blurred that for an instant he thought he had been attacked by some creature from above, a giant hawk-eyed angel wielding a hoary weapon. As his sight cleared, he saw before him a tall raw-boned girl with a broom" (656). In a corresponding scene at the story's end, "the broom" is still in play. When Parker tells Sarah Ruth, by then his wife, that the picture of Christ on his back is in fact a picture of God, she screams, "Idolatry!" and "grabbed up the broom and began to thrash him across the shoulder with it" (674). No broom has been mentioned in the context. "*The* broom" looks back to the earlier broom-wielding scene, as well as another occasion when he brought her apples and "she did nothing to acknowledge his presence. He might have been a stray pig or goat that had wandered into the yard and she too tired to take up the broom and send it off" (660). Hardly the makings of a love story here, and yet from the start a kind of love-hate relationship is going on. Parker becomes another of O'Connor's gentleman callers, a distant cousin to Tom T. Shiftlet and Manley Pointer, yet at the same time their opposite number. Not only do neither of them know anything of genuine love, but both of them know what they want and Parker does not. Parker does not even know why he does what he does. He is driven by twin impulses driving him in what looks like opposite directions: in one his desire to cover his whole body with tattoos, and in the other his desire for Sarah Ruth.

In a second flashback, Parker remembers himself at the age of fourteen, "heavy and earnest, as ordinary as a loaf of bread," and a tattooed man he once saw at a fair, a "small and sturdy" man who "moved about on the platform, flexing his muscles so that the arabesque of men and beasts and flowers on his skin appeared to have a subtle motion of its own" (657–58). The vision had stayed with him. He got his first tattoo at fifteen, quit school at sixteen, lied about his age and joined the navy. All over the world, wherever the navy sent him, he kept picking up tattoos, everywhere on his body except his back, for he "had no desire for one anywhere he could not readily see it himself" (658–59). Yet he was never satisfied. When he would look at himself in a mirror, "the effect was not of one intricate arabesque of colors but of something haphazard and botched. A huge dissatisfaction would come over him and he would go off and find another tattooist and have another space filled up." He felt as if "the panther and the lion and the serpents and the eagles and the hawks had penetrated his skin and lived inside him in a raging warfare." After five months in the navy he went AWOL, "drunk, in a rooming house in a city he did not know," until the navy finally caught up with him, "put him in the brig for nine months and then gave him a dishonorable discharge" (659). It was then that he decided "country air was the only kind fit to breathe," rented a shack, bought an old truck, sold apples by the pound from house to house and met his future wife.

With this recollection, the first flashback resumes, rehearsing the courtship of O. E. Parker and Sarah Ruth Cates (659–64). Sarah Ruth liked none of his tattoos, but allowed that "the chicken is not as bad as the rest," mistaking an eagle for a chicken. Parker was convinced that she "liked him even though she insisted that pictures on the skin were vanity of vanities and even after hearing him curse, and even after she had asked him if he was saved and he had replied that he didn't see it was anything in particular to save him from." He had added, "I'd be saved enough if you was to kiss me," and she, scowling, had answered, "That ain't being saved" (662–63). When she refused to have sex until they were married, Parker "made up his mind then and there to have nothing to do with her," yet in the very next breath we are told that "They were married in the County Ordinary's office because Sarah Ruth thought churches were idolatrous." As Parker confides at the beginning of the story, he "understood why he had married her—he couldn't have got her any other way—but he couldn't understand why he stayed with her now" (655).

SOMETHING BETTER THAN THE BIBLE

Now that they are married, things have gotten worse. Sarah Ruth is jealous of the woman he worked for, a woman he told her was "a hefty young blonde" but was actually "nearly seventy years old and too dried up to have an interest in anything except getting as much work out of him as she could" (655). Still dissatisfied with his tattoos, Parker is dissatisfied with his marriage as well: "Every morning he decided he had had enough and would not return that night; every night he returned. Whenever Parker couldn't stand the way he felt, he would have another tattoo, but the only surface left on him now was his back" (663). Finally the dissatisfaction grows so great "that there was no containing it outside of a tattoo. It had to be his back. There was no help for it" (664). And if it was on his back it would not be for himself, for he could not see it, but for Sarah Ruth. The twin impulses in opposite directions, his love for tattoos and his love for Sarah Ruth, finally turn out to be a single impulse in a single direction. But what will he put on his back? His first thought is a Bible, "an open book with HOLY BIBLE tattooed under it and an actual verse printed on the page." What better gift for a Bible Christian than a Bible? But Parker knows what Sarah Ruth will say—"Ain't I already got a real Bible?"—and he decides that he needs "something even better than the Bible." He begins to lose both sleep and weight over it, becoming "generally nervous and irritable, and he developed a little tic in the side of his face." From here on, Parker is driven, much as Hazel Motes or Tarwater were driven, not just toward another tattoo or toward Sarah Ruth, but toward God. He had had feelings before "as if someone were after you, the navy or the government or religion" (661), and now it is worse: "Once or twice he found himself turning around abruptly as if someone were trailing him" (664).

The moment of truth comes one day while Parker is driving a tractor and hay bailer around the field of the old woman for whom he works. The field is cleared and wide open "save for one enormous old tree standing in the middle of it," a tree the old woman had warned him to be sure not to hit as he picked up the hay:

> As he circled the field his mind was on a suitable design for his back. The sun, the size of a golf ball, began to switch regularly from in front to behind him, but he appeared to see it both places as if he had eyes in the back of his head. All at once he saw the tree reaching out to grasp him. A ferocious thud propelled him into the air, and he heard himself yelling in an unbelievably loud voice, "GOD ABOVE!" He landed on his back while the tractor crashed upside-down into the tree and burst into flame. The first thing Parker saw were his shoes, quickly being eaten by the fire; one was caught under the tractor, the other was some distance away, burning by itself. He was not in them. (665)

No mere "creature from above" this time, no "giant hawk-eyed angel wielding a hoary weapon," but a Moses-like encounter with the living God, enough to make Parker as much of an Old Testament believer as the woman he married.

God is on the scene in classic O'Connor fashion, in the golf-ball size sun before and behind him, and the biblical echoes of Moses and the burning bush are readily apparent, right down to the loss of his shoes. As for Moses in the book of Exodus,

> the Lord appeared to him in a flame of fire out of the midst of a bush: and he saw that the bush was on fire and was not burnt. And Moses said: I will go and see this great sight, why this bush is not burnt. And when the Lord saw that he went forward to see, he called to him out of the midst of the bush, and said: Moses, Moses. And he answered: Here I am. And he said: Come not nigh hither. Put off the shoes from thy feet: for the place whereupon thou standest is holy ground. (Exod 3:2–5)

Just as Parker did not know whether the sun was behind him or in front of him, now he does not know whether to move forward or back: "He scrambled backwards, still sitting, his eyes cavernous," we are told, and the Catholic narrator assures us in an O'Connor-like aside that "if he had known how to cross himself he would have done it." Then he moves toward his truck, "still sitting, still backwards," until "halfway to it he got up and began a kind of forward-bent run," reaches the truck and drives off, knowing that "there had been a great change in his life, a leap forward into a worse unknown, and that there was nothing he could do about it" (665–66).

Parker heads for the city, and a tattoo artist he has used before, knowing now that he has already shouted aloud what, or rather Who, he wants on his back: "GOD ABOVE!" The burning tree has done its work. The Old Testament has pointed him to the New. The footsteps of Moses have led him straight to the God made visible in the person of Jesus Christ, just as Jesus told the Jewish leaders: "For if you did believe Moses, you would perhaps believe me also; for he wrote of me" (John 5:46). So when the tattoo artist asks him, "Who are you interested in," whether "saints, angels, Christs or what?" Parker replies "God." "Father, Son or Spirit?" the artist persists. "Just God," Parker tells him "Christ. I don't care. Just so it's God" (666). And he finds the picture he is looking for in the artist's book by working his way from the back of the book "where the up-to-date pictures were," toward the front: "Some of them he recognized—The Good Shepherd, Forbid Them Not, The Smiling Jesus, Jesus the Physician's Friend, but he kept turning rapidly backwards and the pictures become less and less reassuring." As he nears the front of the book "a pair of eyes glanced at him swiftly." He hurries on, but an "absolute silence" abruptly stops him, telling him "as plainly as if silence were a language itself, GO BACK," and he sees "the haloed head of a flat stern Byzantine Christ with all-demanding eyes," which he knows he must have, "just like it is or nothing" (667). Here in the tattoo parlor just as before on the ground beside his burning tractor, Parker moves forward by going backward, recalling once again the paradoxes so evident in the New Testament: that the way up is down (Matt 23:12), that the poor are the truly rich (Luke 6:20, Jas 1:9), that the last are first (Matt 20:16), that the blind are those who see (John 9:39), and that those who lose their life save it (Mark 8:35).

Parker has the tattoo done, although the eyes will take another day. That night in the Haven of Light Christian Mission, he longs unaccountably for Sarah Ruth: "Her sharp tongue and icepick eyes were the only comfort he could bring to mind. He decided that he was losing it. Her eyes appeared soft and dilatory compared with the eyes in the book, for even though he could not summon up the exact look of those eyes, he could still feel their penetration" (669). The next day, when the eyes of the Byzantine Christ are in place on his back, he does not want to look at them, and when the tattoo artist compels him to with the help of double mirrors, he "looked, turned white and moved away. The eyes in the reflected face continued to look at him—still, straight, all-demanding, enclosed in silence" (670). Fortunately he does not have to look again, and cannot, except with mirrors. His shirt, moreover, covers the face and eyes of Christ like a veil— pulled up momentarily by his cronies in the pool hall, only to be dropped again instantly, "like a veil over the face." Again, "a silence in the pool room which seemed to Parker to grow from the circle around him until it extended to the foundations under the building and upward through the beams in the room"[3]—silence broken by a shouted "Christ!" and a riot that ends with Parker being thrown out into an alley. Then "a calm descended on the pool hall as if the long barn-like room were the ship from which Jonah had been cast into the sea" (671; see Jonah 1:15, "And they took Jonas and cast him into the sea: and the sea ceased from raging").

Like Jonah too, Parker struggles with a call, one that has so far gone unrecognized. In "examining his soul," he sees it as "a spider web of facts and lies," and he comes to understand that "The eyes that were now forever on his back were eyes to be obeyed. He was as certain of it as he had ever been of anything. Throughout his life, grumbling and sometimes cursing, often afraid, once in rapture, Parker had obeyed whatever instinct of this kind had come to him—in rapture when his spirit had lifted at the sight of the tattooed man at the fair, afraid when he had joined the navy, grumbling when he had married Sarah Ruth." The last of these instincts, now firmly in league with the "all-demanding eyes" on his back, impels him to finish what he had set out to do. Sarah Ruth "would know what he had to do. She would clear up the rest of it, and she would at least be pleased" (672).

THE VEIL

Parker goes straight to the house with the pecan tree on the embankment where he and Sarah Ruth live, and knocks on the door. It has no lock, but "she had evidently placed the back of a chair against the knob." Three times her voice from within asks, "Who's There?" and Parker keeps answering, "Me, O. E.," or just "O. E.," or "O. E. Parker" (673). They had played this game before, when they were courting, and Sarah Ruth had asked him,

3. The repeated accent on "silence" in connection with Parker's Christ recalls Ignatius' second century letter to the Ephesians, which O'Connor is likely to have known: "The one who truly possesses the word of Jesus is able to hear his silence as well" (Ignatius, *To the Ephesians* 15.2; *The Apostolic Fathers*. Loeb Classical Library, 1.235).

with "just a hint of flirtatiousness," what the initials stood for. Finally and reluctantly he had revealed his name to her, a name he had never revealed to anyone, "only to the files of the navy and the government," the name that stood "on his baptismal record which he got at the age of a month; his mother was a Methodist." "Obadiah Elihue," he had told her, and in returned she had introduced herself as "Sarah Ruth Cates" (662). The biblical names (all four of them) are unrelated, yet deeply evocative of the Old Testament. Sarah was Abraham's wife, one of the four matriarchs of Israel; Ruth was a foreigner adopted into the line of Sarah's descendants and the royal ancestry of King David (Ruth 4:17–22; Matt 1:5); Obadiah was a writing prophet whose name means "Servant of the Lord"; Elihue, the name of Job's comforter according to Job 32–37, is Hebrew for "My God is He." Parker had guarded his biblical double name as jealously as Hulga Hopewell in another story guarded the privacy of her wooden leg: "When the name leaked out of the navy files, Parker narrowly missed killing the man who used it." Now Sarah Ruth wants to hear it again, as the price of opening the door and letting her husband in.

Meanwhile something is going on with Parker, who "turned his head as if he expected someone behind him to give him the answer. The sky had lightened slightly and there were two or three streaks of yellow floating above the horizon. Then as he stood there, a tree of light burst over the skyline." The "tree of light" recalls both the burning tree that struck Parker on the tractor and the "phosphorescent cross" in the Haven of Light Christian Mission, where Parker had spent the previous night (669).[4] When the question comes a fourth time, "Who's there, I ast you?" he whispers, "Obadiah," and then "Obadiah Elihue," and "all at once he felt the light pouring through him, turning his spider web soul into a perfect arabesque of colors, a garden of trees and birds and beasts" (673). The presence of "someone behind him," in the form of a "tree of light," at last brings order and beauty to a creation that had before seemed merely "haphazard and botched." It is only when Parker goes "back" to his baptism and his baptismal name, "Obadiah Elihue," that his life and his tattoos begin to have meaning. Sarah Ruth lets him in, but the shining moment does not last.

4. To the student of ancient Christianity, the "tree of light" also recalls the "cross of light" in a passage O'Connor might or might not have known, in the apocryphal *Acts of John* 98, where it is personified as "sometimes mind, sometimes Jesus, sometimes Christ, sometimes door, sometimes a way, sometimes bread, sometimes seed, sometimes resurrection, sometimes Son, sometimes Father, sometimes Spirit, sometimes life, sometimes truth, sometimes faith, sometimes grace" (M. R. James, *The Apocryphal New Testament*, 254–55).

When he removes the veil (that is, takes off his shirt) and shows her the Christ on his back, she sees it at first as just another tattoo: " 'No, who is it?' Sarah Ruth said, 'It ain't anybody I know.' " Only when he tells her that it is God does she scream "Idolatry!" and beat him across the shoulders with the broom, "until she had nearly knocked him senseless and large welts had formed on the face of the tattooed Christ" (674).

Oddly, it is Parker, not Sarah Ruth, who first echoes the Old Testament principle that no one may see God: "'What do you know how he looks?' Parker moaned, 'You ain't seen him.'" Sarah Ruth has jumped to the conclusion that because "No man shall see his face," it follows that "He don't *look*," that is, that God does not have a face. Parker knows better, for he knows that the face of God is the face of Jesus Christ. "Just God," he had told the tattoo artist, "Christ. I don't care. Just so it's God." In short, Sarah Ruth's vision of God is veiled, just as much when the veil is lifted as when it is properly in place. From O'Connor's standpoint even her reading of the Old Testament is faulty because she has failed to take account of the New. In similar fashion the Apostle Paul, commenting on Moses' descent from the mountain with a veil over his face so that the Israelites could not see that the glory was fading away (Exod 34:32–35),[5] concluded that

> until this present day, the selfsame veil, in the reading of the old testament, remaineth not taken away (because in Christ it is made void). But even until this day, when Moses is read, the veil is upon their heart. But when they shall be converted to the Lord, the veil shall be taken away. Now the Lord is the Spirit. And, where the Spirit of the Lord is, there is liberty. But we all, beholding the glory of the Lord with open face, are transformed into the same image from glory to glory, as by the Spirit of the Lord. (2 Cor 3:14–18)

For Sarah Ruth, the veil remains "even until this day," that is, right up to the end of the story. What will happen after that is anyone's guess.

5. Paul's interpretation of the Exodus passage is not altogether clear, least of all to readers of the Douay version, where, following a mistranslation in the Latin Vulgate, Moses's face is said to be "horned" as he comes down from the mountain (Exod 34:30, 35). The verb "shone" in the King James translates a Hebrew word referrring to the emission of a "ray" (of brightness), which could also be translated as "horn." Hence, *cornuta* in the Latin, and "horned" in the Douay Bible, a translation famously graven in stone in Michelangelo's statue of Moses. Even so, Paul's words about the futility of trying to read the Old Testament apart from the new revelation in Christ stand on their own.

To some readers Sarah Ruth is almost redundant at the story's end, even though Parker is last seen through her eyes. Given her interest in his biblical name, his utterance of it should have bonded him with her as well as with his own baptismal past, but it does not. It is arguable that she is not even a reliable witness to what she sees and what has just happened, given her stated impression that he had "called himself Obadiah Elihue." She seems to have forgotten that it was she who had to drag it out of him. And the phrase "called himself" oddly recalls what the schoolteacher Rayber wrote in a journal about old Mason Tarwater, in *The Violent Bear It Away*. That is, that his "fixation of being called by the Lord had its origin in insecurity. He needed the assurance of a call, and so he called himself" (341). The old man in his rage repeated over and over what his nephew had written: "Called myself. I called myself. I, Mason Tarwater called myself!" (341–42). It was as if he were "tied hand and foot inside the schoolteacher's head," or pinned in a straitjacket: "Jonah, Ezekiel, Daniel, he was at that moment all of them—the swallowed, the lowered, the enclosed" (378).

Obviously, Sarah Ruth's use of the phrase "called himself" is different because she is referring merely to Parker's name, not to his call from God. Still, the two are not unrelated, and she is in denial about her own role in making him acknowledge his baptismal name, and with it his Old Testament roots. "Obadiah Elihue" is not simply what he "called himself," but who he is. His is not a conversion story, for he, like Hazel Motes, is saved by becoming what he already was, or at least what he had already become at his baptism. It is as true of him as it is of Haze that "In my end is my beginning." Parker's Old Testament roots, above all his encounter on the tractor with the God of Moses and the burning tree, have led him straight to the Word made flesh, the divine Christ whose "all-demanding eyes" look out at Sarah Ruth from his back. God has been at work in his life all along, but he needs Sarah Ruth to demand that he acknowledge it. The tattoo on his back is there to please her, to fulfill what Parker took to be her wishes, just as the New Testament fulfills the Old. Yet Sarah Ruth herself, the resolute Old Testament believer, is not ready to acknowledge it. As the Apostle Paul might have put it, the veil is still upon her heart.

Most readers, the "religious" ones in particular, have been fairly certain that they know something of Parker's future: he is "leaning against the tree" as if crucified with Christ (Gal 2:19–20, 3:13; Rom 6:6), he bears the wounds of Christ, and he is "crying like a baby," signaling that he has been born again (1 Pet 1:23, 2:2). He will be a Christian disciple, perhaps a prophet, perhaps a martyr, an older version of Hazel Motes or Francis

Marion Tarwater. Not so in the case of Sarah Ruth. In contrast to Parker, her future is genuinely uncertain. Either she is a heretic headed straight for hell, or she will simply disappear, like Enoch Emery in *Wise Blood*, having served her purpose in the story.

What these conventional readings overlook is that Parker and Sarah Ruth are still married, and more than that, she is pregnant with his child. O'Connor's stories rarely deal with marriage. Most of her protagonists are either young unmarried men or women, or else middle-aged or elderly widows or widowers. It is likely, therefore, that when a real marriage is in play, it is meant to be taken seriously. Sarah Ruth would have found it difficult to deny the biblical principle that a man "shall cleave to his wife: and they shall be two in one flesh" (Gen 2:24), and "What therefore God hath joined together, let not man put asunder" (Matt 19:6, Mark 10:9). Parker too, in spite of himself, had found marriage to Sarah Ruth irresistable. Even though "pregnant women were not his favorite kind" (655), her pregnancy had not stood in the way of his desire to make her happy. In short, his destiny and hers are inextricably bound together, and were from the start. Their love-hate relationship matches a kind of love-hate relationship between the two testaments that comprise the Christian Bible. The Old Testament prepares for the New, is "fulfilled" (so Christians claim) in the New, and yet the people of the Old Testament, the Jews, did not accept "the Word made flesh" revealed in the New, but put to death the One who claimed to be their Christ. By the same token, some early Christians threatened to dispense with the Old Testament altogether as a mere tribal history of the Jews, or worse, as the work of a inferior and alien God. But the mainstream Christian churches were unable or unwilling to do so, appropriating instead the Hebrew Bible and claimed it as their own.

This is not to say that Sarah Ruth represents the Jews and Parker the Christians in any kind of allegorical way, only that they can no more divorce or get along without each other than the Old and New Testaments can be pulled asunder. Tim Gautreaux implies as much in "Idols," a 2009 tongue-in-cheek pastiche in *The New Yorker*, in which a repentant "Obie" Parker turns out to have bonded with Sarah Ruth, and has all his tattooes painfully burned off! By turning him into a "long-suffering and moralizing carpenter" (79), Gautreaux seems to want to view him as a Christ figure, which he clearly is not, and yet Gautreaux has grasped something that most readings of the story have not grasped: Parker and Sarah Ruth belong together. The more appealing, and more likely, scenario is that somehow the veil over Sarah Ruth's heart will be lifted, even though we do not know how, that they will stay married, and that she will have Parker's child. In the Apostle Paul's words, "Hath God cast away his people? God forbid!" (Rom 11:1). If it is true that the Old Testament is worthless without the New—heresy in fact, in O'Connor's eyes—it is also true that the New Testament is worthless without the Old. Just as Parker's Old Testament vision led him straight to the New, and to the incarnate Christ, so his New Testament faith cannot dispense with the Old, even in the wake of rejection, tears, and wounds "on the face of the tattooed Christ" (674). The "large welts" on Parker's back only confirm Christ's identity as the One "wounded for our iniquities" (Isa 53:5), by whose bruises Obadiah Elihue Parker and Sarah Ruth Cates Parker will both be healed, and the bond between them restored. Rising and convergence indeed, but as so often in O'Connor's fiction, well beyond the story proper.

In her last published book review a few months before her death, while she was still putting the finishing touches on "Parker's Back," O'Connor praised the English version of an abridged Bible for German school children, entitled *The Kingdom of God*. She liked it because "Old and New Testament are tied in together with quotations in such a way as to assist the teacher to show the child that sacred history is a continuous revelation with the seeds of the future contained in the past" (*Presence of Grace*, 176; *The Southern Cross*, January 9, 1964). Whatever else it may be, "Parker's Back" stands as Flannery O'Connor's last touching testimony, as a Christian and a Roman Catholic, to the unity of what she confessed to be Holy Scripture.

Bibliography

Andretta, Helen R. "The Hylomorphic Sacramentalism of 'Parker's Back.'" In *Inside the Church of Flannery O'Connor: Sacrament, Sacramental, and the Sacred in Her Fiction*, edited by Joanne Halloran McMullen and Jon Parrish Peede, 41–63. Macon, GA: Mercer University Press, 2007.

The Ante-Nicene Fathers. Grand Rapids: Eerdmans, n.d.

The Apostolic Fathers. Loeb Classical Library. Cambridge, MA: Harvard University Press, 2005.

Aquinas, St. Thomas. *The Summa Theologica of Saint Thomas Aquinas I–II*. Great Books of the Western World 19–20. Chicago: University of Chicago Press, 1952.

Augustine, St. *Confessions*. Loeb Classical Library. Cambridge, MA: Harvard University Press, 1989.

Asals, Frederick. *Flannery O'Connor: The Imagination of Extremity*. Athens, GA: University of Georgia Press, 1982.

Barth, Karl. *Church Dogmatics* II.2., trans. G. W. Bromiley et al. Edinburgh: T. & T. Clark, 1957.

Boswell's Life of Johnson in Two Volumes. Humphrey Milford: Oxford University Press, 1924.

Bunyan, John. *The Pilgrim's Progress*. London: Penguin, 1987.

Cassell's Latin Dictionary. Revised by J. R. V. Marchant and J. F. Charles. New York and London: Funk & Wagnalls, n.d.

Danker, F. W. *A Greek-English Lexicon of the New Testament and Other Early Christian Literature*. 3rd ed. Chicago and London: University of Chicago Press, 2000.

Drake, Robert. *Flannery O'Connor. A Critical Essay*. Grand Rapids: Eerdmans, 1966.

Driggers, S. G. and Dunn, R. J. *The Manuscripts of Flannery O'Connor at Georgia College*. Athens, GA: University of Georgia Press, 1989.

Edwards, Jonathan. *The Works of President Edwards in Four Volumes*. New York: Leavitt, Trow, 1844.

Eliot, T. S. *The Complete Poems and Plays 1909–1950*. New York: Harcourt Brace, 1958.

Fitzgerald, Robert. "Introduction." In Flannery O'Connor, *Everything That Rises Must Converge*, vii–xxxiv. New York: Farrar, Straus and Giroux, 1965.

Gautreaux, Tim. "Idols." *The New Yorker* (June 22, 2009) 70–79.

Gentry, Marshall Bruce, *Flannery O'Connor's Religion of the Grotesque*. Jackson: University of Mississippi Press, 1986.

Gooch, Brad. *Flannery: Life of Flannery O'Connor*. Little, Brown, 2009.

Gordon, Sarah. *Flannery O'Connor: The Obedient Imagination*. Athens: University of Georgia Press, 2000.

Graybill, Mark S. "O'Connor's Deep Ecological Vision." *Flannery O'Connor Review* 9 (2011) 1–18.

Hawkes, John. "Flannery O'Connor's Devil." *Sewanee Review* (1962) 395–407.

Hawthorne, Nathaniel. *Tales and Sketches*. New York: Library of America, 1982.

The Holy Bible: Douay Version. London: Catholic Truth Society, 1956.

Hopkins, Gerard Manley. *The Poems of Gerard Manley Hopkins*. London: Oxford Paperback, 1970.

Ingraffia, Brian. "'If Jesus existed I wouldn't be clean': Self Torture in Flannery O'Connor's *Wise Blood*." *Flannery O'Connor Review* 7 (2009) 78–86.

James, M. R. *The Apocryphal New Testament*. Oxford: Clarendon, 1924.

Kilcourse, George. *Flannery O'Connor's Religious Imagination: A World with Everything Off Balance*. New York: Paulist, 2001.

Knox, Ronald A. *The New Testament of Our Lord and Saviour Jesus Christ: A New Translation*. New York: Sheed & Ward, 1946.

Lewis, C. S. *Miracles: A Preliminary Study*. New York: Macmillan, 1947.

———. *The Problem of Pain*. New York: Macmillan, 1948.

McMullen, Joanne Halloran. "Christian but Not Catholic: Baptism in Flannery O'Connor's 'The River.'" In *Inside the Church of Flannery O'Connor: Sacrament, Sacramental, and the Sacred in Her Fiction*, edited by Joanne Halloran McMullen and Jon Parish Peede, 167–88. Macon, GA: Mercer University Press, 2007

Michaels, J. Ramsey. "'The Oldest Nun at the Sisters of Mercy': O'Connor's Saints and Martyrs." *Flannery O'Connor Bulletin* 13 (1984) 80–86.

———. "Off on a New Quest for the Historical Jesus." *Books & Religion* 14 (May/June, 1986) 3–4.

———. "Everything That Rises Must Converge: Paul's Word from the Lord." In *To Tell the Mystery. Essays on New Testament Eschatology in Honor of Robert H. Gundry*, edited by Thomas E. Schmidt and Moisés Silva, 182–95. JSNTSup 100. Sheffield: JSOT, 1994.

———. "A 'World with Devils Filled': The Hawkes-O'Connor Debate Revisited." *Flannery O'Connor Review* 6 (2008) 119–34.

———. "Eating the Bread of Life: Muted Violence in *The Violent Bear It Away*." In *Flannery O'Connor in the Age of Terrorism*, edited by Avis Hewitt and Robert Donahoo, 59–69. Knoxville: University of Tennessee Press, 2010.

Musurillo, Herbert. *The Acts of the Christian Martyrs*. Oxford: Clarendon, 1972.

The New Oxford Annotated Bible. New York: Oxford University Press, 1991.

The New Shorter Oxford Dictionary. Oxford: Clarendon, 1993.

O'Connor, Flannery. *Collected Works*. New York: Library of America, 1988.

———. *The Complete Stories*. New York: Farrar, Straus and Giroux, 1971.

———. *Conversations with Flannery O'Connor*. Edited by Rosemary M. Magee. Jackson: University of Mississippi Press, 1987.

———. *The Habit of Being: Letters Edited and with an Introduction by Sally Fitzgerald*. New York: Farrar, Straus and Giroux, 1979.

———. *Mystery and Manners: Occasional Prose*. Selected and edited by Sally Fitzgerald. New York: Farrar, Straus and Giroux, 1969.

———. *The Presence of Grace and Other Book Reviews by Flannery O'Connor*. Compiled by Leo J. Zuber. Athens: University of Georgia Press, 1983.

Old Testament Pseudepigrapha. 2 vols. Edited by J. H. Charlesworth. Garden City, NY: Doubleday, 1983–85.

Park, Clara Claiborne. "Crippled Laughter: Toward Understanding Flannery O'Connor," *The American Scholar* 51.2 (1982) 249–57.

Percy, Walker. *The Message in the Bottle*. New York: Farrar, Strauss and Giroux, 1975.

————. *The Thanatos Syndrome.* New York: Farrar, Strauss and Giroux, 1987.

Pinnock, Clark H. "The Physical Side of Being Spiritual: God's Sacramental Presence." In *Baptist Sacramentalism,* edited by A. R. Cross and P. E. Thompson, 8–20. Carlisle, UK: Paternoster, 2003.

Ragen, Brian Abel. *A Wreck on the Road to Damascus: Innocence, Guilt and Conversion in Flannery O'Connor.* Chicago: Loyola University Press, 1989.

Scott, R. Neil and Streight, Irwin H., editors. *Flannery O'Connor: The Contemporary Reviews.* Cambridge: Cambridge University Press, 2009.

Sessions, William A. "The Hermeneutics of Suspicion." In *Flannery O'Connor in the Age of Terrorism,* edited by Avis Hewitt and Robert Donahoo, 201–12. Knoxville: University of Tennessee Press, 2010.

Sykes, John D., Jr. "Two Natures: Chalcedon and Coming-of-Age in O'Connor's 'A Temple of the Holy Ghost.'" *Flannery O'Connor Review* 5 (2007) 89–98.

Trowbridge, Charles W. "The Comic Sense of Flannery O'Connor: Literalist of the Imagination." *Flannery O'Connor Bulletin* 12 (1983) 77–92.

Updike, John. "Me and My Books." In *More Matter: Essays and Criticism,* 758-62. New York: Fawcett, 2000.

Wilder, Amos N. *Grace Confounding.* Philadelphia: Fortress, 1972.

Williams, Charles. *Descent into Hell.* New York: Pellegrini and Cudahy, 1949.

Wood, Ralph C. *Contending for the Faith. The Church's Engagement with Culture.* Waco, TX: Baylor University Press, 2003.

————. *Flannery O'Connor and the Christ-Haunted South.* Grand Rapids: Eerdmans, 2004.

————. "Hazel Motes as a Flesh Mortifying Saint in Flannery O'Connor's *Wise Blood.*" *Flannery O'Connor Review* 7 (2009) 87–93.

————. "The Heterodoxy of Flannery O'Connor's Book Reviews." *Flannery O'Connor Bulletin* 5 (1976) 5–29.

————. "The Scandalous Baptism of Harry Ashfield: Flannery O'Connor's 'The River.'" In *Inside the Church of Flannery O'Connor: Sacrament, Sacramental, and the Sacred in Her Fiction,* edited by Joanne Halloran McMullen and Jon Parrish Peede, 189–204. Macon, GA: Mercer University Press, 2007.